THE END OF STRESS
AS WE KNOW IT

THE END OF STRESS
AS WE KNOW IT

Bruce S. McEwen
with Elizabeth Norton Lasley

Joseph Henry Press
Washington, D.C.

Joseph Henry Press • 500 Fifth Street, N.W. • Washington, D.C. 20001

The Joseph Henry Press, an imprint of the National Academies Press, was created with the goal of making books on science, technology, and health more widely available to professionals and the public. Joseph Henry was one of the founders of the National Academy of Sciences and a leader in early American science.

The Dana Press, a division of the Charles A. Dana Foundation, publishes health and popular science books about the brain for the general reader. The Dana Foundation is a private philanthropic organization with particular interests in health and education.

Library of Congress Cataloging-in-Publication Data

McEwen, Bruce S.
  The end of stress as we know it / Bruce S. McEwen, with Elizabeth
Norton Lasley.
     p. cm.
Includes bibliographical references and index.
  ISBN 0-309-07640-4
  1. Stress (Physiology) 2. Stress (Psychology) 3. Stress management.
I. Lasley, Elizabeth Norton. II. Title.
  QP82.2.S8 M38 2002
  155.9'042—dc21

                    2002014006

Cover design by Michele de la Menardiere. Cover photograph by Lars Klove/The Image Bank. Author photograph by Ingbert Grüttner.

Illustrations on pages 22, 71, 192, 194, 195, 197, and 198 by Kathryn Born.

Printed in the United States of America

Contents

Foreword

The 20th century was filled with all sorts of brilliant, eccentric physicists who came up with some pretty cryptic sound bites now and then—God not playing with dice, things of that sort. One of them, Niels Bohr, had a great one: "Sometimes the opposite of a great truth is a great falsehood. But sometimes the opposite of a great truth is another great truth." This is relevant to the course of scientific progress. There's a perception that science proceeds in a very directional, linear manner, with an accepted knowledge base and people toiling to inch the edifice away from great falsehoods toward The Great Truth. In reality, though, what scientists often have to do is lurch knowledge toward a great truth to counteract their field lurching too far, nearly capsizing, with an enthusiasm for a different great truth.

Psychology, for example, spent the last century lurching. Early on the field was dominated by William James, who emphasized the great truth that the mind is the organ of philosophizing. This made psychology an armchair sport of thinking about what's going on inside that head. By midcentury, psychology was dominated by a different great truth, one meant as a purgative of philosophical psychology. This one, behaviorism, emphasized how the mind is the organ that produces measurable behavior, behavior that is shaped by rates of positive and negative reinforcement. And soon you had B. F. Skinner proclaiming that a pigeon equals a rat equals a boy, doesn't matter, so long as you can quantify the number of lever presses they make for a reward—just be able to measure the behavioral output and don't get gummed up with that mumbo jumbo of what is going on in that black box called "mind." And psychology has spent recent decades tacking back from that woefully excessive truth.

Medicine has been doing its own zigzagging. One of the most important great truths that Western thinking has ever embraced is the reductionist credo: If you want to understand something complex, break it down into its small component parts. Understand those building blocks, fix the ones that are broken, put them back together, and you're in business. It's a great strategy for fixing Guttenberg's printing press should it have a mechanical problem. Or for fixing your computer. And it has constituted one of the great truths of medicine for the last century. If you want to fix a disease, you must understand the itty bitty things that make you sick—bacteria, viruses, or parasites or a miniscule stretch of DNA containing a mutation.

Now this approach is great. It's gotten us vaccines for yellow fever, smallpox, polio. Drugs that block the precise step in the replication of a virus's DNA. It's gotten us the molecular explanation of genetic disorders like sickle cell anemia and Huntington's disease. And it's gotten us something approximating the sequence of the human genome, the holy text of reductive medicine.

I'm serious that this really is great. Having been a kid in the Jonas Salk era, I'm mighty glad I got his vaccine (or maybe it was Sabin's—let's not even go there). Reductive medical approaches have made staggering inroads against infectious diseases, extending our life spans to unprecedented lengths.

But it's time for many branches of medicine to lurch away from the great truth of reductive medicine to another great truth: You can't understand a disease outside the context of the person with the disease—something that might be called a holistic approach (a term that most medical scientists loathe for purely visceral reasons).

Think about the following: gazillions are spent by pharmaceutical companies to invent new drugs targeting reductive steps in disease. But a huge problem is figuring out why people so often stop *taking* their medicine the second they feel better, guaranteeing that they'll have to do it all over again and that the medicine won't be as effective the next time. Or that there already exist mountains of very good science about what constitutes a healthy lifestyle, but still our leading cause of death is I'll Do It Starting Tomorrow—people continuing to eat poorly, smoke, not exercise, drink in excess.

Other facets of our current picture of health and disease also show just how little of it has to do with reductive science. Consider that a major predictor of your risk for a bunch of diseases is your socio-economic status. Even after controlling for an array of risk factors and protective factors. Even in countries where there's universal health care, where no one's poor. Even for diseases that have nothing to do with how often you go to the doctor. Or that an even better predictor of health than your socioeconomic status is what you *perceive* your socio-economic status to be. Go find a pill to cure the adverse effects of *that* on health.

Or how about that public health prognosticators predict that by 2025 the second leading cause of medical disability on earth will be clinical depression? You're never going to be able to vaccinate people against life in a way that would provide a reductive cure for that disease. Or that if you want to save millions of lives annually in the developing world, forget reductive medicine and get people some clean water. Or that Americans now spend roughly a quarter of their health dollars on alternative medicine, in large part because its practitioners actually do something as retro as *talk* to their patients, spend more than 8.3 minutes with them. Or that being isolated, anonymous, lonely is demonstrably damaging to your health.

We've entered the gilded genomics era just in time to have to admit that most of our ills have to do with extraordinarily ungenomic things like your psychological makeup and patterns of social relations, your social status and the society in which you have that status, your lifestyle. And at the center of this nexus is stress—what stressors we are exposed to and how we cope. Most of us will live long enough and well enough to get seriously ill with a stress-related disease. And given that most of us would rather have this happen later than sooner, it is well worth learning about the links between stress and disease. To that end, you have in your hands a superb introduction to this subject. There is no one better situated to have written such a book than Bruce McEwen.

His own scientific history is interesting. Despite being intrigued with psychology back in high school, he started his research career as a graduate student in the early 1960s as a cell biologist—doing that reductive science stuff. And McEwen has continued making seminal contributions in that reductive realm since then, in showing the effects of stress on the brain and the immune system. This has earned him a trunk-full of accolades: an endowed professorship at one of the most prestigious research institutes in the world, presidency of the international Society for Neuroscience, election to the National Academy of Sciences, the highest honor for an American scientist.

But along the way McEwen also branched off into that more integrative realm of this subject, involving himself in the markedly unreductive issues of what emotions, coping, socioeconomic status, and so on have to do with health. And in that path he has pioneered some extraordinarily important research showing what "allostatic load"—what might be called the cumulative wear and tear of life, a topic covered at length in this book—has to do with disease. What these parallel branches of investigation have produced is the leading living scholar of stress. This book represents a wonderful distillation of that knowledge—clear, readable, as scientifically authoritative as you can find. It is a decidedly unreductive fact that reading the right book can improve your health; this is one such book.

Robert Sapolsky
Stanford, California

Acknowledgments

I wish to thank my current and former students and postdoctoral fellows who taught me at least as much as I taught them. A lot of their hard work and some of their names are referred to in the pages of this book. I also thank many professional colleagues, particularly Don Pfaff, Fernando Nottebohm, Paul Greengard, and Torsten Wiesel at the Rockefeller University, and a host of other neuroscientists throughout the world who have inspired me and provided important insights along with their collaborative energies. I am particularly indebted to colleagues, past and present, of the MacArthur Research Network on Socioeconomic Status and Health (Nancy Adler, University of California, San Francisco, Chair), and particularly Teresa Seeman at UCLA and Burton Singer at Princeton University, for their efforts in operationalizing the concept of allostatic load. I want to acknowledge my mentors: the late Alfred Mirsky, Vincent Allfrey, the late Holger Hyden, the late Neal Miller, and the late Eliot Stellar, who helped to shape my scientific thinking and my concept of the responsiblities of a scientist toward society.

Special thanks to the scientists who gave of their time to review and comment on the manuscript, including John Mason, most recently of Yale University, Carl Sheck of Oregon State University, Stephen Porges of the University of Illinois at Chicago, and Firdaus Dhabhar of Ohio State University.

Finally, the work involved in writing this book was made much easier by the administrative and clerical efforts of Adelaide Acquaviva, Halina Korsun, and Maryse Aubourg, and by the tireless efforts of the editorial team. Heartfelt thanks to Stephen Mautner at the Joseph Henry Press and to Jane Nevins at the Dana Press for their vision, criticism, and enthusiasm.

Bruce McEwen
New York City

THE END OF STRESS
AS WE KNOW IT

CHAPTER 1

A New Way
to Look at Stress

As part of my work as a research scientist, I sometimes give talks on stress, health, and the functioning of the brain. I start by asking who in the audience has used the word *stress* in the past 48 hours. Most people's hands go up. It's clear that we like to talk about stress. The word has been adopted, without change, in many languages, including Japanese, French, and Hindi. We all think we suffer from stress, and, naturally, we all want to avoid it.

But when we use the word *stress*, what do we mean?

For many people, stress is something external. We use the word to mean the trials and tribulations of life, which we generally refer to in a passive sense, saying that we're "under stress." These include job pressures, perhaps, financial strain, and worries about our children. Other people describe stress in terms of the way it makes them feel—the various unpleasant physical sensations that arise in the face of adversity, such as the shortness of breath, heart palpitations, or stomachache that a sudden crisis sets off or the state of fatigue and demoralization that we enter when one such crisis seems to follow on the heels of another.

Increasingly, though, today's meaning of the word *stress* includes all of the above definitions and more. For many of us, it refers to a state of complete overload. External events unite with the discomfort of our own response to overwhelm us and exhaust our ability to cope. As a result we begin to feel tired, edgy, and run down; eventually, this state tips toward illness. In trying to keep up with the ever-increasing pace of the world around us, we start catching colds that we can't seem to shake off. Or in struggling to meet the needs of innumerable friends, co-workers, and family members, we develop a sense of inadequacy that spirals into helplessness and depression. When things get to this point, we are no longer simply under stress—we're "stressed out."

Viewed in this way, stress is indeed an enemy that we can neither fight nor avoid, for how can we control outside events or override the instinctive, involuntary responses of our own bodies?

The answer is that we don't have to view stress this way. In fact, in this final and all-encompassing guise, stress takes the very form that we have the power to prevent. In other words, we don't need to be stressed out. It's true that we cannot always ward off life's adversity or flip a switch to bring our heart rate down when we want to stay calm. But preserving our health in a crisis—even in an ongoing state of crisis—is well within our grasp. Why I believe this to be true, what decades of research tell us about the relationship of stress and health, and how we can fortify our inherent ability to cope are the subject of this book.

The Meanings of Stress

Because the word contains so many meanings, dealing with stress is like fighting the mythical hydra, which had a limitless ability to grow new heads to replace the ones Hercules cut off. This ambiguity is embedded in the very word *stress* and has been a stumbling block right from the beginning.

In *Webster's New World Dictionary*, for example, the first definition of the word is "strain or straining force." For this definition, the first example given is "the force exerted upon a body, that tends to strain or deform its shape," usually measured in pounds per square inch. So right away we can see that stress has two meanings. There's the sense of something being imposed from the outside, such as some uncontrollable force, and there's the negative effect that this force has on its object—the pounds-per-square-inch concept, which we might call the "engineering" sense of the word. Since this is not a book about engineering, I'll convert the concepts into human terms. Stress refers to the pressure that life exerts on us *and* to the way this pressure makes us feel.

The *Oxford English Dictionary* puts the word in human terms straight off, defining stress as hardship, adversity, affliction ("engineering" definitions come later). According to this dictionary, the word *stress* is simply a shortened form of *distress*, and in Middle English, *destresse* and *stresse* were used interchangeably. Stress certainly equals distress in the 14th-century poet R. Brunne's description of the heavenly manna sent to the Israelites as they wandered in the desert:

> That floure ys kalled 'aungelys mete'
> That God gave the folke to ete
> Whan they were yn wyldernes
> Forty wyntyr, yu hard stres.

Distress is an integral component of 21st-century stress as well. There's no doubt that stress can cause wear and tear, both psychologically and physically. In the United States the economic toll of stress-related illnesses exceeds $200 billion annually by some estimates. People suffering from intense or ongoing stress may develop cardiovascular problems, such as heart attacks or the "hardening of the arteries" known as atherosclerosis—a risk factor for both heart attacks and stroke. Chronic stress can take a toll on the immune system, making someone more susceptible to colds and infections; it can also ratchet up the immune response to detrimental levels, resulting in allergies, asthma, and autoimmune conditions. The mind itself can be a casualty of stress if normal feelings of distress and demoralization tilt toward clinical depression or anxiety. There is even evidence that depression and traumatic stress can cause parts of the brain to atrophy. Other stress-related illnesses include diabetes, colitis, chronic fatigue syndrome, fibromyalgia, eczema, and ulcers. The reason for this impressive range is simple.

The major systems of the body work together to provide one of the human organism's most powerful and sophisticated defenses: the stress response, also known as the fight-or-flight response. The stress response helps us react to an emergency and cope with change. To do so, it musters the brain, glands, hormones, immune system, heart, blood, and lungs. Whether we need to fight, stand firm, bolt to safety, or concentrate on a task at hand, the stress response provides the tools—energy, oxygen, muscle power, fuel, pain resistance, mental acuity, and a temporary bulwark against infection—all at a moment's notice. Hence the array of illnesses that can arise when we get stressed out.

Why *do* we get stressed out? Surely the last thing we need when times are tough is to complicate things even further by developing physical or mental illness. So why does the human organism contain a provision for causing illness under duress? The answer, of course, is that causing illness is not the function of the stress response. Rather, the fight-or-flight response evolved with the prime directive of ensuring our safety and survival. It's a powerful system, a dynamic resilience that sharpens our attention and mobilizes our bodies to cope with threatening situations, then returns to baseline, usually with no ill effects. Only when it's overwhelmed or derailed does the stress response system begin to cause disease.

This book was written to emphasize the following paradox: stress protects under acute conditions, but when activated chronically it can cause damage and accelerate disease. In our more jaded moments we view being stressed out as the normal, even inevitable, consequence of life in a fast-paced world. But although stress in the sense of challenging events is inevitable to some degree, being stressed out is not. It is not inevitable or normal for the very system designed to protect us to become a threat in itself. It is this distinction that I find most important to describe and understand—so much so that I feel we need new terminology to use in discussing how stress affects our health.

I believe the whole concept of stress is outmoded, and I'd like to separate it back into its original components. When I use the word *stress* in this book, it will be in reference to outside events only. Science is giving us a better way to understand the stress response, or fight-or-flight response, so I like an alternate term: *allostasis*. And for the last and bleakest definition of stress—when we're besieged to the point where the stress response system turns against us—consider the term *allostatic load*. I will discuss these last two terms in great detail throughout the book, but for now here's a quick overview.

Allostasis Revealed

Allostasis sounds like a disease in its own right, but it's a term that came into being in the early 1980s as a newer and more appreciative way to view the body's swift and efficient methods of dealing with danger. To understand it properly we need to backtrack a bit and invoke another biological term, one that might be more familiar: *homeostasis*.

Homeostasis is often described as an organism's need to maintain a steady internal state. It comes from the Greek roots *homeo*, meaning same, and *stasis*, meaning stable—remaining stable by staying the same.

The word *homeostasis* was first used in the mid-19th century by a French scientist named Claude Bernard. He introduced the thinking that eventually led to the concept, and science, of stress. Bernard emphasized the body's need to maintain a constant state, what he called *le milieu internel*. Many bodily conditions must not only remain constant, they must stay the same, or at least remain within rigidly proscribed limits. Body temperature is one of these: a fever of 100 is a legitimate reason to stay in bed, a fever of 104 a potentially life-threatening situation. Other homeostatic systems include the blood's acid-base balance and oxygen content and the amount of oxygen that reaches the brain. If these things change by much, we die.

Luckily, however, only a few areas of our existence are confined within such narrow straits. Obviously our circumstances are changing constantly; we live in a world of change, and the body must be able to respond. Bernard and the scientists who followed him knew that many of the body's systems can and do operate within an astonishingly wide range of parameters. Heartbeat, breathing, the amount of glucose in the blood, and the amount of energy currently stored as fat are all things that can change quite quickly. Some debate exists in the scientific community as to whether these systems, too, should fall under the heading of homeostasis—they do, after all, help maintain constancy of a sort. But I prefer the newer term, *allostasis*. It comes from the Greek root *allo*, meaning variable, and it emphasizes the point that allostatic systems help keep the body stable by being themselves able to change. Nowhere are these changes more dramatic than in the systems that comprise the stress response.

Allostasis, Fight, and Flight

Allostasis is produced by a swift and intricately organized system of communication. It links the brain, which perceives a novel or threatening situation; the endocrine system (chiefly the adrenal glands), which is primarily responsible for mobilizing the rest of the body); and the immune system for internal defense. Allostasis is often thought of as the fight-or-flight response because, taken to the extreme, it prepares for just those two eventualities. The main idea is to get maximum energy to those parts of the body that need it the most.

To fight or flee, an animal needs an increased flow of oxygen to its muscles, particularly the large muscles of the legs. So breathing accelerates to bring in more oxygen, and the heart rate speeds up to deliver that oxygen through the bloodstream to the major muscles. The blood vessels in the skin constrict so that there will be as little bleeding as possible in the event of injury; this constriction produces the sensation of the hair standing on end. To provide sufficient fuel for the exertion, our glands liquidate stored carbohydrates into the blood sugar. The immune system, too, is involved. Under acute stress, the immune response is enhanced. The infection-fighting white blood cells attach themselves to the blood vessel walls, ready to depart for whatever part of the body is injured. But if a stressful situation goes on too long, the immune response is dampened in favor of the primary systems—the heart and lungs—that need the energy most. Already, you can see the potential for trouble if this system gets stuck in the "on" position.

The classic image of allostasis is that of an animal running away from a predator. As far as humans are concerned, most people have heard the story of the 80-year-old lady who ran out into the street and lifted a car off her cat's tail. For most situations, we would wish that the stress response were a bit more judicious. It seems that allostasis has not caught up with evolution and is not yet convinced that such dramatic physical responses are becoming less necessary. So a council member standing up at a town meeting, a first-year teacher facing a classroom full of unruly children, and a violinist stepping before an audience in a hushed concert hall may feel they are gearing up, involuntarily, to vanquish their opponent or propel themselves away.

But fight or flight is allostasis with a sense of urgency. Remember, the purpose of allostasis is to help the organism remain stable in the face of any change and to provide enough energy to cope with any challenge—not just the life-threatening ones. Take the simple act of getting up in the morning. Some people consider it to be the first major trauma of the day, but even for early birds, moving from sleep to wakefulness and from lying down to standing up makes demands on the body. To ensure sufficient energy to meet these demands, allostasis provides for a higher level of stress hormones in the morning. Even allostatic responses that some people consider noticeably stressful aren't always perceived that way by others. For example, successful musicians, actors, athletes, and politicians know how to channel their stage fright into an energy source that gives their performance an added edge, whereas those unused to performance may freeze up and forget what they're supposed to do.

Nevertheless, most of us notice allostasis at times that we deem to be trying, and it usually seems to kick in when we don't want it to. Increasingly, the situations that ignite the stress response are ones for which neither fight nor flight is an option—working for an overbearing boss, for example, or caring for a family member who is seriously ill. In these situations the stress response cannot help speed us toward a resolution. And so, deprived of its natural result, the very system designed to protect us begins to cause wear and tear instead, and illness sets in.

This is the type of stress, or the state of being stressed out, that I prefer to describe as *allostatic load*—the damage that the allostatic response causes when it is functioning improperly. Some of the ways it

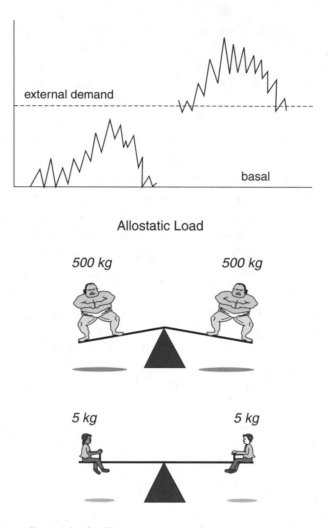

Allostatic Load

FIGURE 1   Allostatic load is like two sumo wrestlers on a seesaw—the seesaw may be in balance, but it's under a strain that may eventually cause it to break.

may malfunction are when it does not shut off at the right time—for example, when someone cannot seem to calm down after a heated argument and still has a pounding pulse hours later; when it does not adapt to a repeated event—when someone meets the same challenge at work, time after time, with the same level of anxiety and, coincidentally, develops a cold; when it chronically, repeatedly, or inappropriately activates the major body systems, causing them to turn on themselves and eventually break down. Why allostasis becomes allostatic load in some people and not others may be partly a matter of genetics. It may also have to do with our emotional reactions to situations. And although science shows that much happens automatically, you're right if you think lifestyle plays a role.

Other Kinds of Allostatic Load

Allostatic load does not always denote a failure of the body's efforts to cope with change or emergency. We can create it for ourselves by living in a way that makes for internal imbalance. Sleep deprivation, for example, leads to elevations in blood glucose and cortisol; chronic elevations of this sort can lead to bone mineral loss and increase the amount of fat that accumulates in the abdominal area (considered the most unhealthy type of fat). Eating a rich diet or overeating produces a metabolic load on the body, thereby increasing fat deposition and hardening the arteries, both risk factors for heart disease and other ailments. Lack of regular exercise is another major contributor to allostatic load: regular exercise increases energy expenditure and boosts the muscles' ability to burn glucose. Exercise works against the bad effects of a rich diet and increased body fat, enhances well-being, and improves sleep.

Quite often, bad habits reflect our *personal* efforts to deal with stress. Eating the wrong things, sleeping irregularly, and not exercising compound the effects of stress to make our lives miserable. We reach for a bag of potato chips and forgo daily exercise while working on a report. Then anxiety over whether the boss will like the report causes us to lose sleep at night. As a result we may put on a few more ounces of fat in the wrong places and move ourselves one step farther down the road of allostatic load.

Anticipation or anxiety—or anticipatory angst, to split the difference—can lead to allostatic load even when it doesn't drive us to make poor lifestyle choices. The human mind is so powerful, the connections between perception and physiological response so strong, that we can set off the fight-or-flight response by just imagining ourselves in a threatening situation. This ability can be a source of power or an invitation to illness. If we use our imagination to gear up for a competition or a presentation at the office, we can command the forces of allostasis to give our performance an added edge. But if we torture ourselves with worst-case scenarios, voluntarily simmering in a toxic broth of dread, we can exhaust our bodies' allostatic systems without ever coming into contact with a predator or an adversary, without even leaving home.

Anyone who doubts the danger of allostatic load should consider one of the most graphic examples, which is found not in an office setting but in the rivers of Nova Scotia. Every year the salmon swim upstream to spawn, battling the adverse current, leaping over rocks, traveling up to a thousand miles to return to their breeding ground. After ensuring the birth of a new generation, the salmon die.

The salmon is the icon of persistence, self-sacrifice, even heroism. But the truth is more prosaic: the fish are killed by their own stress hormones. The stress hormones give them the enormous burst of energy needed for the trek but ultimately reach toxic levels. This is what we call a biphasic action of the stress response: though it can mobilize to accomplish incredible feats, it can also cause damage and death. In the case of the salmon, death serves a useful purpose: it frees up the food supply for a new generation.

We cannot find a comparable purpose in the damaging side of stress on the human body, but there is a lot we can do to prevent allostatic load. The first step is to understand what we're dealing with.

Stress and the Emotions

By articulating the concept of homeostasis and the body's need to maintain a constant internal environment, Claude Bernard laid the groundwork for the scientific study of stress. The first scientist to actually bring the word into the medical vocabulary was a physiologist by the name of Walter Cannon.

As early as 1914, Cannon began talking about stress in all of the senses that we invoke today. He used the word in terms of the emotions, as was common then, in phrases like "great emotional stress" and "in times of need or stress." He also ushered in the more "engineering" concept, discussing the strain that cold, lack of oxygen, or low blood sugar can place on the body. Some of his work even foreshadowed the idea of allostatic load; he proposed that critical stress levels can over-whelm the body's homeostatic mechanisms. A visionary, Cannon urged doctors to study all things that could cause a disturbance in the body's workings—including emotional stress—and how best to relieve them. Still, the connection between emotional stimuli and imperiled homeostasis would not resurface for several decades.

Many scientists working in the area of stress and health believe that Cannon should be considered the father of the field. But there's no denying that in the 1930s a Hungarian scientist named Hans Selye be-gan the research that put the word *stress* on the map, ultimately rein-troducing it into the English language to mean what I try to call allostatic load. Although some of us now regret Selye's choice of words, all of our current understanding of the connections between stress and health stems from his research.

Hans Selye and the General Adaptation Syndrome

Selye's first contribution was simply to recognize the physiological sys-tems involved in the body's response to challenge. As a young medical student at the University of Prague, he noticed that when medical pro-fessors presented case histories of patients with infectious diseases, the patients had many of the same symptoms. Regardless of which par-ticular disease they had, all of the patients had coated tongues, aches and pains, loss of appetite, and inflamed tonsils. In other words, they all felt and looked ill. Selye further noticed that none of these facts interested the presenting physicians, who were concerned only with the symptoms unique to each particular disease. The youthful Selye suggested that studying "sickness" in general should be as important as studying any one sickness in particular—much to his professors' scorn.

But later, in the 1930s, as an endocrinologist at McGill University in Montreal, Selye again encountered the signs of a generalized re-sponse. He was studying the effects of various hormones injected into rats. One of his ovarian extracts produced an unusual trail of dam-age—stomach ulcers, enlarged adrenal glands, and shrinking or atrophy of several parts of the lymphatic system. No known ovarian hormone produced all of these changes at once, so Selye was excited: Had he discovered a new hormone, previously unglimpsed by the medical world? His excitement was short lived. Hormone extracts in those days were crude preparations, and it occurred to Selye that the effects he saw might be due to some toxin or impurity in the extract, not to the hormone itself. To test the idea, he injected the rats with formalin, a chemical used in preserving tissue and a highly painful irritant. The formalin produced the same array of reactions, making it impossible to establish a direct link between the reactions and the mystery hormone, and Selye's hopes that he had found a new hormone were dashed.

As Selye wrote in his book *The Stress of Life,* he was so depressed that he didn't go to his laboratory for several days. But then he began to wonder if his results were the microscopic equivalent of the generalized responses he had seen in patients in Prague. Selye began to experiment, first with other toxins and then with other challenges, including sudden cold, sudden heat, radiation, pain, and forced exercise. Every type of irritant produced the same constellation of responses. Why? Why should the body react in the same way to unrelated or even opposite kinds of stimuli? The evidence was strong that the body must have a consistent, organized mechanism to help cope with a variety of insults. Selye dubbed the mechanism the *general adaptation syndrome,* and he used the phrase to include three meanings of stress, which he called the alarm reaction, the stage of resistance, and the stage of exhaustion. He resolved to make this syndrome his area of study.

Once again, Selye's professors tried to discourage him. The medical mindset at the time emphasized the need to match up one specific disease, toxin, or drug to one specific reaction—and here was Selye planning to investigate the nonspecific, miscellaneous, medically useless stuff that the body does in response to practically everything. But Selye held firm:

> If we could prove that the organism had a general nonspecific reaction-pattern with which it could meet damage caused by a variety of potential disease-producers, this defensive response would lend itself to a strictly objective, truly scientific analysis. By clarifying the function of the

mechanism of response through which Nature herself fights injuries of various kinds, we might learn how to improve upon this reaction whenever it is imperfect.

Selye's research appeared in the journal *Nature* on July 4, 1936, as a 74-line note entitled "A Syndrome Produced by Diverse Nocuous Agents." His next step was to find a better name for his discovery than general adaptation syndrome (along with its unfortunate acronym). Eventually he hit on the word *stress*. Selye himself had concerns about the word's multiple meanings, but stress was the word he chose. And because the word is an Anglo-Saxon monosyllable that has no equivalent in other languages—certainly not in Selye's threefold sense—he shifted it over untranslated. When lecturing in French, he spoke of *le stress*; in Spanish, *el stress*; in Italian, *lo stress*; and so forth.

Throughout the intervening decades Selye and many other scientists, including myself, have sought to understand stress by unraveling the connections among the various bodily systems involved in Selye's syndrome. What do the adrenal glands and the hormones they produce have to do with stress? What are the links, structural and biochemical, between the adrenals and the brain? How does the brain communicate a state of emergency to the immune system, and by what means does it sound the all-clear? What safeguards are normally in place to prevent the stress response from causing damage, and under what circumstances are these safeguards removed?

Recent events have made it urgent for scientists to answer these questions. Since the terrorist attacks of September 11, 2001, the word *stress* has taken on newer, wider, and deeper connotations. No longer just a term used with perverse pride to display the scars or medals of a fast-paced life, stress has come to mean fear for one's safety, health, and livelihood; a loss of the assumption that the world is a safe place; the invasion of horrific images that may at any time reappear on the nightly news; and frequent official broadcasts of unspecific alerts.

In a more practical way it is crucial to disentangle the many connotations of stress. We cannot always control what happens to us. We cannot, and should not, eliminate the fight-or-flight response, for it is a powerful, highly sophisticated resource. But we will be able to find ways of keeping the stress response in balance, so that it works for us and not against us. Our growing understanding of the biological realities of stress will help us achieve this goal in several ways.

First, we can expect to see better-targeted medications. The newer antidepressants like Prozac and its successors are good examples. Because of better understanding of the brain chemistry of depression, these drugs work more cleanly and with fewer side effects. We will see similar improvements in medicinal treatment of stress. At this point, we don't have drugs that work by rebalancing the stress response; doctors rely on antidepressants and antianxiety medications, which have more general, palliative effects. Though this is a good start—and getting any treatment at all is often the first-line defense against allostatic load—the picture should improve. As scientists learn about the balances of hormones and brain chemicals, even the actions of single genes, medications will result that act more quickly, more accurately, and with a much lighter touch.

Second, understanding what goes wrong with the stress response provides a solid platform of research to help explain what goes right. Right now, most of what we know about stress, health, and the brain derives from the problems that result when the stress response malfunctions. This is due to a basic fact of science: medical research tends to focus on disease. For one thing, funding is limited, and the grants understandably go to the research most likely to relieve human suffering. For another, it's easier to study something that goes wrong. When people have a particular disorder, you can do blood tests, scans, and psychological profiles and you can compare them to those of normal people, quantify the differences, and come up with data. If you try to study why someone is healthy, where do you start? What questions do you ask? What test conditions do you set up? Fortunately, decades of study of stress-related diseases have provided new markers to look for in studying healthy people who cope with stress just fine. Also, it's becoming increasingly clear that the brain and body do more than just damage control. Scientists are learning more about anabolic factors—the body's processes and substances that build up, strengthen, and protect.

Stress as Today's Problem

Finally, and most important, as we come to understand allostasis and allostatic load, it becomes increasingly apparent that the best way to deal with stress is by maintaining our physical and emotional health. This means taking a long, hard look at lifestyle.

If stress-related illnesses are not unique to the 21st century, it's safe to say that stress is a 21st-century concern. People certainly had asthma and ulcers 100 years ago, and books and articles are always coming out suggesting that some historical figure really suffered from depression or posttraumatic stress disorder. One could argue that life was harder in the past. For example, diseases that were killers in the early part of the 20th century, such as polio, rubella, and diphtheria, are no longer serious threats to public health. For women the dangers of dying in childbirth or in a household fire have greatly receded. Over the past hundred years, the life expectancy of Americans has increased by 50 percent.

But stress is not necessarily the same thing as *hardship*, and stressors are on the rise. We are besieged daily with more information than a staff of 20 could keep up with, threatening our sense of control over our own lives. Television brings death, illness, and violence into our homes, while keeping us at an ever-widening distance from friends and neighbors who might be able to help should these things visit us in reality. Technology has enabled us to do practically anything while seated, resulting in a decline in exercise and a 100 percent increase in obesity in the past 20 years. The simplicity of travel (compared to the days of horse-drawn coaches, nonexistent roads, and unsanitary inns) means that families journey farther and farther apart. The demands of school, work, and organized play have made gathering around the dinner table together to eat nourishing food an anachronism. Children are using mood-altering drugs (legally prescribed and otherwise) at younger and younger ages, and teenage suicide is at an all-time high.

In short, the 21st century may witness the crumbling of our strongest defenses against allostatic load. For decades scientific research has shown that we can guard against the ravages of stress by following advice our grandmothers could have given us: restful, plentiful sleep, a good diet, and regular exercise, as well as the support of family, friends, religious organizations, and community (isolation is one of the chief contributors to allostatic load), and a sense of control over and contribution to one's own life—often noticeably absent in those who suffer from heart attacks or depression.

This is not a prescriptive book; I do not outline an eight-week plan for stress-free living. This is partly because as a research scientist my work takes place in the laboratory and not in a clinical setting. It's also because the very nature of allostatic load means that there are no quick fixes. To take a powerful mechanism like allostasis, which evolved over millions of years to help us cope, and deform it into a source of disease is not something that happens quickly. It signals an imbalance of long standing. The balance is restored not by plunging into a short-lived program that bears little resemblance to one's life but by gradually and permanently building in new habits based on an understanding of how brain and body work.

My hope for readers is that knowledge will be its own kind of prescription and that, by bringing to light the connections between stress and health, you'll start taking the advice your grandmother could have given you—buoyed by an up-to-date, scientific understanding of why her advice can't be bettered. The following chapters detail specific instances in which allostasis becomes allostatic load and talk about ways to prevent this from happening.

First, let's take a closer look at the magic of allostasis. The first thing to know is that allostasis begins in the brain. To borrow an injunction from Dickens' *A Christmas Carol*: "This must be distinctly understood, or nothing wonderful can come of the tale which I am about to relate."

The Stress Response— or How We Cope

Whether a stressor is a slight change in posture or a life-threatening assault, the brain determines when the body's inner equilibrium is disturbed; the brain initiates the actions that restore the balance. Many creatures without brains have systems to help them cope with changes and challenges in their environment. But as humans and other mammals have evolved, the intertwining of the brain, hormones, and immune system has come to represent allostasis in its most elegant form. As early as the third century B.C., the Greek physician Hippocrates, often called the father of medicine, said: "Men ought to know that from the brain and the brain only arise our pleasures, joys, laughter, and tears. Through it, in particular, we think, see, hear, and distinguish the ugly from the beautiful, the bad from the good, the pleasant from the unpleasant. To consciousness the brain is a messenger."

Hippocrates was tactful in his use of the word *messenger*. Some scientists argue that the brain and its functions are actually the source of consciousness. These pages will not make the case that a human being is tantamount to a series of biochemical relays; whether our being has a reality separate from that of the body is a debate far beyond the scope of this book. But one thing is clear. At least throughout our mortal life span, our identities are inextricably fused into the physical integrity of the brain. A blow that damages brain tissue can hack away at the columns on which our humanity rests—the individuality of memory, for example; our ability to empathize and envision; our adroit use of spoken and written language. A disruption in the brain's delicate biochemical balance can threaten our very selves, as anyone who knows the heartbreak of schizophrenia or Alzheimer's disease can attest.

Of course we think through the brain; that much is obvious. Thoughts form the basis of humanity's greatest achievements—science, poetry, exploration, commerce, government, technology, philanthropy. Take an early example. When our hunter-gatherer ancestors changed over to an agricultural lifestyle, one or more enterprising individuals had to come up with the idea to cultivate crops and domesticate animals. To put the idea into practice must have taken lots of planning, as well as a certain amount of trial and error in figuring out when and where to grow the crops and which animals were the most suitable. Those early entrepreneurs undoubtedly had to overcome resistance from their fellow tribesmen (and from the animals). They probably had to keep faith during a few meager harvests. But eventually the shift to agrarian living was complete. It was a major transition point for humanity, encapsulating analysis, conceptual thinking, goal setting, problem solving, and deferral of immediate gratification for a long-term gain—all of which come under the auspices of the brain.

But the things about stress that interest all of us, particularly its effects on health, are not generally associated with mental functions— ulcers, for example, or high blood pressure, or whether a tense job situation can aggravate asthma. These turn out to be the brain, after all— some less obvious aspects of its operations.

The Brain Behind the Scenes

Where, for example, do great ideas come from? Tellingly, Hippocrates, in his paean to the brain, did not start by citing triumphs of reason such as problem solving. Instead, he led off with a different list entirely: pleasures, joys, laughter, tears. In other words, emotions. Emotions are the wellspring of ideas. Whether resulting from arduous mental effort or popping into one's mind while taking a shower, ideas appear in response to a desire. Desires, in turn, result from needs. And both begin in the brain.

Let's go back to the hunter-gatherers. In their forays they must have experienced fatigue from roaming farther and farther afield; hunger and thirst when supplies ran short; and pain from sore feet, aching backs, and any injuries they might have sustained. At first glance, there doesn't seem to be anything even remotely cerebral about the physical need to avoid hunger and pain. It's true that we first notice the sensation of hunger in our stomachs. But, in fact, hunger is a state created by the brain. The brain keeps tabs on the stomach through a series of nerves and chemical messengers. When it's time to eat again, the brain activates that empty feeling, those thoughts, if you're a hunter-gatherer, of a nice thick mastadon steak. Similarly, you feel pain at the site of an injury, but that's due to specialized nerves that send the alarm to your brain. When you touch something that causes pain, the brain responds by moving the affected body part if possible (the hand-off-the-hot-stove reaction) and by initiating the sensation of pain. Then other parts of the brain, in turn, perceive the pain, and this is where emotions begin to come in.

According to both Hippocrates and modern science, the brain distinguishes "the pleasant from the unpleasant, the bad from the good"—in humans at any rate. We know that animals avoid pain. Though we can be reasonably sure from their behavior that they don't like it, there's no way to tell whether animals have a subjective emotional reaction to pain. Humans perceive pain as unpleasant; it triggers states to which we ascribe emotional labels, such as fear, anger, the resolve to avoid the pain in the future, and sometimes the desire for revenge. Research has shown a biological correlate to the first stage of this process—the unpleasantness of pain.

Isn't pain, by definition, something unpleasant? Not necessarily. In a 1997 study, researchers at the University of Montreal asked volunteers to dip their hands in hot water first while conscious and then under hypnosis. While in the hypnotic state, the subjects were told that the pain would be either more or less unpleasant than the first time, and their brain activity was observed by means of a positron emission tomography (PET) scanner. After the study, the subjects reported that their experience of the pain did change according to the hypnotic suggestion. Interestingly, the PET scans showed a corresponding change in activity in an area of the brain called the anterior cingulate, thought to be involved in emotions. But activity in the part of the brain that perceived the pain, the somatosensory cortex, was unaltered. Because the emotional interpretation of the pain as unpleasant took place in a different location from the mere awareness of the pain signal, the researchers concluded that the emotional aspect, or the "affect," is a separate component of the pain experience.

Human beings, of course, have finer, more complex emotions than aversion to pain. The hunter-gatherers, for example, probably worried that they would not be able to find enough food. They would have known the grief of losing loved ones to famine or to a hunt that had gone dangerously wrong. They would have enjoyed the feelings of fullness after a feast (caused by brain chemicals called endorphins) and the fellowship and celebration that ensued. Agriculture was invented in part to provide a reliable food source but probably also to make the concomitant pleasures more consistently available. Perhaps the breakthrough was inspired by even loftier motives. Maybe it was proposed by a tribal nerd whose talents didn't lie in hunting and who longed to distinguish himself in some other way or by an artistic soul who preferred to spend her time painting on cave walls. The underlying circuitry of the subtler emotions, such as ambition and artistry, has not yet been mapped out, but they are brain children nonetheless.

Even that least brainy emotion of all, love, begins in the brain, although we still talk of love in terms of our hearts and no one ever sent his Valentine a box of chocolates in the shape of a brain. Like the other emotions we've discussed, love is based on an array of needs—some more noble and idealistic than others. Astute readers may observe that some of these needs seem to be more associated with the glands. This raises an important point. Emotions are a function of the brain's interconnection with the rest of the body. They may originate in the brain, but the real horsepower comes from the brain's link with the glands—hormones, otherwise known as the endocrine system. Scientists don't know whether the drive to create a work of art is fueled by hormones, but more basic emotions, such as love, anger, and fear, certainly are. And the interconnections are most clearly understood as they occur in the stress response.

The Stress Response: Once Around the Circuit

The brain decides what is threatening and what is not. When we face an audience, a classroom, or a shadowy figure in a dubious alley, the brain does a quick search. Have we been here before? If so, how did we feel? What was the outcome? Can we cope with the situation now? If there's doubt as to any of these questions, the stress response goes into high gear.

Anyone who has to get up and give a talk in front of a strange audience, or one filled with critics or enemies, is likely to feel anxious and dread the worst. The opponents are likely to deal only verbal blows, or throw vegetables at the very worst, but the speaker still has the same responses as a prey animal trying to escape from a predator. A creature in danger has to do one of two things—defeat the adversary or get away. So many things have to happen at once. A central aspect of the stress response is the concept of shifting energy from long-term to immediate needs. For example, the lungs need oxygen and the muscles need fuel. It's also in the animal's best interest not to be overly sensitive to pain at this point or to lose too much blood. On the other hand, digestion, growth, and sexual reproduction are not of paramount importance now. When you hear that a major storm is on the way, you start looking for candles, you fill the bathtub in case the water is cut off, you nail a board over that cracked window. You don't start wallpapering the dining room or filling out an application for a home equity

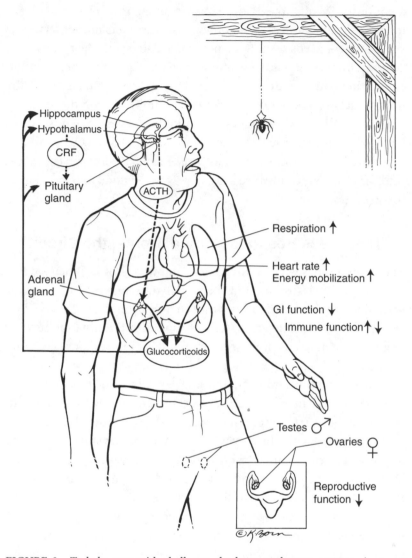

FIGURE 2   To help cope with challenge, the hormonal stress response increases heart rate and respiration, energy reserves, and hormones like glucocorticoids; lower-priority functions, like gastrointestinal function and reproduction, are decreased. The immune system is stimulated in the short term but can be suppressed by prolonged, severe stressors. ACTH, adrenocorticotropic hormone; CRF, corticotropin-releasing factor; GI, gastrointestinal.

loan. The complexities of the stress response—and their potential for causing trouble—are due to the same type of priority setting.

Allostasis begins deep in the brain, where a structure called the hypothalamus sounds an alert to the adrenal glands, far away at an outpost on top of the kidneys. The adrenals answer by pouring out the first of the major stress hormones—epinephrine, more commonly known in the United States as adrenaline—for the classic fight-or-flight response. The pulse begins to race as the adrenaline steps up the heart rate, sending extra blood to the muscles and organs. Oxygen rushes in as the bronchial tubes in the lungs dilate; extra oxygen also reaches the brain, which helps keep us alert. The hair stands on end because adrenaline constricts the blood vessels that supply the skin, thus preventing too much bleeding should the opponent deal an injurious blow. Adrenaline also triggers a substance called fibrinogen, which speeds up blood clotting, as a further defense against loss of blood. Finally, adrenaline mobilizes the body to release glucose from energy stores such as glycogen and to break down and release fatty acids from stored fats, thus providing a ready source of energy. During this stage of the fight-or-flight response, the brain releases natural pain-killers called endorphins to keep our hypothetical animal functioning during the crisis.

To marshal these emergency forces as quickly as possible, the hypothalamus uses a direct communication link—a circuit of nerves going straight to the adrenals. This phase, in which adrenaline plays a leading role, is the immediate response to stress. It was probably adrenaline that endowed the old lady with sufficient strength to hoist the parked car off her cat.

Next, the brain brings in the elite force: the hypothalamic-pituitary-adrenal axis (HPA axis for short). This is the second wave of defense, which the brain summons using hormones as couriers. The HPA axis is the cornerstone of allostasis and of allostatic load. Here the nervous system, glands, and immune system are brought together and held in balance—or not. When the HPA axis is functioning properly, we have the energy and focus to deal with a crisis. When unremitting stress makes the axis tilt, the result might be an asthma attack or a cold that won't go away.

The HPA axis is responsible for the adjusting phase of the allostatic response. It kicks in when the hypothalamus secretes a substance called corticotropin-releasing factor, which moves through specialized blood vessels to the pituitary, an almond-sized gland at the top of the brain. The pituitary in turn produces adrenocorticotropic hormone, which travels through the bloodstream to the adrenal glands. And the adrenals produce the second of the major stress hormones, cortisol, into the circulating blood.

Cortisol is one of the so-called steroid hormones made from cholesterol. (This is one of the helpful things that cholesterol provides to the body.) Cortisol's first job is to replenish energy stores depleted by the adrenaline rush, and it does so by converting a variety of food sources into storage forms such as glycogen or fat. Cortisol also makes us more active—and hungry. Yet too much cortisol blocks the actions of insulin to stimulate muscle to take up glucose. An excess also enhances the storage of energy in an unsightly manner—fat, particularly abdominal fat, which is thought to pose more of a health threat than fat around the thighs and hips. Cortisol promotes the loss of protein from muscle and converts it to fat, and it causes minerals to be lost from bone.

Cortisol has a double-edged effect on the immune system. Too much of it suppresses immune function and makes us more vulnerable to infections. Yet in the short term, a burst of cortisol helps the immune system respond to an infection or injury. It sends the white blood cells, the body's main line of defense against injury and infection, to their battle stations. In fact, cortisol actually changes the texture of these cells, causing them to become sticky and to attach themselves to blood vessel walls and to the body tissues where their protection may be needed, such as a wound or site of infection.

Cortisol also signals when the level of immune activity is adequate. It sends this message via the brain, which relays the information through the hypothalamus to the pituitary gland; the stress response is then adjusted accordingly. Cortisol's checks-and-balances effect is what makes it such a successful treatment for problems resulting from a hyperactive immune system, such as rashes or allergies, and for autoimmune conditions in which the immune system attacks the body's own healthy tissue. When we put cortisone cream on a rash or take steroids orally to fight inflammation, we are only supplementing what our own cortisol normally does.

Stress Hormones

The stress hormones, adrenaline and cortisol, are points at which the HPA axis may tip out of balance. Too much adrenaline and the resulting surges in blood pressure can damage the blood vessels of the heart and brain, creating rough spots or scars known as "lesions" where sticky plaques build up and restrict blood flow through these organs. This "hardening of the arteries" is a major risk factor for heart attack and stroke. When we can no longer rise to a challenge but instead become weakened by it, the predicament may be due to the fact that our cortisol isn't functioning properly. The hormone may be overactive or underactive even in its immediate response, or it may continue to flood the body even when an emergency has passed. At this point the stress response turns into allostatic load. Since cortisol works as a brake on the immune system, excessive quantities can actually suppress immune function; this is why many people under chronic stress are more susceptible to colds and other types of infection. On the other hand, too little cortisol can allow the immune system to get out of hand, resulting in inflammation, allergies, and autoimmune disorders.

The brain, too, is vulnerable to cortisol, not only when the amount is inappropriate but also when the timing is off. Cortisol normally obeys the body's inner clock, the so-called circadian rhythms that respond to light and dark, morning and night. As daylight-oriented creatures, humans rise in the morning, and to go from lying in bed to standing in the shower is a big enough change to require extra energy. Even people who don't find it stressful to get out of bed still receive a boost from their stress hormones. Cortisol acting in the brain and adrenaline acting outside it also aid us throughout the day, forming chemical links with brain cells in ways that affix important things in our memories. Thanks to quick surges of these hormones, we remember where we were and what we were doing when President Kennedy was killed or when terrorists flew airplanes into the World Trade Center and the Pentagon.

Ideally, the tide of cortisol is highest in the early morning, ebbing in the afternoon and reaching a low at night. But in people with severe depression, cortisol levels remain moderately elevated around the clock, particularly in the evening. There's no denying that a flat cortisol rhythm is a bad thing. Increased abdominal fat, loss of muscle mass, and bone demineralization are some of its more common nasty effects. Abnormal patterns of cortisol secretion have also been found in sufferers of posttraumatic stress disorder (PTSD) as well as the state that many people describe as burnout.

These facts are ominous because some patients with chronic severe depression, as well as some PTSD sufferers, have memory loss and other cognitive problems as a result. The abnormal secretion of cortisol that accompanies these conditions may work together with elevated brain cell activity in two key brain areas, the hippocampus and amygdala, to cause atrophy of brain cells and even permanent damage. The hippocampus and amygdala are crucial not only in stressful situations and in the regulation of immunity but also in "higher" thought functions such as learning and memory.

Later chapters discuss in detail how a chronically activated stress response damages the cardiovascular, immune, and nervous systems. In fact, so much of this book will discuss problems related to allostatic load that I'd like to take this opportunity to affirm my main philosophy: allostasis, when functioning smoothly, is what empowers us to handle and adapt to changes in our environment. Even if we perceive those changes as stressful, the intricate, elegant system of allostasis exists for the very purpose of helping us cope. Distorting this process to the point where it causes harm is a comparatively recent development in the history of life on this planet. It is a uniquely human problem in which our thoughts and emotions exert a powerful influence, for good or bad.

Stress Emerges from the Sea

For nearly three-quarters of geological time, the continents were rocky, inhospitable, uninhabited lands. Life on earth began in the ocean; in the waters of the pre-Cambrian age, about 1,500 million years ago, the first bacteria, called the prokaryotes, appeared. The needs of these organisms were comparatively simple. Maintaining homeostasis was a matter of keeping a consistent internal environment while temperature and pressure changed in the surrounding water. They also had to avoid irritants and toxins. In these early one-celled creatures, homeostasis was maintained by something called the heat shock response. This most ancient of homeostatic switches is triggered not only by heat but by anything a cell considers stressful, including extreme cold or pressure, bacterial or viral infection, and exposure to various toxic metals. The heat shock response activates the genes that produce the proteins responsible for the cell's in-house quality control. These heat shock proteins include the quaintly named chaperone proteins, which detect, repair, or dispose of other proteins that may be structurally or functionally unsound.

Heat shock proteins appear in many-celled organisms, such as humans, as well as in prokaryotes, and they continue to play a role in stress. Nikki Holbrook, now at Yale University, has shown that the hormonal response to stress is linked to the "primitive" heat shock mechanism. Working with rats, she has shown that mild stress, such as temporary immobilization, activates heat shock proteins in the adrenals and some blood vessels.

Allostasis on a larger scale, as characterized by the HPA axis, evolved over several hundred million years. To be strictly accurate, what we call allostasis has been around that long; its step-by-step development is submerged beneath the waters of prehistory.

Living things remained in the all-nourishing ocean for another billion years after the prokaryotes, together with their heat shock proteins, made their first appearance. During this time, life forms became more complex, evolving from single cells to groups of cells. Coral and sponges began to colonize the ocean floors; jellyfish and marine worms began to swim about. These creatures had specialized aggregates of cells, called organs, to help them circulate blood, respire, reproduce, and digest food. To direct these separately functioning units and keep them working in the interests of the whole, networks of nerves appeared to carry impulses, electrically and through specialized neurochemicals—the hormones.

Hormones have been found in creatures as primitive as algae. A hormone called diiodotyrosine, a relative of thyroid hormone, is found in coral; and thyroid hormone is fairly ubiquitous among invertebrate species. Thyroid hormone stimulates cell energy metabolism and promotes the generation of heat. The octopus, one of the most complex and "smartest" of invertebrates, has thyroid hormone and other hormones, short protein chains known as peptides that are produced by nerves. In ocean-going invertebrates, the hormones, acting as couriers between the nervous system and the rest of the body, serve as the main mechanism for regulating homeostatic systems like heart rate and circulation.

At this point in evolution, we can discuss stress only in terms of allostasis—actively maintaining a stable internal milieu and avoiding what scientists call noxious stimuli. In invertebrates, neurohormones do act as signal chemicals in learned behavior that help the animal avoid dangerous situations. But since both the brain and the endocrine system are still primitive in these animals—in particular, there are no brain structures that even foreshadow the seats of emotion in humans—invertebrates likely do not experience fear as such. Perhaps, originally at least, they did not even need fear, since their predators had not appeared.

It was in the Silurian period, 400 million years ago, that stress made its debut in more modern senses of the word. From a human point of view, life began to get more challenging and competitive. The first invertebrate predators appeared—giant marine scorpions up to 5 feet long. One of these may have been the first creature to venture up onto the barren rock of the earth, a semiaquatic arthropod pioneer whose descendants would include crabs, lobsters, and eventually insects. The land, meanwhile, was changing. Plants, which had also progressed from microscopic algae to more complex forms like seaweed, managed to grow on the inhospitable crust of the earth, crumbling the stone into soil with their roots and forming the first layer of field and forest.

Back in the ocean, predators even more terrible than the giant sea scorpion emerged: fish. These creatures had backbones; the more sophisticated ones, called the teleosts, had symmetrical fins that propelled them swiftly and surely through the water and fearsome jaws for snapping and devouring prey. ("Teleost" comes from the Greek words for "complete" and "bone.") These swimmers were so successful that the next stage in evolutionary history, the Devonian period, is called the Age of the Fishes. Five hundred million years ago, fish dominated the world. Not surprisingly, it was in the teleost fish, particularly the best studied of them, the salmon, that stress in many of its modern senses truly made its debut.

Fish as Exemplars of Stress

Teleosts exemplify the true fight-or-flight response. Salmon, for example, have need of both fight and flight. Though they started off as predators, as evolution proceeded, they also became prey to larger fish, birds, bears, and humans. In preparation for any challenge from the environment, salmon have the same set of responses as humans do—involving the brain, cardiovascular system, glands, and immune system. And in salmon, as in humans, these responses pivot around the HPA axis.

The HPA axis makes its appearance very dramatically in teleost fish like the salmon. Earlier fish, such as the lamprey, which may be the most primitive vertebrate alive today, have a few brain regions and hormones that may be slightly similar. But in the salmon the entire system is suddenly fully operational, and the ensuing 400 million years of evolution have not made many substantive changes. A salmon has a hypothalamus, a pituitary gland, and kidneys containing adrenal-like tissue that produces cortisol. Salmon have very well defined immune systems, including white blood cells called T cells, which search out and destroy invaders such as bacteria, and they have B cells, which form antibodies for future protection. In salmon, as in humans, cortisol replenishes glucose reserves and inhibits the immune system. Salmon have the so-called autonomic nervous system, which regulates involuntary processes by sending its branches into the organs, blood vessels, and glands. They also have a rudimentary limbic system, the counterpart of the brain structures that process emotions in humans.

According to Carl Shreck, zoologist at Oregon State University, salmon present a paradigm shift in the concept of stress—from just any threat to homeostasis to a condition that specifically activates the stress response systems, particularly the HPA axis. A bacterium safeguards its homeostasis by producing heat shock proteins, but in salmon an event or situation can be called stressful only if it sets in motion the precise chain of nervous system and hormonal responses associated with stress. Not everything that endangers a salmon sets off the HPA axis. For example, the metal cadmium, a common pollutant in heavy mining areas, is lethal to fish. Even though there is no greater threat to homeostasis than death, fish that die from cadmium exposure do so without showing any of the classic signs of stress; the metal acts as a general anesthetic and simply puts them into a permanent sleep. So cadmium, deadly though it is, cannot be considered to cause stress in the modern sense of the word. But copper, an equally lethal toxin, is an unqualified stressor. It kills the fish by driving up cortisol levels and sending the HPA axis into overdrive.

Interestingly, salmon will swim right into waters laced with cadmium, but they have been observed to avoid copper if they can. This distinction brings in another aspect of stress as we know it—not only the fight-or-flight response, as evinced by HPA activation, but also the beginnings of fear. Salmon will avoid anything that sets off the HPA axis. "Virtually anything that can 'scare' the fish can cause the full range of stress responses," says Shreck, "a bad smell or slapping the water to sound like a bird striking the surface. Humans may never know how (or even if) salmon experience fear, but if the HPA axis is triggered, the perception of risk is there as well."

If the salmon's fight-or-flight response is invoked repeatedly by circumstances, the final aspect of stress emerges: allostatic load, when the systems designed for protection and adaptation become overwhelmed. Overcrowding is a stressor for salmon, stimulating all of the stress responses—overactivating the adrenal glands and stifling the immune system. Overcrowding also halts the maturation process in young salmon. Salmon are born in fresh river water and swim downriver to the ocean where they live as adults. The transformation of the fish from river dwellers into creatures that can live in saltwater is called smoltification. Recall that under conditions of extreme stress growth is a luxury that is postponed until the crisis has passed. Among overcrowded fish, smoltification does not occur.

The most striking example of allostatic load in salmon, though, is the one stressor that the fish do not try to avoid: the trek back upriver to the waters of their birth, where they spawn the next generation. The journey can be as much as 1,000 miles, depending on the species. The salmon take their time, averaging 25 miles a day, but they don't swim constantly; sometimes they rest in the river for a month or so. The trip can take up to nine months and is initiated by a rise in cortisol.

Migrating salmon show signs of severe stress. When they begin their migration, they stop feeding and the digestive tract atrophies. By the time they spawn, the high levels of cortisol have exhausted their stores of energy and devastated their immune systems; most dying salmon show massive infection. Prolonged exposure to cortisol is the presumed cause of death.

The whole reason for the migration is to produce the next generation of salmon, so in the cortisol-soaked salmon, unlike other chronically stressed animals, reproduction is not a luxury system to be put on hold. Far from it; the sex glands continue to mature and the sex hormones skyrocket. In fact, biologists consider death by cortisol to be programmed into the salmon. With their energy reserves depleted, adult salmon could not make it back to the sea without feeding again. The waters where they spawn, such as those in the Pacific Northwest and Alaska, are fed by snowmelt and are too poor in nutrients to feed both the adults and the hatchlings. So it's in the best interest of the species for the adults to die after laying and fertilizing the eggs, and cortisol brings about this necessary turn of events. (In a grisly variation on the theme, some biologists think that the salmon may indirectly become food for the hatchlings themselves, as their decomposing bodies increase the microscopic organisms that nourish zooplankton, on which the newly hatched salmon feed.)

Allostasis as a Coping Mechanism

Death by cortisol is the most clear-cut example of the "bad" side of the allostatic process; it's also the most extreme. In most species, allostasis kicks in to help the animal adjust to changes in the environment. John Wingfield, a zoologist at the University of Washington, suspects that elevations in cortisol actually produce the behavioral changes through which birds, reptiles, and mammals cope with their world. This brings us back to one of our central dogmas: allostasis is what equips us to deal with stress—a concept played out again and again in the animal kingdom.

Many situations that we might consider stressful don't even evoke the stress response in animals. "It's a mistake to think that birds and animals are constantly battling the elements," observes Wingfield, an expert on the stress response in birds. "Many situations are a normal part of a wild animal's experience and don't affect circulating cortisol levels." For example, a creature as seemingly delicate as a goldfinch can withstand near-freezing temperatures without showing any rise in cortisol. Commonplace disturbances that trigger the fight-or-flight response include a prolonged severe storm or the loss of eggs to a predator. In these cases stress hormone levels quickly return to normal.

Unpredictable events, however, can trigger the stress response in a more lasting way, leading to adaptive changes in behavior. Animals whose feeding or nesting areas are repeatedly destroyed by storms or predators can react several ways. They can cease territorial and hierarchical behavior. They can hide or move away from whatever is threatening them. They can alter their metabolism to use fuel reserves during the disruption, and they can seek out and colonize a safer location.

Elevation of stress hormone levels provokes these behavioral changes. During severe storms, sparrows may abandon their nests and territory, showing elevated levels of corticosterone (similar to cortisol). This sad scenario is played out poignantly in Antarctica, once again showing the two-sided nature of the stress response. The king penguins of the Antarctic lay their eggs on the ice, sometimes miles inland from the ocean that provides their food. The birds take turns guarding their young; one parent forages in the ocean for up to several weeks, while the other stands over the chick. In a 1988 study a French research team periodically captured the birds for brief periods and measured their blood cortisol levels. The researchers found that initially the fasting parent penguin could draw on its reserves of fat without any increase in cortisol. But as fat stores were depleted, cortisol levels rose to mobilize body proteins for energy. This is a short-term, emergency measure, of course. Eventually, if the penguin's mate does not come to its relief, the penguin will abandon the nest and return to the ocean rather than risk starving to death. This grim decision is triggered, or at least accompanied, by an even steeper rise in cortisol.

Allostasis in terms of the HPA axis induces many other adaptive changes in animals. In mammals it facilitates feeding and foraging, exploration, avoidance behavior, and learning retention. In some toad species the tadpoles react to the stress of living in a dried-up pond by speeding up the rate at which they become land dwellers; this metamorphosis, too, is a function of increased corticosterone. If the stress continues after the tadpole becomes a toad, the amphibian's growth can be impaired. But the initial response, which turns it into an animal more suited to life on land, gives it a fighting chance.

So if allostasis is a robust dynamic coping mechanism that's been around for 500 million years, how did humans—during the blink of an eye in geological time—manage to turn it into a recipe for stress-related disease? The issue is neatly implied in the title of a book by neuroendocrinologist Robert Sapolsky of Stanford University: *Why Zebras Don't Get Ulcers*. A zebra's stress response kicks in when the zebra is chased by a lion; when the zebra escapes (or gets eaten), the stress response shuts off. In between predation attempts, the zebra is at ease; it doesn't flood itself with stress hormones wondering when the next lion is going to show up.

Animals can experience allostatic load in a quite "human" fashion when subjected to repeated or ongoing stress. In Hans Selye's experiments of the 1930s, rats exposed to a variety of stressful treatments got ulcers, and monkeys and dogs can get them too. Animals can show stress-related wear and tear even in the wild. But in general they tend not to experience allostatic load because once a stressful situation is over, the stress response subsides. For the most part, only humans can keep the HPA axis going indefinitely. We can do this because of how our faculties of perception, thought, and emotion are produced in the brain and how they are connected to the stress response.

The Power of the Brain

Stress begins in the brain. As far as we know, only humans can become stressed out from things that exist in idea only, such as by performing a mental rehash of an old argument until it sparks the release of adrenaline and activates the autonomic nervous system, causing a rise in fibrinogen and aggravating a case of clogged arteries.

Viewed against the power at its command, the human brain is an unimpressive-looking organ. It weighs about 3 pounds, occupies about the same volume as half a gallon of milk in a plastic bag, and consists of convoluted grayish tissue. The brain's massive processing power comes from its 100 billion cells called neurons, each one making contact with about 10,000 others. Messages are sent among these neurons through direct electrical charge and by means of chemicals, mainly neurohormones and others called neurotransmitters. Although most of these neurons are present at birth, the interconnections are formed based on input from the outside world, in a phenomenon known as plasticity. Whatever a child is exposed to—love, music, reading, violence—will become incorporated into both the functioning and the very structure of that child's brain.

The brain evolved from the inside outward. Paul MacLean of the National Institute of Mental Health uses the concept of the "triune brain." The oldest part of the nervous system—the spinal cord and the brain stem just above it—he calls the proto-reptilian brain. It's the engine room where the fundamentals chug away—like heartbeat, respiration, blood pressure regulation, muscular reflexes, thirst, and reaction to temperature change. Next comes the old mammalian brain or old cortex, an area that surrounds the brain stem and includes the so-called limbic system. From the limbic system arise the needs and reactions that eventually become emotions—searching for food, fighting, mating, and bonding with offspring. The most recent part of the brain is the cortex. Every vertebrate has one, but in humans the cortex is much larger and more highly developed. MacLean calls the human cortex "the brain of reading, writing, and arithmetic." The cortex controls all voluntary muscles and allows the brain to function as an integrated whole. The forward part, the prefrontal cortex, houses the functions most directly associated with thought: self-awareness, abstract thinking, and many kinds of memory.

Memory is one of the most important aspects of allostasis, since in order for us to perceive something as stressful we must remember that it—or something like it—has caused us trouble in the past. The degree of trouble—just how unpleasant the event was—equates to the level of emotion we feel in desiring to avoid it again. And these two things, memory and emotion, began not in the abstract contemplative neocortex but earlier in the limbic system.

The term *limbic system* was originally used to mean the center of emotions. In the intervening years scientists have begun to tease out not only the structures but also the circuits through which emotions are processed, so the concept of a single emotion center is a bit passé. Two structures in particular that are part of the limbic system and that play important roles in both emotion and memory are inseparable from the stress response: the hippocampus and the amygdala.

Stress, Emotion, and Memory

The hippocampus is a 2-inch-long, banana-shaped formation (its name is from the Greek word for sea horse) located deep in the brain on a level with a line drawn from the eye to the ear. Declarative and episodic memories—those that help us keep track of episodes or events in our daily lives and remember what happened to us, whom we met, and what we read or heard—take shape in the hippocampus. Spatial memory, which helps us orient and find our way, is also a function of the hippocampus. In birds and animals that store food for the winter and must remember where they stored it, the hippocampus is enlarged. Studies in humans show a similar role. For example, London taxi drivers spend two years or more in a course they call "The Knowledge" to pass a difficult examination about the streets of their city. In one imaging study, when London taxi drivers were asked to imagine a route from, say, Paddington Station to Covent Garden, their hippocampi revealed intense activity. More recently, the same investigators reported that the hippocampus of a London cab driver is larger than average and may even increase in size with the length of time on the job.

Because daily life for humans centers on verbal communication, verbal memories assume paramount importance in this structure. The hippocampus seems to be more associated with memory formation than memory storage—damage to the hippocampus leaves memories of the past intact.

The human brain is particularly good at storing memories with strong emotional content, positive or negative, such as memories of where we were and what we were doing when we proposed marriage or learned about an award, a promotion, or a bonus. By the same token, strong memories often occur when there is bad news, such as the death of President Kennedy or the terrorist attacks of September 11. Most people remember exactly what they were doing when they heard of these events.

Emotional memories can form instantaneously, in part because the hippocampus acts as a monitor of reality, comparing the outside world with the brain's representations of it. A sudden change will send the hippocampus into action and will also involve the amygdala if there is fear or even strong positive emotion involved. Working with the amygdala, the hippocampus forms conscious memories of emotional events. Thus we remember where we were and what we were doing during times of great emotional significance. We don't have to reinforce these memories through study, as we might have to do with information that's less personally resonant, like the names of all of the presidents in chronological order.

A powerful emotion can sear a memory into the brain's very structure, and this takes place in the foundry of the amygdala. The amygdala, named after the Greek word for almond, is an appropriately almond-shaped structure adjacent to the hippocampus. A frightening experience activates the amygdala immediately, without having to travel up to the ivory tower of the thinking, reasoning cortex. Down in the iron-works of the amygdala, stress hormones cast perceptions, memories, emotions, and sensations into a sometimes unbreakable mold. Even before memories are formed, the amygdala activates the stress hormone pathways through a massive infrastructure of nerves, galvanizing the nervous system to reactions such as combat or escape.

Joseph LeDoux of New York University calls the amygdala the "low road." The presence of this low road is why we are all here. It's a built-in survival mechanism that prompts us to escape first and ask questions later. To use Sapolsky's imagery, a zebra would not survive long if it habitually said to itself, "Hang on—maybe that's not a lion; maybe it's just a patch of dead grass." The zebra is infinitely safer assuming the straw-colored shape is a lion and running for its life. So the visual stimulus goes straight to the amygdala; only later does it work its way up through the visual cortex for processing and analysis.

A memory manufactured completely in the amygdala will be a nameless nonspecific sense of fear or dislike; many phobias and inexplicable aversions take shape here. The hippocampus brings such a memory into consciousness by providing context, such as time and place. In his book *The Emotional Brain*, LeDoux tells a story well known in neuroscience circles, which illustrates the difference between memories arising from the amygdala and from the hippocampus.

A woman had amnesia resulting from damage to her hippocampal system; she was unable to form new memories. Her doctor had to reintroduce himself, shaking hands with her every day because she never remembered having already met him. One morning he slipped a straight pin between two of his fingers, which pricked the patient as they shook hands. The next time they met she would not shake hands with him. Consciously, she remembered neither the doctor nor the pin; her damaged hippocampus had not supplied her with the details of who, what, and where. But the anonymous intelligence of the amygdala remembered the pain and gave her an equally important message: "Don't!"

Normally, humans spend very little time at the mercy of primal inaccessible memories. That's because the amygdala and the hippocampus have connections to the rational, analytical, "thinking" part of the brain, the cortex, and the cortex has powers of its own. For example, the cortex is one of the places where a process called extinction takes place. In classic Pavlovian conditioning, if a rat learns to associate the sound of a buzzer with a mild shock, the buzzer by itself will soon be enough to trigger the full range of fear responses. But if the rat hears the buzzer often enough without getting a shock, it will eventually lose its fear. This is extinction, and it's different from forgetting. Extinction is an active learning process, a repatterning of a new memory over an old one that takes place in the smartest brain area of all, the prefrontal cortex.

In humans the formidable prefrontal cortex is capable of overcoming instinctive amygdala-driven fears; we invoke its powers when we deliberately put ourselves in scary situations—by riding on roller coasters or visiting the reptile house at the zoo. Still, extinction is a slow process. More circuits, and bigger ones, go from the amygdala to the cortex than come back the other way. This imbalance is probably why psychotherapy is such a lengthy procedure. But LeDoux notes that evolution may ultimately even out the score: primates have more brain circuits going from the cortex back to the amygdala than do any other species. So it's possible that one day humans will evolve into a species where reason truly predominates.

In the meantime, though, the linkage of thoughts, emotions, and the stress response can be, like everything else having to do with stress, a double-edged sword. By using healthy coping mechanisms such as exercise, calming music, good company, and enlightening books, we can recruit our mind power to overcome the physiological responses to stress. But stress invariably creates negative emotions. Brooding and worrying about the stress we're under, in addition to whatever is causing the stress in the first place, can add to allostatic load. To really bring about an end to stress as we know it, we will need some help from the scientific community. And the first step is to understand just how the impressive, elegant mechanism of allostasis can go awry and cause disease.

Stress and the Emotional Connection

As early as 1914, Walter Cannon spoke of stress in its emotional aspect as well as its "engineering" sense (strain or force exerted on an object). But Hans Selye, in his early papers on the general adaptation syndrome, avoided the word *stress* entirely, precisely because it was popularly associated with nervous strain. In his groundbreaking 1936 *Nature* paper, "A Syndrome Produced by Diverse Nocuous Agents," the word *stress* did not appear. Throughout the 1940s, Selye used the word in the sense of an outside agent or force. Only in a 1950 book did he begin toying with the idea of stress as a response within an organism. At this point he began to reject use of the word *stress* to refer to outside stimuli and suggested *stressor* instead. (Selye took credit for inventing this word as well as for ushering his view of stress into the English language and for carrying it, like a missionary, into foreign lands.)

By the time *The Stress of Life* came out in 1956, Selye was willing to pay lip service to the idea of psychological stress. He began by saying: "The soldier who sustains wounds in battle, the mother who worries about her soldier son, the gambler who watches the races—whether he wins or loses—the horse and the jockey he bet on: they are all under stress." In saying this he went beyond putting psychological stress on a par with physical stress: in observing that the gambler experiences stress whether winning or losing, Selye acknowledged that happy experiences, too, can make certain demands on the body. But for the most part, even in *The Stress of Life*, Selye stuck to his final definition of stress as the nonspecific response of the body to any demand, and almost all of those demands were engineering ones—heat, cold, fatigue, pain. According to John Mason, the scientist who was soon to take up the research baton, Selye never liked to muddy his general adaptation syndrome with emotional stress—and he was not alone.

Selye's research was methodical and tidy. The events and stages of the general adaptation syndrome, and the list of nocuous agents that produce it, were precise and quantifiable. In the 1930s and 1940s, emotions were none of those things; they were considered, by their very nature, unscientific. Methodical quantifiable science would ultimately advance into the realm of the emotions, but that day had not yet arrived. Most conspicuously absent was a demonstrable link connecting the emotions, the stress response, and the brain.

I have made the claim that stress begins in the brain, giving the statement the same ring of scientific certainty as the idea that the earth revolves around the sun. But the scientists of Selye's day did not accept the brain as the master coordinator of the stress response. One might argue that stress has to begin in the brain. For the physiological mechanisms of fight or flight to be successfully sprung, an animal has to first perceive the intruder—by seeing, smelling, or hearing it—then call up past experience to decide whether to run away or prepare to dine. Not executive-level decision making, perhaps, but a process associated with the brain nonetheless. But even this logical sequence of events was not universally accepted. At the end of the 19th century, William James, the father of modern psychology, proposed an alternate view. He suggested that there is only one basic state of physiological arousal and whether we describe it as love, rage, or terror depends on what's going on in our surroundings. If we experience heart palpitations, shortness of breath, and lightheadedness in the presence of a lover, we describe our affliction as love; but the same symptoms evoked by a prowler are ascribed to fear. James's philosophy is pithily summed up with the maxim, "You're not running because you're scared; you're scared because you're running."

Nor were emotions considered to be the province of the brain. Despite what Hippocrates said about laughter, tears, and rage originating in the brain, the brain was not considered an emotional organ until the 1950s when Paul McLean of the National Institute of Mental Health identified the structures he called the limbic system. In the 1980s, Joe LeDoux of New York University teased out the circuits revealing the amygdala as the crux of the fear response, and Wayne Drevets and Mark Raichle of Washington University, St. Louis, used brain imaging techniques to show that the amygdala and other structures were active during emotional responses.

But even leaving out emotions and supposing that William James was wrong and that the stress response does begin once something is acknowledged as dangerous, the scientists of Selye's day were still at an impasse. They knew that the horsepower for both the stress response and the emotions was provided by the endocrine system, under the supremacy of the so-called master gland, the pituitary. They knew that the early phase of the fight-or-flight response was activated by the brain through a direct hookup of nerves—called the sympathetic nervous system—to the major organs. But the phase that Selye was now calling stress—the general adaptation syndrome—worked through a chemical signal originating, or so his contemporaries thought, in the pituitary and activating the adrenal cortex, resulting in the production of cortisol. This relay—the pituitary-adrenal part of the hypothalamic-pituitary-adrenal axis that recruits the endocrine glands and immune system—scientists were unable to attribute to the brain: no network of nerves running from the brain to the pituitary had been found.

So how could Selye's methodically characterized syndrome be triggered by something arising in the shadowlands of the mind? Suppose, for example, that a mouse could picture a cat in its tiny mind and, in doing so, could activate its whole range of stress response mechanisms. This would mean that somewhere in the mouse's brain a signal was produced and ferried, through unknown channels, to the endocrine system. It might also imply the reverse—that the hormones unleashed by the mouse's original encounter with the cat had left some sort of trace in the mouse's brain, so that a subsequent "thought" of the cat activated the same responses as the real thing. This in turn would mean that the brain must have some means of receiving input from the glands. Here the scientific community balked. If there was one thing researchers knew about the brain in the 1930s and 1940s, it was that it was part of the nervous system and not an endocrine gland.

New Look at an Old Idea

Many scientists were willing to accept the brain-emotion-body link at least conceptually, however. As early as the fourth century A.D., the Greek physician Galen established his theory that in every person one of four bodily fluids predominated, resulting in a particular personality type. A surfeit of blood resulted in romantic tendencies, while too much yellow bile made for choler, or a quick temper; phlegm led to apathy and black bile to melancholy. The terminology persisted well into Shakespeare's time. In *Richard II*, when the Duke of Norfolk and the soon-to-be usurper Henry Bolingbroke accuse each other of treason, King Richard replies:

> Wrath-kindled gentlemen, be ruled by me:
> Let's purge this choler without letting blood.

During the 18th and early 19th centuries, as more became known about the biological and anatomical realities of the brain and body, the branch of medicine that would become known as psychosomatic medicine fell into disfavor. But in the latter 19th century, women plagued with symptoms that had no discernible cause were well known to Sigmund Freud, and beginning in World War I, army physicians recognized similar unattributable illnesses in soldiers traumatized by battle. These diseases became known by such names as functional neurosis, hysteria, and shell shock.

Some scientists thought that further investigation was warranted. In a 1928 address to the Massachusetts Medical Society, Walter Cannon said:

The doctor is properly concerned with the workings of the body and their disturbances, and he should have, therefore, a natural interest in the effects of emotional stress and in the modes of relieving it. The field has not been well cultivated. Much work still needs to be done in it. It offers to all kinds of medical practitioners many opportunities for useful studies. There is no more fascinating realm of medicine in which to conduct investigation. I heartily commend it to you.

Hans Selye's achievements, which delineated so carefully the physiological mechanisms of the stress response, cast a wide enough ripple through the scientific community to attract the attention of researchers who were attuned to Cannon's way of thinking and who could grasp the significance of the generalized adaptation syndrome for psychology and psychosomatic medicine. One such free spirit was John Mason, a young intern and resident at New York University, although he did not consider himself to be psychologically oriented at the time. "In the late 1940s I wanted to be a surgeon," says Mason. "But I kept coming up against the role that psychology played in the illnesses of my surgical patients. Four of my first five peptic ulcer patients were New York City taxi drivers, which I didn't think was likely to be a coincidence. As I evaluated patients with other classic psychosomatic disorders, such as ulcerative colitis or hypertension, a simple inquiry into their recent medical history often led to a session in which they aired their family problems or other sources of stress."

When Mason told his mentors in the surgical ward of his newfound interest, he drew about the same reaction that Selye had when he proposed to study the general adaptation syndrome. "They looked at me a bit fish-eyed and suggested I study psychiatry," Mason remarks.

Mason took courage, though, from a 1948 publication by Sir Geoffrey Harris, an anatomist at the University of Oxford. Harris had put the H in the HPA axis. His research showed that a tiny network of blood vessels led from the base of the hypothalamus to the pituitary gland just below it. Now, for the first time, there was a plausible route by which the brain could send communications to the endocrine system, via the pituitary. Harris called his discovery the portal-hypophysial capillary system (hypophysis being an old term for the pituitary gland), and he proposed that through this system the brain secreted hormones of its own and activated the endocrine glands.

How the Brain Uses Its Chemical Messengers

Scientists already knew that the nervous system relayed signals throughout its own territory using chemical messengers known as neurotransmitters. The first neurotransmitter, acetylcholine, was discovered in the 1920s by a German physiologist named Otto Loewi. Loewi was studying the vagus nerve, which originates in the "old brain," the brain stem, and sends projections into the intestines, lungs, and heart. The vagus nerve slows the contractions of the heart muscle, and Loewi wanted to find out how. He put a frog's heart, still beating and with the vagus nerve attached, in a dish filled with fluid and electrically stimulated the vagus nerve until the heart stopped. Then he took the fluid surrounding the first heart and added it to a dish with a second heart; this time the fluid itself, minus the vagus nerve, was enough to still the heart. Loewi concluded that when the vagus nerve was stimulated, it produced some chemical that had the heart-stopping effect; within about five years he had identified the chemical as acetylcholine. Research throughout the next few decades showed that acetylcholine is one of the chief neurotransmitters in the brain.

"The medicinal properties of certain drugs that block acetylcholine receptors were recognized and employed in medical practice for hundreds of years before anyone had ever heard of neurotransmitters," observes Solomon Snyder of Johns Hopkins University in his classic work, *Drugs and the Brain*. One such drug was the plant belladonna, which could be medicinal or deadly depending on the dose. Snyder wrote:

> Extracts of the belladonna plant have been used since the days of Hippocrates to treat intestinal disturbances, slowing down intestinal contractions and reducing acid secretion in the stomach. In the Middle Ages, these belladonna alkaloids were also used as poisons; lethal doses were observed to cause memory loss, disorientation, and destruction of other mental faculties before the victim finally succumbed. In fact, Carolus Linnaeus, the founder of modern botanical nomenclature, named the plant Atropa belladonna after Atropos, the oldest of the Three Fates, who was said to cut the thread of life after her sisters had spun and measured it.

The active ingredient of belladonna, atropine, was isolated in the mid-1800s; in the 1930s it was shown to block a receptor for acetylcholine.

Because memory loss and dementia ensue when atropine blocks this receptor, scientists surmised that acetylcholine plays an important role in memory. In fact, acetylcholine-containing nerves are thought to handle information processing in the cerebral cortex, where higher brain functions such as memory take place. The loss of memory and even self, so devastating to those whose loved ones have Alzheimer's disease, is due in part to the death of neurons that supply acetylcholine.

Many more neurotransmitters were identified up through the 1960s using the same basic approach as Otto Loewi's. The procedure was to test the substance for its effect, usually on the heart or intestinal muscles of a frog, purify it, establish its chemical structure, make it synthetically, and finally show that the synthetic material had all the properties of the natural factor. Neurotransmitters identified this way include adrenaline, known for its role in the early phase of the stress response; gamma amino butyric acid, an "inhibitory" neurotransmitter that tells other neurons to become less active; and glutamate, an "excitatory" neurotransmitter that tells neurons on the receiving end to speed up. Also discovered were dopamine and serotonin, well known to many science enthusiasts for their roles in mood and behavior.

Not What—But Where

Neurotransmitters have many different roles in the brain and cannot be labeled according to any one function. For example, serotonin is not intrinsically a sedative or an antidepressant, even though low levels of serotonin are usually found in persons suffering from depression, and antidepressant drugs work in part by making serotonin available to nerve cells for longer periods. Serotonin plays many other roles in the brain depending on where it is being used and which of the many types of receptors are responding to it; it can play a role in appetite, libido, and the effects of drugs, depending on where in the brain it is functioning.

For anyone interested in stress and the brain, the interaction between neurotransmitters and their receptors is one of the most important relationships in biology. When a neurotransmitter hooks up with the right receptor, the result can be an emotion, a memory, a jolt of pain, the relief of pain, activation of the HPA axis, or a signal that the fight-or-flight response is no longer needed. Receptors are most often described using a lock-and-key analogy: the neurotransmitter (the key) leaves the neuron sending the message and attaches to a receptor (the lock) in the receiving neuron, where it triggers a further series of events in that cell. In reality, there's more to it than that. A receptor is actually a highly complex molecule designed to respond to a specific neurotransmitter in a specific way. For example, there are 14 different receptors for serotonin that scientists know about, to say nothing of the ones we don't know about.

The neurotransmitter-receptor relationship is not limited to the brain, however. The term *neurotransmitter* is commonly used to refer to any of the brain's chemical messengers. But that word is correct only when the messenger travels from one neuron to another. When such a messenger acts on a gland, it is more correctly described as a neurohormone. Sir Geoffrey Harris's 1948 discovery of the portal hypophysial capillary system—that is, the tiny blood vessels connecting the brain and the pituitary gland—opened up the possibility that neurohormones exist, but more than 20 years went by before the first one was identified.

The delay was due partly to the skepticism that greeted Harris's publication but also to the enormous difficulty of isolating neurochemicals that were present—if they existed at all—in tiny amounts. To appreciate the scarcity of these chemicals, consider that Harris's entire capillary system takes up about as much space as the eraser on the end of a pencil. Two researchers named Roger Guillemin and Andrew Schally began to collaborate on the search for these chemicals in the 1950s, but in one of the most famous duels in the history of science, they became enemies and spent the next two decades in bitter competition searching for hypothalamic hormones. Guillemin and Schally searched through truckloads of brain tissue collected from slaughterhouses, trying to follow the classic discovery method that had revealed the neurotransmitters—injecting extracts into rats to observe the effect on the pituitary, working out the chemical structure of the extract, and then synthesizing the chemical to see if the imitation had the same effect as the original.

In a photo finish about a month apart in 1971, Guillemin and Schally each published their finding of a hormone produced by the brain that stimulates a gland—not the pituitary in this case but the thyroid gland. The new discovery techniques led to the identification of other hypothalamic hormones, such as gonadotropin-releasing hormone, which regulates the sex glands, and growth hormone. Finally, as recently as 1983, Wylie Vale of the Salk Institute (a protegé of Guillemin) announced his team's discovery of the hormone everyone was waiting for: corticotropin-releasing factor, the one that kicks off the stress response. Sir Geoffrey had been proven correct, and the picture of how mental stress activates the stress response was finally becoming clear.

Meanwhile

Back in the 1950s, however, John Mason didn't need the actual chemical structure of the releasing hormones to tell him that he was onto something with his ulcer-riddled cab drivers. In 1953 he set up a department of neuroendocrinology—the study of the interactions between the nervous and endocrine systems—in the new neuropsychiatry division of the Walter Reed Army Institute of Research in Washington, D.C. Also in the 1950s, revolutionary new techniques were making it possible to detect extremely small amounts of hormones, such as cortisol, in blood and urine—so that hormone levels could be tested before, during, and after stress.

The first thing Mason did was to go through the list of stimuli that Selye so quaintly described as nocuous. These included heat, cold, pain, fatigue, fasting, and something called nervous stress. Reading through Selye's studies carefully, Mason concluded that what Selye referred to as mere nervous stress probably meant immobilization—placing the rat in a cylinder that prevented it from moving freely. (The word *mere* also conveyed to Mason an unwillingness by many scientists to regard psychological stress, in addition to flesh-and-blood stimuli, as a factor that could influence endocrine function.)

Mason decided to repeat some of Selye's experiments and try to separate out psychological stress to see if that stress by itself could activate the general adaptation syndrome. The difficulty was in separating nocuous stimuli from nervous ones. Mason thought that even a rat would experience mental stress while being subjected to heat, cold, pain, or fatigue. With the immobilization experiment, on the other hand, there was no guarantee that the rat's distress was solely psychological; perhaps it was experiencing an "engineering" stress such as muscle strain from not being able to move. So how could he tell what sort of stress the rats were actually experiencing?

Mason chose to study the stress of fasting, and he used monkeys for his subjects. If lab monkeys are not fed, they will show the adrenal and immune abnormalities associated with the stress response. Mason had observed that in most fasting experiments the monkeys were housed in cages next to other monkeys acting as subjects for other unrelated studies. When the fasting monkeys had to watch their lab mates being brought dinner as usual, they became greatly upset. They also became agitated whenever their caretaker came into the lab, as if demanding to know where their food was.

Were the monkeys experiencing psychological stress—that is, were they anxious and angry from missing out on their meals? Or were they suffering from the bodily physiological stress of hunger and poor nourishment? Mason resolved to find out. To eliminate the mental strain of the experiment, he developed a placebo food—pellets that looked, smelled, and tasted like the monkeys' usual diet but without the nutritional content. These monkeys did not show any of the psychological signs of stress as measured by their stress hormone levels. Since fasting per se did not raise their levels of stress hormones, Mason concluded that when studying the effects of "physical" stress on the HPA axis the accompanying psychological stress was a powerful factor to which attention must be paid.

Mason and colleagues at Walter Reed get the credit for firmly establishing how psychological stimuli can affect the output of stress hormones. They perfected an experimental setup called the avoidance session, in which monkeys are trained to avoid a mild electric shock by pressing a hand lever when they hear a clicking sound. They demonstrated that the anticipation of a shock was more of a stressor than the shock itself. Monkeys who received shocks randomly, without being able to prevent them with the lever, quickly became accustomed to the sensation (which was not strong enough to be painful) and stopped showing hormonal responses. Mason also showed that novelty, uncertainty, and unpredictability—combined with the "responsibility" of having to press the lever—were particularly effective in elevating stress hormone output. Moreover, he found that suddenly changing the rules for a task, so that the previous responses were no longer effective in avoiding the shock, led to disorganized behavior and elevated stress hormone production. Thus, frustration is also a driving force for the release of stress hormones into the bloodstream.

How Hormones Affect the Brain

While research was going on into the means by which the brain could activate the endocrine glands, many researchers, including myself, were studying the other side of the coin: how hormones made their way back to the brain, affecting health and behavior. Earlier I said that, when an animal has a close encounter with danger, the memory is strong enough to ignite the stress response in advance the next time the same situation arises. This would suggest that stress hormones leave a biochemical trace in the brain. But this concept also met with resistance. Scientists still believed that the brain was a relatively isolated system that picked up oxygen and fuel from the blood but was otherwise cordoned off from the rest of the body. The brain was certainly not believed to contain receptors for chemicals produced by the glands.

Scientists were familiar with some of the effects of the stress hormone cortisol before we had any reason to believe that it acted in the brain. In the 1940s, Philip Hench of the Mayo Clinic in Rochester, Minnesota, identified cortisol as a substance that calms inflammations as well as conditions such as asthma, a discovery that won Hench a Nobel Prize in 1950. Cortisol was also known to regulate the metabolism of carbohydrates, such as glucose (hence the name glucocorticoid to refer to this class of hormones). But next to nothing was known about its action in the brain itself.

My interest in stress and stress hormones arose from my own explorations into how the external world around us, as well as our own experiences of it, can change the brain. This interest began while I was still in high school, studying science with a teacher named Lawrence Conray. Out of four of us from my high school class who went on to major in chemistry at Oberlin, three are still science professors at academic institutions—a testimony to the contributions of good high school teachers!

Then at Oberlin, when I was thinking about going to medical school, I had the good fortune to study psychology with a young assistant professor named Celeste McCullough. Her lectures linked up psychology and behavior with the brain's mechanisms in a particularly interesting area—the visual system. After a dull year with chemistry and calculus, I took an intriguing and refreshing course with Professor McCullough in which we explored the physics of visual perception and the mechanisms of seeing color; basically, we looked at paintings, such as those by impressionist and pointillist artists. This area, which was her specialty, awakened my interest in the brain.

Professor McCullough taught for only a few years before going on to work with the Air Force, but in that time she made a lasting impact with her research, not an easy thing to do at a small private college like Oberlin. She described a phenomenon called the McCullough effect, which is something that happens when you stare at a crisscross pattern consisting of two different colors, say, red horizontal lines crossed with green vertical ones. If you shift your eyes to the same design in black and white, you'll see the complementary colors: green horizontal and red vertical lines. This afterimage is considered to be a conditioned reflex because the effect becomes stronger with repetition. Professor McCullough also stirred the imaginations of a few other students who went on to become noted neuroscientists, including Larry Squire of the University of California at San Diego, whose research has contributed much of what we know about memory in the brain, and Bob Wurtz of the National Eye Institute, who has provided a good chunk of the wiring diagram for how the brain processes visual information.

I lost track of Dr. McCullough, but a few years ago, after I had given a talk on allostasis and allostatic load at Arizona State University, a gray-haired lady came up to me and said, "Dr. McEwen, I'm sure you won't remember me, but my name is Celeste McCullough." I remembered her, all right! I gave her a big bear hug and said that I'd been waiting 40 years to thank her for firing up my interest in the brain.

Unlike Hans Selye and John Mason, I didn't have to pursue my interests over the objections of my mentors. After deciding on a career in research instead of medicine, I did my doctoral work at Rockefeller University in New York City, where I spent a lot of time listening to Professors Alfred Mirsky and Vincent Allfrey talk about a subject that was then in its infancy: the possibility that environmental factors could influence the expression of genes, particularly genes in the brain. This was heady stuff in the early 1960s. James Watson and Francis Crick had determined the double-helix configuration of DNA only in 1953, for which they won a Nobel Prize in 1962. Scientists were just beginning to understand RNA, the interim molecule that makes protein from the instructions contained in DNA.

Many people tend to think of genes as diminutive unexploded bombs that contain inherited diseases or traits desirable or undesirable. It's true that we can inherit genes that make us vulnerable to certain diseases ranging from cancer to depression. In some diseases, called autosomal dominant disorders, a gene truly is a time bomb—as with Huntington's disease or cystic fibrosis—in that someone who inherits the "bad" gene will eventually develop the disease. Many characteristics of personality, such as a propensity for risk taking, are also proving to be at least in part genetically based.

But genes are not mere carriers; their role is far more fundamental and more complex. Everything that happens in the body and many things that happen in the mind are the result of a gene being activated. The manufacture of structural proteins like bones and muscle, and of enzymes, antibodies, hormones, and neurotransmitter receptors, takes place when the information in the relevant gene is "translated" into a protein; at this point the gene is made reality; it is, as scientists say, expressed.

Hearing my professors talk about gene expression in response to the environment was intriguing. Those conversations, combined with a latent interest from Celeste McCullough's classes, stayed with me after I left Rockefeller University to do postdoctoral work at the University of Minnesota. I was just beginning my studies there when Alfred Mirsky told me about an opening at Rockefeller in a field that was then becoming known as behavioral science. I packed my bags and went back to Rockefeller in 1966, to begin studying how hormones regulate genes in the brain to bring about behavioral changes.

Finding Hormone Receptors in the Brain

The first challenge was to establish whether hormones could get into the brain at all and, if so, how. We started by studying female sex hormones, the estrogens, because everyone knows that sex hormones influence behavior, and some scientists at the time were fairly certain that this occurs through direct action on the brain. Studies already conducted at Rockefeller University had shown that if you took a female rat whose ovaries had been removed and injected estradiol (one of the estrogens) directly into the hypothalamus, the rat would come into heat. Since the signal for this change couldn't be coming from the ovaries, which had been removed, the hormone must have exerted a direct effect on the brain.

Just how this might happen was becoming clear thanks to another group of scientists who were working with cells in the uterus. These scientists used radioactive material to "label" the estradiol and then added it to a culture dish containing cells from the uterine wall. The hormone, glowing with the radioactive tag, could be seen binding to receptors inside the cell, then traveling into the cell nucleus. Here the receptor, with hormone attached, stimulated the expression of genes that enable the uterus to grow and develop sufficiently to support a fetus.

Was it possible that estradiol made a similar connection inside cells in the brain? There was a way to find out. A third group had established methods for identifying and measuring the protein receptors that bind estradiol. One of my graduate students, Richard Zigmund, set about using these methods to look for estrogen receptors in the brain. He zeroed in on the hypothalamus, already established as an estrogen-sensitive area by another Rockefeller colleague, Donald Pfaff, and made a finding that would once have been startling but by now was what we suspected: the hypothalamus contains estrogen receptors just as the uterus does. Subsequently, several labs, including ours, showed that when estradiol comes in contact with cells in the hypothalamus, its action is comparable to its effect on uterine cells; the hormone "turns on" several genes that make changes in the cell's functioning. In the case of the hypothalamus, one of these changes is the production of receptors for a neurotransmitter called oxytocin, which plays an important role in female sexual behavior.

So now we had shown that sex hormone receptors did exist in the brain and that, when the hormone bound to the receptor, a gene turned on that changed how the brain operated. The next question was whether a similar setup existed to explain the actions of stress hormones. To find out, the head of my laboratory, a famous psychologist named Neal Miller, suggested that I get together with another Rockefeller colleague who was on a parallel track. This was Jay Weiss, who was studying stress in a situation called learned helplessness.

In learned helplessness the stressor cannot be escaped. When rats are given a tone followed by a mild shock in one particular part of their cage, they quickly learn to move to the other side as soon as they hear the tone. When the rats move and then get shocked anyway—when they learn rules that are then suspended—it isn't long before they lose their ability to cope altogether. Even if the rules of the game are restored and the tone again precedes the shock as expected, the rats just huddle where they are. They haven't forgotten what to do. Rather, they have learned that they cannot escape the shock—in other words, they've learned that they are helpless. Learned helplessness has been extensively studied in many species and is thought to be a model of depressive illness in humans. One of the hallmarks of clinically depressed people is that they can't make changes to improve their lives; they are convinced that nothing they do will make any difference. Rats with learned helplessness, and humans with some kinds of depression, show apathetic behavior and high levels of cortisol.

The twin findings of elevated cortisol and depressive-type behavior led Jay to wonder, like me, if and how stress hormones acted in the brain. He and I decided to use the same methods that we were using for estradiol to study whether a radioactive form of the stress hormone corticosterone is taken up and retained in the brain.

We expected to find radioactive corticosterone uptake and retention in the hypothalamus, because the hypothalamus is the linchpin of the stress response. To our astonishment, although some corticosterone was taken up by cells in the hypothalamus, we found remarkable uptake and retention of corticosterone in another brain region, the hippocampus. Soon after that, Linda Plapinger and I extracted and characterized the cortisol receptors from the nucleus of cells in the hippocampus.

These experiments provided a scenario for the long-standing question of how stressful experiences could "get back" into the brain. Finding out what stress hormones do once they reach the brain, and when these processes are helpful versus harmful, would take many years to answer. We are still working on it and even coming up with additional questions, all of which I will discuss in further detail in Chapter 7. But about 1970, our research indicated that we had begun to close the loop. Harris, Mason, Guillemin, Schally, and Vale had shown how the brain could perceive a stressful event and initiate the hormonal responses to help the body cope. Now research began to show that the brain could, in turn, be influenced by these changes. And the revelation that the brain could be the target as well as the initiator of the stress response opened the door to understanding many of the problems and illnesses associated with allostatic load.

Allostatic Load: When Protection Gives Way to Damage

In the late 1980s the U.S. Department of Agriculture, under pressure from animal rights activists, suggested a change to the guidelines for the care of laboratory animals, which the USDA oversees. The department proposed that research monkeys housed individually (to meet the requirements of whatever study they were in) would henceforth be given an hour or so a week in a large enclosure with other monkeys. It was thought this would be a good way for the animals to relax, socialize, and enjoy themselves.

"Actually this is a good way to give a monkey a heart attack," says Robert Sapolsky at Stanford University. When unacquainted monkeys first meet, they need time to squabble and test each other, eventually establishing who's who. A few hours a week would not be enough; the animals would be returned to their individual cages before coming to an understanding. So the social hour would become a weekly brawl never to be resolved, beginning anew every time the monkeys got together—a setup likely to generate the very stress-related problems it was designed to prevent.

Sapolsky, a pioneer in the field of stress research, had previously studied wild monkeys that had been thrust into a cage all together for shipment to the United States. Many arrived dead, not from any noticeable injury but from the trauma of being trapped in a hostile environment. He and several other scientists convinced the USDA not to carry out the proposed change, and the stressor of social disruption never became a federally mandated animal-handling guideline.

This story illustrates the first of four ways in which the allostatic response can turn coat and become allostatic load: being activated too frequently when a person or animal is subjected to repeated, unrelieved, or unremitting stress. This does not involve a malfunction per se; even the most finely tuned stress response in the healthiest of individuals can begin to cause damage if activated again and again over a long period. In other words, chronic stress can cause illness, putting a strain on the heart, undermining the power of the immune system, and triggering processes that may lead to diabetes and other chronic illnesses. And as Sapolsky says in the preface to his book, under conditions of extreme and unusual stress (in some zoos, for example), zebras can sometimes get ulcers.

Allostatic Load Scenario Number One: Unremitting Stress

Chronic stress takes its toll most immediately on the heart. When the fight-or-flight response swings into action, one of the most important things the animal (or person) must do is to move quickly. So the first of the stress hormones, adrenaline, courses through the sympathetic nervous system to step up the heart rate, increasing blood pressure to drive more oxygen to the large muscles of the arms and legs. But these sudden surges, when activated too often, cause damage to the blood vessels in the coronary arteries. The sites of damage are places where the arteries become clogged with the sticky buildup that sets the stage for atherosclerosis.

In humans, too many sudden escalations in blood pressure can trigger myocardial infarctions (heart attacks) in blood vessels that have become clogged. Studies with primates show that stress can aggravate the clogging-up process. Jay Kaplan of Bowman Gray University made into an experiment the social disruption the USDA had proposed for laboratory monkeys. After weeks and months of shuffling the groups around, forcing the monkeys repeatedly to scramble for position, the resulting elevations in blood pressure sped up the process of athero-sclerosis and increased the risk of heart attacks. (Sapolsky and other scientists cited Kaplan's work when protesting the USDA's suggestion.)

Studies of social disruption in monkeys have parallels in the world of human doings. A striking example was observed in the British Civil Service (a fount of information about stress-related diseases) during the years of privatization under then-Prime Minister Margaret Thatcher. In a classic series called the Whitehall studies, blood pres-sure was found to be lowest among the highest grade of employees and highest among the rank and file (food for thought for those who believe that stress plagues only fast-track yuppies). But one study fo-cused on a department that was undergoing privatization during the years of Margaret Thatcher; in this department researchers found in-creases in body mass index, need for sleep, incidence of stroke, and cholesterol.

The British privatization effort was more radical than anything that has happened here in the United States. Thatcher took some big entities that had been parts of the government, including the telephone company and the electric utilities, and turned them into private com-panies, selling stock to investors and severing all ties to the govern-ment. Before, these groups were run as bureaucracies with a public mission, with civil service types of incentives and penalties—basically, a job for life if you did your work and kept your head down. After, they were private companies run for the benefit of their shareholders, with private-sector incentives and penalties—make more money and do things cheaper and better or you'll be fired. Privatization had essen-tially propelled the civil service employees into a situation very much like the one that confronted the monkeys in the social disruption stud-ies. The known social order, in which people knew their place and each person's place was secure, went up in smoke. Suddenly employees had to compete and produce, often for the first time in their professional lives.

Something similar occurred in Russia and Eastern Europe following the collapse of communism in 1989. A study that examined morbidity and mortality rates (that is, illness and death) showed a dramatic increase in both rates in virtually all Eastern European countries. Cardiovascular disease and hypertension were to blame for many deaths, but, interestingly, suicide and homicide also increased. In the former Soviet Union the change was most dramatic; the life expectancy for men dropped from 64 to 59 years. Once again, the status quo had been hopelessly jumbled, and people were no longer sure of their jobs, their homes, their government, or their place in society.

Of course, the situation in Eastern Europe and Russia is unlike that in the United Kingdom in many ways, making it difficult to pinpoint exact causes. In the U.K., all civil service employees had jobs and access to health care, something that was not the case in Russia and Eastern Europe. Moreover, when the causes of mortality were examined in the Eastern European studies, cardiovascular disease and alcoholism ranked very high. But, interestingly, so did deaths from accidents and violence in the form of murder and suicide. One could still argue that, in the wreckage of the former Soviet Union, health care and emergency services were in disarray, making death from such causes more likely than in a stable country like the United Kingdom (Margaret Thatcher notwithstanding). But the fact remains that instability takes a heavy toll on life and health.

Lowering Resistance to Illness

The immune system also suffers from unremitting stress. Most people can probably think of a time when they were under stress and always seemed to be getting a cold, and it's not their imagination. The connection between chronic stress and susceptibility to upper respiratory infection has been well explored by scientists. In times of sudden acute stress the immune system's activity is stepped up to prepare to deal with injury. But under conditions of chronic stress the immune system is temporarily squelched.

This effect is not always temporary, though, depending on just how chronic the stress is. Sheldon Cohen of Carnegie Mellon University asked some 300 volunteers to complete a questionnaire about stressful events in their lives and then inoculated them with common cold viruses and watched to see who would begin to show symptoms. The ones who fell sick were the ones who had reported stress that lasted for a month or longer, usually in the form of unemployment or ongoing difficulty with family or friends. This type of chronic stress carried an increased risk of catching a cold compared to subjects who reported stress of less than a month's duration.

Working with Jay Kaplan, Cohen studied the same connection in primates. Male cynomolgus monkeys were randomly assigned to stable or unstable social conditions and at the end of 15 months were exposed to an adenovirus, one of the common cold viruses. Unlike the results of Kaplan's experiments with social disruption and cardiovascular disease, this time colds were not a direct response to upheaval; the animals in the unstable groups were not more likely to become infected. But the ones with lower social status in both groups were.

Clearly, then, frequent overactivation of the stress response can overwhelm the body's ability to manage it properly. People who have had excessive stress in their lives, as measured by multiple episodes of living at the poverty level, show earlier aging, more depression, and an earlier decline of both physical and mental functioning. And individuals who were abused as children suffer an increased risk of depression, suicide, substance abuse, and earlier illness and death from a wide range of diseases.

Allostatic Load Scenario 2: Inability to Adjust

There are also situations in which, though the stress itself is not lengthy or severe, the body responds in a way that is inappropriate. Often we perceive a situation as stressful not because it imperils our survival but because it is unfamiliar and a bit challenging—a new job, perhaps, or a newly assumed position of leadership in the community. Once the alarming becomes commonplace, we cease to activate the fight-or-flight sequences. In some people, though, when an initially threatening experience becomes business as usual, the stress response doesn't get the message.

Clemens Kirschbaum and colleagues at the University of Trier subjected a group of 20 male volunteers to some of the most threatening events imaginable—public speaking and mental arithmetic in front of an audience for five consecutive days. The investigators measured the cortisol in saliva samples taken from the subjects on each day. Most of the men became comfortable "on stage" by the second day, and their cortisol levels diminished accordingly. But seven of them showed no discernible difference in their reported discomfort or in their cortisol levels between days 1 and 2 and only a very slight decrease by day 5. Perhaps not coincidentally, a personality questionnaire revealed that the still-stressed men had low self-confidence and self-esteem. In short, the men were not able to habituate to an experience that was no longer novel. Although no particular diseases or symptoms were matched up to this group (which Kirschbaum dubbed "high responders"), it's likely they were overexposing their bodies to stress hormones under many circumstances in daily life that other people might not consider stressful. And we know, for example, that frequent jumps in blood pressure are a risk for cardiovascular disease.

One study turned up a closer correlation between people's stress levels in the lab and in their day-to-day lives. Karen Matthews and colleagues at the University of Pittsburgh studied a group of employed middle-aged men and women. Again, volunteers were put through the torture of public speaking in a laboratory while plugged into equipment that monitored their vital signs. In the ensuing 24 hours, the participants wore a cuff that recorded their blood pressure every half hour; at the same time, they reported how they felt. Those whose blood pressure shot up during the public-speaking test showed the same elevation when they reported feelings of stress throughout the day. But on other days when they weren't feeling stressed, the same people did not show elevations in blood pressure during the test. Thus our reactions to situations depend very much on our current emotional status and what other things we are experiencing.

Allostatic Load Scenario 3: Not Hearing the "All-Clear"

Most of us can probably remember repeatedly rehashing an argument or other stressful scene, getting worked up all over again until our friends grew tired of hearing about it. For some people this condition is chronic; they continue to mount an allostatic response long after the stressful event has ended, and here there is evidence that genes may play a role. Bill Gerin and Tom Pickering of the Hypertension Center at Cornell University gave an arithmetic test to more than 500 undergraduate volunteers, measuring heart rate and blood pressure before, during, and after the test. They were interested in seeing whether differences in cardiovascular response could be attributed to the students' race, sex, or parental history of hypertension. It turned out that none of these factors had anything to do with cardiovascular response while the test was going on. But afterwards, a certain percentage of the students still showed elevated blood pressure. Even though the stress was over, their systems were not able to recover and return to baseline. Most of these subjects had two parents with hypertension, suggesting they were genetically ill disposed to let go of a stressful situation.

Failure to shut off the sympathetic nervous system and the hypothalamic-pituitary-adrenal (HPA) axis when appropriate may also be a function of aging, as animal studies show, although there is less evidence for this in humans. In some aging laboratory animals, stress-induced secretions of both cortisol and adrenaline return to baseline more slowly than in normal animals. In humans the "negative feedback" effects of cortisol (by which it tells the brain to ease off on some aspects of the stress response) don't work as well in the elderly.

Stress Hormone Overdose

All of the above three scenarios involve long-term overexposure to adrenaline and cortisol, whether it's because the stress itself goes on too long, because the system cannot accommodate the fact that the situation should no longer be stressful, or because the shutoff processes are not functioning. Stress hormones do more than raise blood pressure and stifle the immune system. For example, cortisol is often chronically elevated in depression, and some women with a history of depressive illness have decreased bone mineral density. This is because bone formation is one of those long-term luxuries that get played down as part of the fight-or-flight response; cortisol actually interferes with the processes by which bone is formed. Prolonged exposure to cortisol has been shown to create allostatic load in women undergoing intense athletic training; though exercise may not seem stressful to the athlete, when carried to an abusive extreme it elevates both the sympathetic nervous system and the HPA axis. Results can include weight loss, lack of menstruation, and anorexia, a condition often related to exercise extremism.

Chronically elevated cortisol can also dampen the effects of insulin, and indeed chronic stress—defined as feelings of fatigue, lack of energy, irritability, demoralization, and hostility—has been linked to the development of insulin resistance, a risk factor for type II or non-insulin-dependent diabetes.

It's also possible that overactivation of the stress response over a lifetime may undermine the whole process of allostasis itself, causing the systems to wear out and become exhausted. One particularly vulnerable link is the hippocampus, which helps turn off the HPA axis after stress and is also a nexus of memory and cognition. Because the hippocampus is rich in receptors for cortisol, using levels of this hormone to play its "checks-and-balances" role in the stress response, it is one of the first targets when levels of cortisol get too high. According to the so-called glucocorticoid cascade hypothesis, when the hippocampal region of the brain is flooded with cortisol, the resulting wear and tear leads to both an improperly functioning HPA axis and cognitive impairment.

The hippocampus's major role in episodic and declarative memories means that it is involved in remembering daily events and information, such as shopping lists and names of people, places, and things. The hippocampus is also important for the memory of context—the time and place of events, particularly those that have a strong emotional significance. Excessive levels of stress hormones interfere with the formation and retrieval of these memories, including those associated with context. This may add even more stress by blocking the informational input needed to decide that a situation is not a threat. For example, suppose someone averse to office politics finds himself in the deep end of a dicey negotiation. High levels of cortisol may leave him unable to remember who's likely to be in his camp and who isn't and which names go with which faces. (Cortisol works in another part of the brain, too: the amygdala, which plays a prominent role in forming long-term memories associated with fearful or traumatic events. The amygdala is also involved in what we might call anticipatory angst, the fears and anxieties that we harbor regardless of whether there is legitimate reason to worry. So increased stress hormone levels in the amygdala can make us fret even more, augmenting the stress we are already under.) Finally, the hippocampus is involved in the shutoff of the stress response. In sum, damage to this brain structure can both weaken our ability to perceive that something is not genuinely stressful and prevent the stress response from being shut off, thereby ratcheting up stress levels even higher.

Allostatic Load Scenario 4:
Too Little Is as Bad as Too Much

The idea of checks and balances in the stress response brings us to the final way in which the protective systems of allostasis can trigger the damage of allostatic load: when the stress response is insufficient, resulting in underproduction of the stress hormones, particularly cortisol, wear and tear can also result (see box on next page). How can this be? Surely if there are no stress hormones, there must be no stress and consequently no stress-related illness. But like most of human physiology, it isn't quite that simple. Cortisol acts somewhat like a thermostat; in fact, it clamps down on its own production. It slows the production of the two hormones that touch off the HPA axis: corticotropin-releasing factor in the hypothalamus and adrenocorticotropic hormone in the pituitary. Cortisol also reins in the immune system and reduces inflammation and swelling from tissue damage.

When one of the participants in a checks-and-balances arrangement isn't doing its job, the others may go overboard in doing theirs. In some people, allostatic load takes the form of a sluggish response by the adrenals and a subsequent lack of sufficient cortisol. The most immediate result is that the immune system, without cortisol's steadying hand, runs wild and reacts to things that do not really pose a threat to the body. Allergies are one example of this process. In most people the

---

Disorders Linked to Over- and Underproduction of Cortisol

Overproduction	*Underproduction*
Cushing's syndrome	Atypical/seasonal depression
Melancholic depression	Chronic fatigue syndrome
Diabetes	Fibromyalgia
Sleep deprivation	Hypothyroidism
Anorexia nervosa	Nicotine withdrawal
Excessive exercise	Rheumatoid arthritis
Malnutrition	Allergies
Obsessive-compulsive disorder	Asthma
Panic disorder	
Chronic active alcoholism	
Childhood physical and sexual abuse	
Functional gastrointestinal disease	
Hyperthyroidism	

---

immune system does not put things like dust and cat dander on a par with pathogenic (disease-causing) bacteria. But in people prone to allergies, the immune system goes on red alert in the presence of such usually innocuous substances, throwing everything it's got at the irritants: uncontrollable sneezing to expel the invaders, mucous secretion to entrap them, swelling caused by the influx of white blood cells to the infected area, pain, redness, and general misery. All of these symptoms are reduced by the action of cortisol.

Asthma is another example in which the small tubes called bronchioles in the lungs swell and constrict. Once again, the oversensitized system is trying to ward off things that are not actually harmful (such as dust, cold, and exercise), in this case by barring the portals of access to the lungs. Allergies and asthma are both considered inflammatory diseases, and they are classic signs of the type of allostatic load signaled by the underproduction of cortisol. People who suffer from these conditions notice that their symptoms worsen when they are under stress. Other kinds of inflammatory disorders are the so-called autoimmune diseases, in which the immune system fails in its prime directive—distinguishing "self" from "nonself"—and goes after the person's own body tissue. These conditions, too, are normally prevented by cortisol (and often treated with cortisol by doctors). Rashes are a prime example of the immune system attacking healthy skin; one type, atopic dermatitis, in children is a sign of both stress and an underresponsive HPA axis. Other autoimmune disorders, often exacerbated by stress, are rheumatoid arthritis, in which the joints are chronically inflamed, and multiple sclerosis, a degenerative disease in which the immune system destroys a part of the nervous system known as the myelin sheath.

A feeble HPA response can often manifest itself in conditions not always immediately associated with the immune system. Fibromyalgia, for example, is a condition of chronic pain that most doctors consider psychosomatic (and some consider imaginary, though the patients certainly don't). The connection with the immune system and cortisol becomes clear when we consider that pain is a part of the inflammatory response; pain warns us that there's a problem and encourages us to leave the affected area alone until the problem is resolved. But in many chronic pain states, as with other inflammatory disorders, there is no apparent threat. Rather, the system is responding in a maladaptive way, which the available supply of cortisol is too low to prevent.

Influencing the Course of Allostasis— For Good or Evil

It's important to remember that allostatic load is more than the experience of being under stress. It also reflects our lifestyle and ways of coping with daily life. What we eat, if we smoke, how well we sleep, and whether we exercise all feed into the final common path that is the production of cortisol, adrenaline, and other cast members in the allostatic scenario.

To a certain degree, we ourselves can determine whether allostasis will slide into allostatic load by the ways in which we cope with stress. If we make poor choices, we can tilt the scales in favor of stress-related illness. For example, smoking (a front-line defense for many) elevates blood pressure and accelerates clogging of the coronary arteries, thereby raising the risk of both heart attack and stroke. Finding solace in high-fat snacks, such as doughnuts or potato chips, can also lead to health problems. A high-fat diet accelerates atherosclerosis and increases cortisol secretion. Increased cortisol, in turn, steps up the accumulation of body fat, which is a risk factor for cardiovascular disease, stroke, and diabetes.

On the other hand, if we counteract stress with a brisk walk or a visit to the health club, we can increase the odds in our favor. Exercise prevents the buildup of body fat, protects against cardiovascular disease, and reduces chronic pain and depression. We can also protect ourselves by seeking company and support. Sheldon Cohen, who studies the relationship between stress and upper respiratory disease, has reported that people with many social connections get fewer colds. Ronald Glaser and Janice Kiecolt-Glaser of Ohio State University have shown that isolation can undermine the activity of the immune system.

With so many ways of going wrong, it may sound as if the fight-or-flight response is a fragile thing, but actually it's quite resilient. In the past 10 years, research into the effects of stress on the cardiovascular, immune, and nervous systems has shown in detail what can happen when allostasis gets out of kilter, while at the same time indicating just how resilient these systems really are.

CHAPTER 5

Stress and the Cardiovascular System

T he idea that stress can affect health gained a new level of acceptance in the 1980s, when the phrase *type A personality* made its debut. The most popular stereotype was that of a top-level male executive. He (for, indeed, he was likely to be a "he") bore the success of the company on his shoulders. He worked 14-hour days and dined on steak and martinis. And by the time he reached his late forties, he'd had at least one heart attack.

Although the type A designation has given way to a more refined view of the factors that make individuals vulnerable to heart disease, the cardiovascular system is a good arena for observing the double-edged sword of allostasis in action. The heart is exquisitely sensitive to the demands of allostasis and the strain of allostatic load. When we are stimulated, whether or not we perceive the situation as stressful, our bodies need extra oxygen, as well as fuel in the form of glucose. So the heart beats faster, driving more blood—which carries both oxygen and glucose—through the body.

Though we've been talking in terms of the fight-or-flight response, it's worth remembering that not all challenges from the environment are quite so extreme. Elevations in blood pressure help us deal with myriad nonemergencies: going from sleeping to waking in the morning, getting out of bed and preparing to stay conscious while going through the day with our heads higher than our feet (which requires increased blood flow to the brain), and running to catch a bus. In short, changes in blood pressure enable us to be active and respond to what's going on around us. But as we've seen, repeated surges in blood pressure can become an illness known as hypertension. Hypertension is a risk factor for heart attacks, especially when the condition known as atherosclerosis is present.

The word *atherosclerosis* comes from the Greek words *athero*, meaning paste, and *sclerosis*, meaning hardness. Remember those jars of paste we used in grade-school art projects, the rims encrusted with hard yellowish chunks? Now imagine this crust sticking to the arteries. The medical term is *plaque*, or a buildup of fatty materials and other debris. The process starts as fatty streaks develop under the lining of major blood vessels of the heart and brain, containing cholesterol and other fats; this process leads to the formation of what are called *atheromatous plaques*. Plaques are created at sites of stress on the blood vessel wall, such as junctions where larger vessels branch off into smaller ones. The deposits not only begin to clog the blood vessels but also serve as sites for the formation of blood clots, or thrombi, when pressure from the heart causes the plaque to rupture. The result is blockage of the flow of oxygen within the heart, which sets off a heart attack, or to the brain, which triggers a stroke.

Another phase of the allostatic response can lead to hypertension. One of the intricate ways in which the stress response protects us is by increasing a protein in the blood called *fibrinogen*, which speeds up the clotting process. This prepares us for combat by ensuring that bleeding will be held to a minimum if we are injured. However, hypertension is associated with increased levels of fibrinogen, and too much fibrinogen is a risk factor for increased blood clotting and a heart attack or stroke.

Both atherosclerosis and obesity are forms of allostatic load that arise when the coordination between the two major stress hormones is thrown out of kilter. When the body requires increased fuel for fight or flight, adrenaline and cortisol work together to keep the energy supply in balance. Adrenaline supplies energy by ordering the release of glucose from the liver and fatty acids from fat reserves. Cortisol sees to it that these energy stores are replenished. If our levels of cortisol are chronically high, due to stress or poor sleep, for example, too much energy goes into the storage bin called fat. The two places where fat is most likely to accumulate are the blood vessel walls, which raises the risk for atherosclerosis, and around the abdomen. In fact, an increase in waist-to-hip ratio is a risk factor for cardiovascular disease, because if fat levels are high enough for the midriff to expand, then fat is probably building up in the blood vessels as well.

We can make the situation worse by turning to high-fat foods as a coping strategy. When we grab a bag of potato chips or eat a hamburger and french fries while writing a report and neglect our daily exercise, we take in more calories than we expend. Excess calories, coupled with high cortisol from feeling under stress, can lead to the buildup of fat in those two very unhealthy places—blood vessel walls and the abdomen.

The archetypal high-powered executive is a good candidate for at least one of the conditions in which allostatic load affects the heart. Dominance, in particular, has its price. In the Bowman Gray social instability studies, it was the dominant monkeys in the unstable hierarchies that showed accelerated atherosclerosis. Interestingly, the atherosclerosis was slowed down by drugs known as beta blockers, which seal off the receptors through which adrenaline acts. But the effects of allostatic load on the heart are not limited to the classic type A personality. Other studies by Bowman Gray show that, in females at least, being low on the totem pole can give rise to health problems. Shively and Clarkson studied female monkeys and found increased atherosclerosis in the subordinates; this increase was correlated with reduced ovarian activity and parallels the increase seen after removal of the ovaries. Then there are the Whitehall studies, which followed groups of British civil servants: the people in the lowest job categories had the highest blood pressure; the ones at the top had the lowest.

Perhaps the central issue isn't who reports to whom but who is facing a loss of control. Control is a pivotal issue in the development of allostatic load. In a study by Cornell University and New York Hospital, a group of male volunteers wore a small blood pressure monitor for 24 hours. Those who reported "job strain," defined as high psychological demands coupled with lack of control, had the highest blood pressure—not only during the workday but also in the evening and even while sleeping. They also showed atherosclerosis.

At any rate, regardless of one's professional or social status, perceived stress and loss of control make their effects known almost immediately on the heart. Personality can also figure in. For example, hostility is another factor that raises the risk of heart disease. The coping mechanisms that we choose can make matters worse. If we habitually seek consolation in a few beers, a cheeseburger, and an ice cream sundae, we are tipping the scales in favor of a triple bypass. Alcohol and smoking increase the risk of hypertension, and a diet high in fat raises cortisol levels, which may be elevated already. If, on the other hand, we take out our frustrations on the tennis court or the treadmill, we can help keep the stress response on our side.

The Three Faces of the Autonomic Nervous System

The heart is vulnerable to allostatic load because of its central location in the wiring of the stress response system. When the body gears up to respond to a stimulus, whether it be the sound of a clock radio or the shadow of a mugger, blood flow and the expenditure of energy have to be shifted to the appropriate places immediately. The heart can go from beating 50 times per minute at rest to 150 or faster during strenuous activity. This ability to shift is brought about by a direct hookup of nerves connecting brain and body, known as the autonomic nervous system.

The autonomic nervous system links the most primitive part of the brain, the brain stem, with the rest of the body through a neural pathway that intertwines among a variety of target organs: the eyes, salivary glands, larynx, heart, lungs, stomach, intestines, kidneys, and genitals. The autonomic nervous system is the classic exemplar of

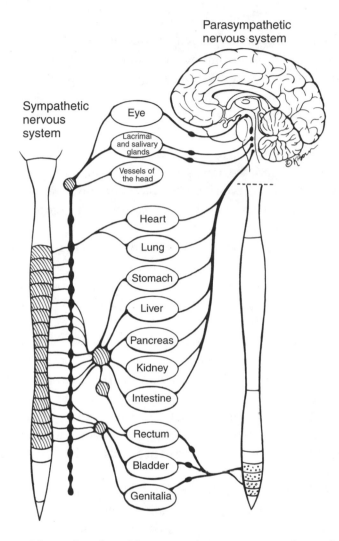

FIGURE 3   The two branches of the autonomic nervous system often work in op-position; for example, the sympathetic nervous system (left) increases heart rate and blood pressure, while the parasympathetic nervous system (right) decreases them.

allostasis: it's a system that is activated in response to external demands placed on the individual. It prepares the individual for the burst of activity needed to deal with the environmental challenge, but it also provides for recovery, restoration, and growth when the encounter is over.

This yin-yang ability is made possible by three separate but complementary components. First, the sympathetic nervous system turns on the power. Then, the visceral afferent system, a network of nerves running from the organs back to the brain, acts as a network of microphones through which the brain can pick up messages from the body. Finally, the parasympathetic nervous system restores the status quo.

The sympathetic nervous system is responsible for many of the sensations most immediately associated with stress: pounding pulse, sweating, and the feeling of hair standing on end. This is because in response to signals from the environment, such as a change in temperature, noise, or pain, the sympathetic nervous system speeds up the heart, constricts the blood vessels, dilates the eyes, and slows the digestive system. To do this, motor neurons originating at the base of the brain and connecting to the target organs carry orders for movement or change: speed up; secrete more of this or that. The neurotransmitter used for this is adrenaline. (Adrenaline is the preferred term for epinephrine, which, of course, is produced by the adrenal glands, but it's also produced by sympathetic nerves in blood vessels and many organs and in the brain.)

The churning sensation in the stomach, the discomfort brought about by those sudden heart palpitations, aren't much use as danger signals if we aren't aware of them. To send these sensations back to the brain for processing, another system of nerves go *from* the heart, stomach, and other organs *to* the brain, acting as a set of microphones through which the brain can "hear" what's going on in the body. This network of feedback is called the *visceral afferent system*. It's largely responsible for what we call our feelings—"feelings" in this case referring to the perception of stress signals from the body. Recalling the theory of William James, many sensations can be interpreted as either passion or terror, depending on whether we have glimpsed an *inamo-*

rata or a murderer. But feelings, ferried into our awareness by visceral afferent nerves, are major determinants of both stress and the effects that stress has on us.

Finally, the parasympathetic nervous system makes the autonomic nervous system an allostatic system in the classic sense by providing the ability to shut off the emergency responses and reestablish the priorities of the body or maintain the internal milieu that Claude Bernard described in the 19th century. The parasympathetic nervous system restores the status quo by slowing down the heart, dilating the pupils, facilitating digestion, and relaxing the sphincter muscles. (During sexual arousal, both the sympathetic and the parasympathetic systems are activated at the same time, which may be one reason this state has exerted such influence through the ages!)

A smoothly functioning parasympathetic system is essential to a healthy allostatic response. Stress, says neuroscientist Stephen Porges of the University of Illinois at Chicago, "reflects the subjugation of internal needs in response to external needs." Once the challenge from the environment is met, the parasympathetic nervous system makes sure that the body's priority shifts back to satisfying those internal needs. But when the challenge comes up too often or goes on for too long, or when some abnormal condition disturbs the allostatic response, the parasympathetic nervous system is blocked from serving the ongoing needs of the body, and the result is allostatic load.

Putting the "Vagal Brake" on the Heart

If we accept that a problem with the autonomic nervous system points toward stress, the heart acts as the compass needle. The shift back and forth from sympathetic to parasympathetic activity provides for the astonishing range of performance of which the heart is capable. It's the parasympathetic nervous system, specifically the vagus nerve, that slows the heart back down. The vagus nerve itself is an intricate neural pathway, not just one nerve. And difficulties ensue when this control mechanism, which Porges calls the "vagal brake," is disrupted.

In mammals the vagal brake is on most of the time, keeping the heart from going into overdrive and making sure that stress responses don't become engaged to the detriment of the body's health. But the vagal brake is more than just a clamp to keep the sympathetic nervous system in check; it's an elegant mechanism that can make its own minute adjustments to allow for efficient adaptation to events. Having the brake on in general is a safeguard against becoming overexcited. But in situations that require a sudden shift without being serious enough to warrant involvement by the sympathetic nervous system— a change in attention, perhaps—the vagal brake can also be removed to provide a subtle increase in heartbeat and respiration. In this way, we can step up our general level of functioning without having to bring in the fight-or-flight response, with its more sweeping physiological changes and its risk of wear and tear on the body.

A poorly functioning vagal mechanism is a sign of allostatic load— a detectable and quantifiable one, moreover. Porges has found that a healthy heart, even at rest, shows a normal irregularity in its beating: a slight increase during inhalation, when the vagus nerve's control is weakened, and a decrease during exhalation, during which the vagal influence reasserts itself. This irregularity is variously known as heart period variability or respiratory sinus arrhythmia (named after the sino-atrial node, the heart's pacemaker, where the vagus terminates— not the sinuses that get clogged up when you have a cold). Scientists measure the quality of the vagal brake by taking the information provided by an electrocardiogram, or EKG, and using analytical methods to time the period between heartbeats. A healthy beat-to-beat irregularity is a sign of a well-functioning vagal brake. Porges has used this analysis to develop what he calls the vagal tone index, a good indicator of how the vagal brake helps us cope. A lower vagal tone, signified by a temporary decrease in heart rate variability, means that the vagal brake is off, stepping up the heart rate to deal with the stressor. A chronically low vagal tone means that the brake is off all the time, or nonfunctional. A person without a vagal brake lives in an unending state of emergency. He or she is always experiencing allostatic load.

From the very beginning of life, the vagal tone can indicate either allostasis or allostatic load. For example, in a study of healthy newborns, Porges found that the stress of circumcision resulted in a massive but temporary decrease in vagal tone, which righted itself immediately after the procedure. The vagus released its control over the heart to cope with the demands placed on the baby's system and reestablished control after the crisis had passed. Though the low vagal tone was a sign of the stress of circumcision, it also meant that the infant's nervous system was coping well with the challenge.

In high-risk newborns, however, the vagal brake did not function as well. Porges compared healthy full-term newborns to newborns with complications such as respiratory problems or premature birth. The vagal tone index of the high-risk newborns was about one-third that of the healthy babies; high-risk newborns also had less variability between heartbeats. This means that the high-risk babies essentially didn't have a vagal brake. So not only were they trying to cope with their conditions and the associated medical treatments, they also were poorly equipped to deal with the strenuous demands of their hostile new environment. Their parasympathetic nervous systems were less able to make the shift between addressing external demands and satisfying the baby's internal needs.

Studies have found that low heart period variability can actually increase the risk of death from heart disease in a normal population. Psychobiologist Richard Sloan of Columbia-Presbyterian Medical Center believes that vagal control of the heart is a built-in protector against heart disease. In an analysis published in *Psychosomatic Medicine*, he reviews how reduced heart period variability ("heart period" being the elapsed time between heartbeats) is associated with coronary artery disease in adults. For example, reduced variability is negatively correlated with coronary atherosclerosis (that is, the lower the variability, the greater the severity of atherosclerosis) and increased risk of death after a heart attack.

But the vagal brake does more than protect us from having heart attacks: it may also play an intrinsic role in coping with stress in other ways. Not being able to use the vagal brake judiciously is a signature of several psychological conditions thought to contribute to heart disease. Many studies have confirmed a relationship between hostility and the risk of developing heart disease; depression and anxiety both predict the development of heart disease and are linked to complications, even to greater likelihood of death, following a heart attack. And a poorly functioning parasympathetic nervous system hovers behind all three conditions.

Porges believes that regulation of the heart by the parasympathetic nervous system is more than just a buffer against the surges in blood pressure that can lead to heart disease. He believes that the vagal brake evolved when mammals came on the scene, to help these more complex animals cope with a world that was more challenging, often more hostile, than it was when all of its creatures were reptiles. In the 21st century the vagal brake may buffer humans not only from stimuli likely to set off the fight-or-flight response but also from the demands the world makes on us both emotionally and socially. In short, the vagal system helps us develop appropriate emotional and social behaviors for living in the world—stress-filled or otherwise—of humans.

Evolution of the Vagal Brake

Earlier, talking about the discovery of neurotransmitters, I said that the first known neurotransmitter was acetylcholine and that Otto Loewi identified it as a chemical that could stop a frog's heart kept in a dish with the vagus nerve intact. Acetylcholine is the chemical messenger of choice for the vagal system, which sends nerves to the sino-atrial node in the heart. These nerves send acetylcholine into receptors in the heart designed to receive the neurotransmitter.

According to Porges, the ability to slow down the heart is the oldest stage in the threefold evolution of the vagal system. If it seems odd that evolution should provide for a way to slow the heart, consider the life of a reptile. Reptiles are stationary creatures and when they move, they tend to do it slowly. When they direct their attention to some novel stimulus, their response is to freeze. Behaviorists call this "orienting." Reptiles also spend a lot of time motionless, waiting for their prey to appear, rather than going out and hunting for it. In addition, many reptiles are semiaquatic and spend long periods underwater, where slowed heart rate and hence decreased metabolic demands are advantageous. When reptiles orient and cease motion altogether, upon a signal from the brain their heart rate slows down. This slowdown in heart rate is known as bradycardia, and while it is accomplished by the vagus nerve, it is an adaptation older than, and separate from, the vagal brake. Basically, then, when the environment makes demands on a reptile, the reptile's body responds by slowing the heart via the vagus nerve, thus conserving energy.

The parasympathetic nervous system is a mammalian innovation that seems to have evolved in response to a more demanding world, to which mammals must react differently. Mammals do freeze as a part of orienting to a stimulus, but then they must make a decision—to pounce on the object if it turns out to be dinner, to run if it is a foe, or to decide that the novelty is irrelevant and go their way. The choice of fight or flight will involve movement, usually sudden and intense; the mammal may make sounds or advance on the newcomer with intimidating body positions and facial expressions. In short, in times of challenge a mammal must expend energy, not conserve it; thus arousal in a mammal is characterized by increased heart rate, not bradycardia, and by mobilization of the sympathetic nervous system. To eliminate the chance of the heart slowing down when it's supposed to speed up, the sympathetic nervous system works through a series of nerves independent of the vagus.

Last in evolution comes the vagal brake. Unlike reptiles, which can't quickly gear up again, people may have to make slight, but immediate, adjustments—settling down to enjoy a good book only to hear the doorbell ring, for example. So the vagal mechanism exerts a fine-tuned control over the heart. As mammals we can meet lesser environmental demands by simply removing the brake, thus increasing the driving power of the heart without invoking the more drastic sympathetic nervous system. If the situation calls for a true fight-or-flight response, the sympathetic system kicks in, but even then the brake can be put back on, allowing the vagus to exert a soothing, calming influence by slowing the heart and fostering the internal needs of the individual.

In short, the vagal brake combines the best of both worlds relative to the two earlier stages of autonomic system evolution. Mammals and especially humans, living in ever more complex environments, must be able to respond to gradations of stimuli. For humans as well as reptiles, there are times when slowing down the heartbeat is advantageous. To cope with more drastic situations, though, both previous stages of the autonomic system remain fully operational in humans and can swing into action in times of extreme emotion and stress.

The Vagal Brake and Human Emotion

By the time Walter Cannon began bringing the idea of stress to the awareness of the scientific community in the early 20th century, both stress and emotion were discussed chiefly in terms of the fight-or-flight response—that is, the sympathetic nervous system and its activation and, later, the hypothalamic-pituitary-adrenal (HPA) axis. But even before Cannon's time, scientists had expounded a view of emotions that took into consideration both "feelings" (from the visceral afferent nerves) and, though they might not have known it, the calming effects of the parasympathetic nervous system.

As early as 1865, Claude Bernard suggested that the heart could respond to many forms of stimulation and sensory influence. In 1872 none other than Charles Darwin stated that the heart and the brain influenced each other through the vagus, which was then called the pneumo-gastric nerve; Darwin added that "when the mind is strongly excited, we might expect that it would instantly affect in a direct manner the heart." In Darwin's day the multiple routes of the autonomic nervous system had not yet been mapped out, but his idea acknowledges the importance of reciprocity—the concept of the two-way system of response, on the one hand, and perception on the other. The fact that the vagal system is a two-way street means that the vagal system—and thus the heart—can be affected by many aspects of an individual's internal state, including emotions.

The system becomes most elegant in mammals. In mammals, unlike other animals, the vagus—which, remember, is not a single nerve but a system with many branches—takes two separate routes between the brain stem and the rest of the body. Half of this network begins in an area of the brainstem called the dorsal motor nucleus. Most of the cells here send projections, or axons, into organs lower down in the body, such as the stomach and intestines, but some of them do reach the heart. This network, called the dorsal vagal complex, brings about

bradycardia, the slowing of the heart that cannot be modified by removing the vagal brake.

Under some extreme conditions, humans do exhibit bradycardia.
An extreme and somewhat bizarre example is voodoo death. This phenomenon, described in 1942 by the insightful Walter Cannon, refers to
people who drop dead from some sudden, overwhelming emotion.
Cannon's paper recounted anecdotal evidence from primitive peoples
in which a wizard or medicine man would curse a tribesman for some
offense and the delinquent would obligingly die—hence the reference
to voodoo. In the 1970s George L. Engel of the University of Rochester
found modern-day parallels, collecting newspaper and magazine articles about sudden death due to traumatic or highly exciting life
events. These included the death of a loved one or the threat that a
loved one might die; acute grief; loss of status or self-esteem; and, interestingly, reunions or happy endings and the removal of threat or
danger.

Cannon assumed that such death was due to massive outpouring
of adrenaline and a skyrocketing heartbeat—in other words, sympathetic nervous system activity. But a gruesome series of experiments in
the 1950s challenged this assumption. Curt Richter of John Hopkins
University placed both lab-reared and wild rats in water tanks until
they drowned, monitoring their hearts throughout. The lab rats, more
accustomed to human doings, survived for several hours, but all of the
wild rats died within 15 minutes; some even dove straight to bottom of
the tank and died immediately. Analysis of their hearts showed that the
trusting laboratory rats met Cannon's expectations, showing a surge in
sympathetic activity and eventually dying from exhaustion. The wild
rats, on the other hand, showed a very different pattern. Their hearts
slowed, to the point where they actually stopped. The trauma was so
massive that they fell back on the most primitive survival strategy of
all: they "played dead" and their heart rates plummeted. This is the
bradycardia observed in reptiles. Rats defeated by stronger competi-
tors also die of the same syndrome. Mammals, including humans, still
retain this last-ditch mechanism for self-protection. Scientists believe
that in cases of voodoo death the more recent evolutionary adapta-
tions have failed and control over the heart is relinquished to the oldest

intervention of all—immobilization and bradycardia, which ultimately results in death.

Voodoo death is an extreme and rare example of how stress affects the heart; most people don't respond to bad news by having their hearts stop beating. Sudden accelerations of the pulse due to violent emotions are a much more common threat to cardiovascular health. The usual safeguard is the other half of the vagal system, which originates in the nucleus ambiguus (named for the difficulty scientists had in establishing the structure's borders). In this system, which is called the ventral vagal complex, cells from the nucleus ambiguus send motor projections to the larynx, esophagus, heart, and lungs. (Both dorsal and ventral complexes receive input from the amygdala and the hypothalamus, which puts them in readiness to participate in the stress response. Though a similar dual origin in the brain stem is seen in reptiles, the systems are not as distinct as in mammals.)

The ventral complex has a faster and more subtle effect on the heart because, unlike its counterpart, the nerve fibers are covered with a substance called myelin. Myelin is a fatty sheath produced by certain cells in the brain; it surrounds the extensions of nerve cells, the axons, along which signals travel. Myelin acts as an insulating layer that speeds messages along the axons—myelinated axons carry messages much faster than nonmyelinated ones. According to Porges, the ventral vagal complex is not merely a cushion against the violent emotions likely to accelerate the pulse, such as anger or terror; it sets the stage for the healthy expression of emotions and for human social interactions as well. For one thing, it sends its nerve projections not only to the heart but also to the facial muscles, as well as the muscles that coordinate sucking, swallowing, and vocalizing. These activities cement the most fundamental human interaction of all—communication between mother and child. Later in life, humans rely heavily on facial expression and tone of voice not only to show emotion but for smooth and effective interaction. Behaving in a conciliatory manner, for example, can prevent a situation from escalating into a fight-or-flight-type scenario, and voice and expression are key components. And of course, control over one's own physiological responses—which is afforded by a well-functioning vagal brake—can help prevent mortal combat.

People whose vagal mechanism doesn't work well may be less able to meet the complex demands of the modern world. For example, working with Jane Doussard-Roosevelt and colleagues, Porges found that infants who were less able to regulate the vagal brake were more likely to have social behavioral problems a few years later.

The investigators studied 24 children (12 boys and 12 girls), initially between seven and nine months of age. The babies were tested with the Bayley Scales of Mental Development, in which the child is asked to perform tasks considered suitable to its age. These tasks place fairly strong demands on the child's attention and social interaction. EKG electrodes on the infant's chest provided information on heartbeat, which the investigators used to measure the beat-to-beat variability and to determine the vagal tone index. When the children were three years old, their mothers completed the Child Behavior Checklist for Ages 2–3, a rating scale of 99 items describing behavioral and emotional problems.

Infants whose vagal tone decreased the most during the Bayley test—in other words, those who were best able to take the vagal brake off when appropriate—had the fewest behavioral problems as three year olds. Further, the infants who showed large decreases in vagal tone fared better as three year olds with regard to three specific measurements: social withdrawal, depressed behavior, and aggressive behavior. Once again, social behavior often requires a subtle shift in metabolic resources to come up with the right response for the situation, while the more extreme fight-or-flight response would not be warranted. In the infants subjected to the Bayley test, the vagus nerve released its grip on the heart to help the child gear up for the task—the same way the vagal tone decreased in healthy infants during circumcision. Release of the vagal brake is a healthy response to stress and, when functioning properly, provides an advantage in social development. A logical inference is that children who cannot engage and remove the brake when necessary are forced to rely on cruder coping mechanisms, such as the fight-or-flight response, and it isn't surprising that such children show behavioral problems down the line.

Taking It Personally

Porges's vagal brake theory, or polyvagal theory, as he calls it, explains rather neatly why so many people manifest allostatic load in the form of heart disease. The vagal brake operates with a light touch. In the absence of this type of subtle, finely tuned mechanism, the body must respond to challenges more drastically, by falling back on the fight-or-flight response. And since the vagal brake keeps the heartbeat within reasonable limits, a malfunction here results in faster pulse and higher blood pressure.

It's also intriguing that poor vagal tone is associated with other characteristics known to be associated with heart disease. The best studied of these traits is hostility, probably due to widespread public awareness of the type A personality and its consequences. Many studies attest to the concurrence of hostility with heart disease, though they don't focus on the vagal brake per se. Following the logic of the vagal brake theory, these results suggest that people with stress-related cardiovascular problems respond to situations with an inappropriate level of sympathetic nervous system activity—possibly because more subtle bodily responses provided by the vagal brake are not functional.

For example, hostile people are prone to surges in blood pressure even in situations not necessarily anger provoking. Mary Davis of Arizona State University designed a study in which subjects discussed a controversial topic with a "confederate," a person chosen by the investigators who presented an opposing view. People who scored higher on a hostility profile showed greater increases in blood pressure during the discussion. Davis found a telling dichotomy in these subjects: though their blood pressure was higher, their cardiac output was lower than that of other, more easygoing, participants. In other words, the hearts of the hostile people were beating harder but moving less blood, indicating that blood pressure was going up in a maladaptive way, without any corresponding increase in readiness to deal with a challenge. In patients with coronary heart disease, hostility is also linked with increased platelet formation, possibly increasing the likelihood of blood clotting and therefore of heart attacks and strokes.

In the spring of 2000 a prospective study showed that "proneness to anger" may lead to heart disease. A prospective study is one in which researchers examine the traits of a large population and check back several years later to see what has happened. Janice Williams and colleagues at the University of North Carolina at Chapel Hill surveyed almost 13,000 men and women, both black and white, who were part of an ongoing project called the Atherosclerosis Risk in Communities study. They found that being anger prone placed subjects at greater risk of both ongoing heart disease and fatal heart attacks even when other risk factors, such as hypertension, were absent.

Hostile people are likely to add to their allostatic load by making poor coping choices. For example, smoking, which is a "displacement" behavior for people under stress and also an addiction, leads to a condition known as left ventricular hypertrophy—a small but definite increase in the mass of the heart's left ventricle and a sure sign of incipient heart disease. For a 24-hour period, Paolo Verdecchia and colleagues at the Beato G. Villa Hospital in Italy monitored the everyday or "ambulatory" blood pressure of 115 heavy smokers and 460 nonsmokers who had hypertension. Although blood pressure as tested at the clinic was nearly identical for the two groups, the smokers had significantly higher daytime ambulatory blood pressure, while nighttime pressure did not differ. The smokers also had a faster heart rate, and echocardiographs showed that the mass of the smokers' left ventricles was greater by about 10 percent.

Lack of control and low self-esteem can lead to the same condition even in people who are not hostile. There is a wealth of information, in addition to the Whitehall studies, showing that job stress can lead to heart trouble. Robert Karasek, now at the University of Massachusetts, has studied the so-called demand control model. He has found that people who have demanding jobs but no sense of control or reward—workers who must keep pace on an assembly line, for example—are at increased risk of coronary heart disease and accompanying psychological symptoms, such as depression and exhaustion. Karasek and colleagues reported in the *Journal of the American Medical Association* that such workers also show left ventricular hypertrophy.

Lifestyle and the Heart

Habits that we can learn to control, such as diet, exercise, alcohol consumption, and sleep, can profoundly influence whether the allostatic response works for us or against us. For example, nicotine can stimulate the release of adrenocorticotropin (ACTH), the neurohormone released by the pituitary, which activates the HPA axis, perhaps resulting in an unusually excitable stress response.

Alcohol consumption can also throw off the stress response, though not by directly compromising the cardiovascular system. Studies in rats show that alcohol activates the HPA axis, with females secreting more ACTH than males, while long-term treatment with alcohol can blunt the HPA response. In human alcoholic patients, concentrations of cortisol in the blood are almost twice as high during withdrawal as upon recovery. Even people who are not themselves alcoholic, if they have a family history of alcoholism, show a hypersensitive cortisol response to experimental stimulation.

Sleep is another area in which the stress response can be aided or hindered. Sleep deprivation increases sympathetic nervous system activity and makes the vagal brake less effective, leaving the body more vulnerable to the damaging effects of stress, like blood pressure surges that can cause a heart attack. Sleep deprivation also results in elevated cortisol the next evening. Abdominal fat deposition and cardiovascular disease are later consequences of this scenario when carried to the extreme.

But to safeguard the cardiovascular system, it's most important to watch our habits when it comes to those old standbys—diet and exercise. A diet rich in fat not only puts on pounds and increases cholesterol but also overstimulates the sympathetic nervous system and elevates cortisol.

Body Fat and the Insulin Connection

Being very overweight puts a strain on the heart, and excess body fat, particularly in the abdominal area, is more than a condition that poses a health risk. It's also an accepted sign of allostatic load. In primates, psychological stress can speed up the rate at which fat is deposited in

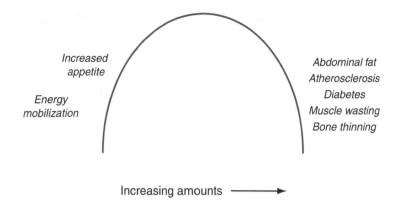

Increasing amounts ⟶

FIGURE 4   Protection versus damage: metabolic systems and cardiovascular health. Normal levels of stress hormones secreted in response to a stressor increase appetite and mobilize energy reserves, but prolonged elevation can lead to unhealthy conditions.

the body. In humans, obesity—as measured by an increased waist-to-hip ratio—tends to show up in the people most vulnerable to stress: in males at the lower end of the socioeconomic scale, according to a Swedish study, and in lower civil service grades in both men and women in the Whitehall studies. And as I've mentioned, scientists consider it a given that when fat is accumulating around the abdomen, it's probably building up in the blood vessels too.

When it comes to allostatic load, obesity is a vicious circle. Stress can make us put on fat more easily, particularly if we help out by seeking consolation in doughnuts, potato chips, or alcohol, putting a strain on the heart and upsetting the stress response—thus leading to more stress and more fat deposition. The demoralization that tends to accompany obesity, particularly in a culture obsessed with thinness, can lead to additional stress, calorie consumption, and weight gain.

The intricate connections between stress, obesity, diet, and inactivity work together to produce yet another stress-related illness, one that we may not immediately associate with the heart: the insulin deficiency known as diabetes. Diabetes, of course, is not a cardiovascular disease like atherosclerosis; it is a metabolic disease—a disorder in the body's use of energy. In addition to being a potentially serious disease itself, diabetes is a risk factor for atherosclerosis, especially when conditions such as hypertension and hypertriglyceridemia (high levels of fatty acids in the blood) are present, which is frequently the case.

The blood carries energy throughout the body in form of glucose, or blood sugar. The hormone called insulin gets the glucose out of the circulating blood and into the muscles and organs that need it. In diabetes the body either does not produce enough insulin (a situation known as type I or insulin-dependent diabetes) or does not use the hormone properly even when supplies are plentiful (type II or non-insulin-dependent diabetes). The result is that the cells do not receive enough fuel in the form of glucose. A person or animal with type II diabetes becomes increasingly resistant to the body's own insulin. Obesity and lack of exercise are risk factors for diabetes, and stress seems more and more to play a role as well. (Stress may also be a factor in type I diabetes, now thought to be an autoimmune condition. More about that later.)

Insulin is produced by the pancreas. High levels of glucose in the blood, such as might follow a meal, signal the pancreas to increase production so that the enormous dinner just eaten can be put to use. Insulin is not the only hormone that regulates blood glucose, however. A steady supply of glucose is of the utmost importance not just to the cells of the muscles and organs—which can, in a pinch, use energy from fats and proteins—but to the brain. Because the brain is so well protected by the blood-brain barrier, fuel can enter only in the form of glucose; other molecules are too large. So to ensure that the brain has a constant supply, several other hormones, including glucagon (also produced by the pancreas) and the stress hormones adrenaline and cortisol, can step in to regulate blood sugar.

The stress hormones can have some undesirable effects on glucose metabolism. Under conditions of stress, when the body assumes that more fuel will be needed to deal with whatever is going on, cortisol triggers the breakdown of protein and its conversion, in the liver, to glucose. Adrenaline also raises levels of blood glucose. Through mechanisms not entirely understood, prolonged elevation of stress hormones can result in insulin resistance and can also lead to the buildup of fatty materials like lipids and triglycerides in the blood. Obesity can have the same effect (and excess cortisol can promote fat deposition, increasing the likelihood of obesity).

Type II diabetics have entered into another type of vicious circle in which the increased production of insulin is related to increased production of stress hormones, particularly cortisol, which acts directly to desensitize insulin receptors in the body's cells. Because of the lack of response from the insulin receptors, glucose begins to build up in the blood, and the resulting high glucose levels spur the pancreas to secrete still more insulin; the stress hormones also increase. Both obesity and poor diet can exacerbate insulin resistance.

Lifestyle Choices

The effects of allostatic load on the cardiovascular system may make for disturbing reading, but there is a ray of hope. Cardiovascular health is the area in which our conscious choices can have the most impact.

No one will claim that obesity, diabetes, and even hostility are lifestyle choices that we make. Obesity in particular, which is both dangerous and widespread enough to rank as a public health concern, is becoming increasingly understood as a disorder. At the end of 2001, the U.S. Surgeon General published a *Call to Action to Prevent and Decrease Overweight and Obesity*, outlining strategies that communities can use to address the problem of obesity. These include requiring physical education and more healthy food options in schools and providing safe and accessible recreational facilities for citizens of all ages.

The Surgeon General also noted that in 1999 an estimated 61 percent of U.S. adults were overweight, along with 13 percent of children and adolescents. Obesity among adults has doubled since 1980, while overweight among adolescents has tripled. Research continues to show the overlapping paths that lead to weight gain—the condition is more than the straightforward result of eating too much—and treatments remain elusive.

But even people whose weight doesn't approach clinical obesity should watch their diets to make sure their stress response is functioning optimally. Other measures to ward off allostatic load, such as getting regular exercise and plenty of sleep, are attractive because they're comparatively simple and because they help eliminate those risk factors that *can* be eliminated. Counseling and even medication to reduce depression, anxiety, and hostility are also worth considering, since these conditions are points of entry into heart-related allostatic load. In the next two chapters we'll talk about the effects of allostatic load on the immune system and the brain—areas in which opportunities for intervention are just beginning to open up.

CHAPTER 6

Stress and the Immune System

In the *The Hot Zone*, Richard Preston's account of a plague that almost hit the United States, an American scientist is testing a virus that he fears may be the annihilator known as Ebola. He has cultured the suspect organism on a slide, along with the blood of a patient known to have died from the disease. To this mixture he has added chemicals that will make the blood glow if it produces antibodies to the virus. Now as he peers through his microscope in the darkened laboratory, the blood begins to glow, signifying that the virus is indeed Ebola. The patient from whom the blood was taken died six years earlier on the other side of the world in Nairobi; the blood has been frozen in a laboratory outside Washington ever since. But still it knows the virus. It has encountered this foe before.

The procedure involved a fairly straightforward chemical reaction. It is by no means the most dramatic event in *The Hot Zone*, as anyone who has read the book can attest. But for immunologists and anyone fascinated with the human body, the brightly glowing slide illuminates one of the most intriguing aspects of blood: it has its own kind of intelligence, enabling it to recognize and neutralize a threat, both at the time of invasion and for many years afterward—in many cases a lifetime. That's because the blood carries the messengers of the immune system, the body's powerful and intricate chemical bulwark against onslaughts from the hostile world.

The immune system orchestrates the body's defenses against infection and injury, fighting off such intruders when possible and healing the damage that occurs when any invaders get past the front lines. Immune cells, generated in the bone marrow and carried by the blood, obey the prime directive of deciding what is a healthy integral part of the body and what is not—in scientific parlance, distinguishing "self" from "nonself." Anything that's nonself is marked for destruction. The immune cells are the white blood cells, as opposed to the red blood cells that deliver oxygen to the body's tissues. Red blood cells derive their color from the iron atom to which the oxygen is attached.

When someone sustains an injury or develops an infection, the first thing that happens is a local inflammatory response. At the site of injury, sensory nerves carry a message—pain—to alert the brain that there's a problem. Immune cells stationed at the site trigger changes in nearby blood vessels, resulting in redness and swelling. These cells also summon the white blood cells, which destroy invaders such as bacteria and form antibodies should the same foe appear in the future. Other local responses include trying to physically eject the intruder, through coughing and sneezing if it came in through the respiratory system or vomiting and diarrhea if it has invaded the digestive tract.

But if the situation is more than the local forces can cope with, the immune system alerts the hypothalamus, which initiates a global response. The hypothalamus raises the body temperature to make the body as a whole an uninhabitable environment for microbes. It also sets the hypothalamic-pituitary-adrenal (HPA) axis in motion to deal with the infection as it would with any stressor, and this is where cortisol comes in. Cortisol replenishes energy stores and—initially—boosts the immune response by sending the white blood cells to their battle stations in the skin and other tissues. Once the immune response has reached a certain level of intensity, though, cortisol also works to switch it off.

Shoring Up the Defenses

The immune system plays an important role in helping us deal with stress. As far as nature is concerned, any fight-or-flight scenario is fraught with risks of injury. Even in stressful situations unlikely to result in physical damage, such as being summoned for jury duty, our bodies still prepare to chase down a wooly mammoth for dinner or turn and run away if the mammoth takes exception to the plan. So the immune system gets ready to deal with injury to the skin, muscles, and tissues and to fight any infection that might result by rushing large numbers of protective immune cells to vulnerable places in the body.

As a card-carrying member of the stress response, the immune system follows the same good news/bad news pattern seen in other areas of allostasis: short-term protection that can lead to wear and tear if the system is chronically overactivated. Acute stress can enhance the response of the immune system, sending white blood cells to their battle stations and helping them arm themselves. Ongoing stress, on the other hand, has a tendency to suppress the immune system, thus setting the stage for infection. This means that we can take steps to help keep the immune system operating on the protective end of the spectrum. How to do this is not as clear as with, say, cardiovascular disease. But there's reason to hope that taking the usual steps to avoid allostatic load—eating healthy foods, getting enough exercise—can help keep the immune system functioning optimally.

The two-edged effect of the immune system fits neatly into the overall view of allostasis and allostatic load that I've described. But the idea of stress playing a beneficial role in immune activity has only recently begun to gain acceptance by the scientific community. In past decades, scientists have tended to concentrate on the suppressive effects that external stress can have on the immune system. The attitude was due, in part, to clinical observations throughout history. Doctors have known for centuries that both physical and emotional stress can undermine our ability to fend off illness. Two thousand years ago the

Greek physician Galen observed that "melancholic" women were more likely to develop cancer than were "sanguine" ones. In the 12th century the Torah scholar and physician Maimonides spoke of the link between emotions and health, urging physicians to keep their patients cheerful and free of anxiety. Between Maimonides and the 20th century, scientists argued in favor of either a strictly anatomical explanation of the link between emotions and health—that all illnesses, even mental ones, result from disease or damage to organs such as the brain—or a view that attributes even "real" diseases to purely psychological causes, as do Freudian analysts.

The biological connections between the brain and the immune system are quite intimate and go well beyond the crosstalk that takes place when there is an injury or invader. Two crucial systems are biologically connected to the immune system. Studies in the 18th and 19th centuries showed a latticework of autonomic nerves in the major structural components of the immune system, such as the bone marrow (where all blood cells are manufactured) and the lymph nodes. Stimulating these nerves experimentally affects the number and type of immune cells that are produced as well as their activity level. So when the sympathetic nervous system pumps in adrenaline to gear up for the emergency, or the parasympathetic nervous system uses acetylcholine to signal the restoration of everyday functioning, it seems likely that the immune system should follow suit.

The brain is also linked to the immune system indirectly, through the HPA axis and the action of cortisol. At first glance, this connection seems to support the idea that stress has only suppressive effects on the immune system. But cortisol—which comes into play if the immune system summons a global response—has that wonderful dual action ability to shut off its own production to prevent the stress response from getting out of hand, and the same mechanism calms the activity of the immune system as well. Cortisol also acts on immune cells directly in ways that are not entirely understood. Its "suppressive" effects have been well known since the Mayo Clinic's Philip Hench won a 1950 Nobel Prize for showing that cortisol can calm the inflammation that accompanies asthma. Many people have experienced similar effects of cortisol when they take it in the commercially prepared form known as cortisone to quell inflammatory conditions such as rashes, asthma, and rheumatoid arthritis.

"Bad News" Piles Up First

Research into more general life experiences confirms the ancients' observations suggesting that stress can dampen the immune response. For example, Sheldon Cohen at Carnegie-Mellon University has found that chronic kinds of stress, including unemployment and social isolation, can render a person more susceptible to the common cold. Dr. Cohen has also found that when research monkeys housed in unstable social structures are exposed to the virus that causes colds, they are more likely to become infected and develop symptoms than are monkeys in a stable, supportive environment.

At Ohio State University, Ron Glaser, Janice Kiecolt-Glaser, and colleagues have studied extensively the connection between chronic stress and health. In studying a group of medical students, they found that loneliness, as measured through targeted questionnaires, can impair the immune system. In other studies the Glasers found that people with little social support who were caring for spouses with Alzheimer's disease fared worse in tests of immune system activity given after one year than those with stronger support systems. The team has also shown that marital strife can undermine the body's defenses. In a study of 90 newlywed couples who agreed to discuss areas of conflict for a 30-minute videotaped session, the ones who behaved in more negative or hostile ways showed elevated levels of adrenaline and adrenocorticotropic hormone, as well as signs of depressed immune system activity, over the next 24 hours.

Another situation that can weaken the immune system is bereavement, perhaps the ultimate social stressor and cause of isolation. Under certain circumstances, the death of a loved one may actually increase one's own risk of dying. In one study the parents of Israeli men killed in the Lebanese war were followed for 10 years. The loss of a son did not automatically lead to the parent's death, but bereaved parents who were widowed or divorced died in significantly higher numbers in the course of the 10-year study. Apparently the social deprivation resulting from the loss of the spouse was a factor in coping with the death of a child.

A question hotly debated by researchers, physicians, alternative practitioners, and charlatans is whether stress reduction programs, such as support groups, can improve the outlook for patients with cancer. As this book went to press, the scientific literature was evenly divided on the subject: five studies showed that participation in support groups increased life expectancy, usually moderately; five showed no increase.

Most recently, Pamela Goodwin and colleagues at the University of Toronto examined group psychotherapy for women with metastatic breast cancer and showed that the women's quality of life was improved but not their length of life; the therapy participants did not live appreciably longer. In the first such study, which came out in 1989, support group participants survived breast cancer about 18 months longer than nonparticipants—an increase of 25 percent, unachievable by any treatment modality. David Spiegel, lead author and professor of psychiatry at Stanford University School of Medicine, observes that in the intervening years social support has vastly improved for cancer patients, even those not enrolled in a formal support group. This may be enough to explain the lack of a survival benefit in the recent Goodwin study: it's not that the group therapy patients aren't living longer, but that the nonparticipants *are*; they're closing the gap.

It's possible that allostatic load influences the progression of cancer by suppressing the immune system. Most researchers accept that the immune system patrols for cancerous cells as it does for viruses or bacteria, though this is not a fact etched into the marble halls of scientific wisdom. Several teams are studying specific immune system interactions. One study shows that in rats the stress of a mild shock to the foot can inhibit the action of so-called natural killer cells, immune cells thought to attack cancerous cells. Studies examining more general effects of stressors show that inescapable shocks can speed up the growth of tumors in rats. At Stanford, Robert Sapolsky has shown that the higher levels of cortisol that accompany aging can make rats more susceptible to tumors.

It stands to reason that what strengthens or weakens the immune

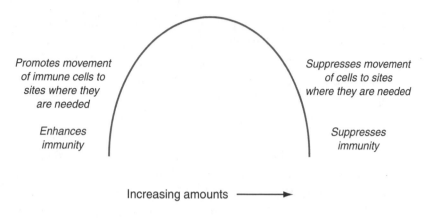

Promotes movement
of immune cells to
sites where they
are needed

Enhances
immunity

Suppresses movement
of cells to sites
where they are needed

Suppresses
immunity

Increasing amounts ———▶

FIGURE 5   Protection versus damage: immune function. Normal levels of stress hormones enhance the immune response, but if the stress response is repeatedly overactivated or prolonged, immune function is impaired.

system will do the same to a patient's experience with illness. Teaming up with Dr. Sapolsky, Dr. Spiegel has recently shown that women breast cancer patients whose cortisol was higher in the evening, when it should be lower, had a shorter life expectancy. If future studies do show that stress reduction, support, and psychotherapy can prolong the lives of people with cancer, scientists will need to ascertain exactly how the emotional benefit translates into biochemical reality.

Finding a Protective Role for Stress

In the shadow of a mountain of evidence, the basic theory that stress suppresses the immune system took shape, and scientists scrambled for an explanation. The most likely seemed to be that immune system activity is a metabolically costly "luxury" process that can be put on hold during times of emergency, like putting off building an addition to a house if a hurricane is approaching.

This philosophy didn't make sense to some scientists, however. One was Firdaus Dhabhar, who was just graduating from Dartmouth Medical School. "The prevailing idea was that 'stress is bad,' and I wasn't satisfied with it," says Dhabhar. "From an evolutionary standpoint, it seemed unlikely that the physiological stress response should have only negative effects—that nature would evolve a mechanism designed to suppress the immune system during a stressful event, just when an active immune response might be most needed." He also took exception to the notion that immunity was metabolically costly, since getting sick in a time of crisis is certainly more costly than rousing the immune system. One other fact did not add up. Cortisol does have antiinflammatory—immune-suppressing—effects when given to patients exogenously, in the form of creams or injections. But exogenous cortisol, which is given in whopping doses, may not mirror the precise effects of the minute concentrations found in the bloodstream. Dhabhar suspected that the immune system swings on the HPA axis in the classic allostasis/allostatic load continuum. He joined our lab at Rockefeller University and, in the tradition of Hans Selye and John Mason, set out on a path of research that led away from the accepted medical wisdom—toward the idea that stress might enhance immunity.

First, Dhabhar noticed that most clinical studies described chronic stress, not acute stress. Also, most scientists measured immune system activity in the circulating blood, where they found fewer white blood cells, and natural killer cells that were less active, in patients reporting higher levels of stress. "On the face of it, having fewer white cells would seem to be a bad thing," Dhabhar acknowledges. "But there were two questions: If the white cells weren't in the circulating blood, did that mean they'd been destroyed? And if they hadn't been destroyed, where were they?"

These questions led to a series of experiments that helped establish the concept of protection in the short term versus wear and tear in the long term. Dhabhar showed that acute stress did indeed result in a rapid and significant decrease in many of the white blood cells that play important roles in immunity. However, the decrease was reversible. The white cells resumed their normal concentrations once the stress was resolved. They had not been obliterated by stress at all; they had only moved. The white cells' mobility is as impressive as their canny distinction between friend and foe. These infection-fighting forces circulate throughout the body in the blood; at a moment's notice they can arrive at the site of an invasion, whether it be the mucous membranes in the nose or injured bones of the left ankle. According to Dhabar's findings, the white cells had done more than just show up in the approximate location of the injury. Their conspicuous absence in previous studies was due to the fact that they had actually left the circulating blood and attached themselves to the tissues and structures where their presence would be most needed, such as the lymph nodes and skin. Furthermore, this process was initiated by the release of cortisol into the bloodstream. In view of these findings, our lab proposed that acute stress causes the immune cells to leave the blood and take up strategic positions in areas where they may be needed. We came to describe this migration as "stress-induced trafficking" and held it forth as an example of how acute stress actually enhances immune activity.

Stress Gets the White Cells Rolling

The picture of a positive role for stress took shape in a series of studies from our lab, led by Dhabhar, on a type of immune response known as delayed-type hypersensitivity (DTH). The DTH response involves two kinds of white blood cells, macrophages and helper T cells, working together. Macrophages gobble up foreign particles and hold up chunks of the offending protein, called antigens, like flags on a flagpole. This signal attracts the so-called T helper cells, which recruit an army of other immune cells to kill the infectious agent wherever they find it. T helper cells have another job: to stimulate still other kinds of immune cells—the B cells—to make antibodies to the foreign agent. These antibodies can be activated in case the intruder ever comes back. DTH is one way the immune system works against certain infections and tumors, and it's also seen in some types of allergic responses, such as poison ivy.

Using this model we found that, in the short term, stressful events and the accompanying release of stress hormones can enhance the immune system. The findings are best summed up in the title of Dhabhar's dissertation lecture: "A Hassle a Day Keeps the Doctor Away!" We immunized rats with a chemical antigen—a substance that will provoke an immune response—applied to their backs. We then gave the animals' immune systems time to "learn" the antigen and form antibodies to it (the "delay" in the DTH). When animals were reexposed to the antigen applied to the ear—a site that we chose because it sticks out and is easy to measure—the ear showed a robust immune response in the form of redness, swelling, and immune cell activity.

Next we added acute stress into the mix by briefly restraining the rats in clear, well-ventilated Plexiglass cylinders. The cylinder does not cause pain; it does not squeeze or put pressure on the rats; it just prevents them from moving about as they would normally like to do. This is thought to be psychological stress for rats. When rats that are briefly stressed in this way have the antigen reapplied to their ears, the DTH response is enhanced; the redness is distinctly visible and the tissue of the ear actually thickens. In examining the tissue we see a dramatic increase in the number of immune cells. The immune cells traffic to the ear during stress. Even after a week or two of a daily restraint session, the animal is still able to traffic its immune cells out of its bloodstream and into the ear. This means that the stress has amplified the response that the immune response "learned" the first time the antigen was applied. Extending this finding to the fight-or-flight scenario, the stress of being wounded can boost the immune response already in place to deal with any bacteria that creep into the wound, reducing the likelihood of infection.

With three weeks of stress, though, we begin to see a suppression of the immune response, and after five weeks of repeated stress the immune cell trafficking and DTH response are both seriously impaired. So the findings also support previous research into the immune-dampening effects of *long-term* stress. But if we let the animals recover for a week, the system begins to bounce back, so the change is not irreversible.

These studies confirm our whole notion of allostasis versus allostatic load, or protection versus damage. Cortisol's role in the process is almost certain. For example, giving the rats a drug that interferes with the production of cortisol also impairs the immune cell's trafficking ability. And activating the cortisol receptors in the immune cells with an experimental chemical can restore the trafficking ability even to animals whose adrenal glands (and cortisol supply) have been removed. Dhabhar, who is now at Ohio State University, is investigating precisely how cortisol exerts its effects on immune cells. Early results show that it may activate cell adhesion molecules, which help the immune cells stick to blood vessels in the tissues to which they migrate; cortisol may also turn on the genes that encode for these molecules.

By now you can see, generally speaking, how cortisol contributes to the protection versus damage cycle of immune system activity. In conditions of acute stress, cortisol promotes the trafficking of immune cells out of the blood and onto "lookout" positions such as the skin and lymph nodes. If the cells don't spot any signs of infection, they eventually return to the circulating blood. Then, once the stressful stimulus goes away or is satisfactorily dealt with, cortisol helps to send the all-clear to the immune system. Finally, cortisol acts directly on receptors in the hypothalamus in the built-in negative feedback loop that I've described, which the hormone uses to halt its own production.

The Other Side of the Coin

In some people, ongoing stress does not impair the immune system: it has the opposite effect, goading the immune system until it attacks targets that don't really pose a threat—in other words, initiating an allergy or asthma attack—or that are actually part of the body, resulting in autoimmune disease. It's important to keep in mind the protective effects of stress and cortisol when considering these diseases because some evidence shows that these conditions may arise or worsen when these protective effects are lacking.

Inflammatory disorders such as allergies occur when the immune system goes into attack mode in response to something that doesn't bother most people—pollen, dust, cold weather, even exercise—producing such symptoms as redness, pain, sniffling, and itching.

Autoimmune diseases are the same idea taken a step further; the immune cells actually fail to distinguish self from nonself and begin attacking healthy tissue. In multiple sclerosis (MS), for example, the immune system destroys the patient's myelin sheath, the fatty insulation that surrounds some nerve fibers and helps to speed communication from the brain. Without myelin the nerve signals run into bare patches that block their transmission, like skaters suddenly running out of ice. Motor nerves are myelinated, which is why impaired movement and disability so often are consequences of MS; the visual pathways in the brain and the nerves that control bowel and bladder are also vulnerable myelinated nerves.

Other autoimmune diseases are rheumatoid arthritis, in which the immune system attacks cartilage, and juvenile or type I diabetes. (This form of diabetes is different from mature-onset or type II diabetes, which is characterized by a resistance to one's own insulin.) In juvenile diabetes the immune system destroys the cells in the pancreas that produce insulin, leaving the patient dependent on insulin injections.

Stress has been shown to worsen all of these conditions, and a growing body of evidence points to stress as a contributing factor in whether they develop in the first place. This state of affairs is partially due to an insufficiently responsive HPA axis and an underproduction of cortisol, which allows the stress response, and with it the immune system, to run amok. A sluggish HPA axis has been implicated not only in asthma but also arthritis, fibromyalgia, chronic fatigue syndrome, and the skin rash known as atopic dermatitis. Scientists know how the process of asthma unfolds: the airways in the lungs constrict when exposed to certain stimuli. In more than 80 percent of cases the stimulus is an allergen, like pollen or animal dander, but asthma attacks can also be triggered by cold air, exercise, and certain respiratory infections. Like many allergies, asthma is caused by immune system cells, which initiate the inflammatory response that makes it so difficult for asthmatics to breathe either in or out.

So much for the "how." The "why" is less clear. In people without asthma the lungs don't react in this way to irritants such as dust or cat dander. Most researchers assume that the development of asthma stems from a combination of inherited genes and the presence of allergens and other irritants in the patient's environment. Which leads us to wonder: Could one of those environmental factors be stress?

Maybe, according to the literature. Sheldon Cohen of Carnegie-Mellon University observes that asthma has been considered since the

1920s to be partly psychosomatic, meaning a condition that has its origins in both psychological and physical causes, not an imaginary state that the sufferer needs to "snap out" of. Anecdotal reports from patients attesting to a link with stress are borne out by studies showing that in people who have asthma stressful experiences such as watching emotionally charged films or performing mental arithmetic causes the airways in the lungs to constrict.

The idea that stress plays a role in asthma is plausible in several ways. First, the autonomic nervous system is directly hardwired into the airways of the lungs. Some studies show that in asthmatics increased activity of the vagus nerve—the normally helpful pathway through which the parasympathetic nervous system keeps a grip on the heart rate—may assist the immune cells in constricting the airways. Particularly in children with asthma, a high degree of vagal activation is linked with stressful stimuli and constriction of the airways. Other studies show that activation of the sympathetic nervous system, through the neurotransmitter noradrenaline, makes the airways constrict and is exaggerated in people with asthma.

There's another way that stress might contribute to asthma. Dr. Cohen, who pioneered research into stress and susceptibility to upper respiratory infections, observes that respiratory infections are one of the most reliable triggers for asthma. In both children and adults with asthma, viruses can aggravate the condition, irritating the airways, causing inflammation and sensitizing the cells involved in the allergic response. Exposure to upper respiratory viruses in early childhood may affect the young immune system, setting the stage for asthma to develop.

Finally, there's the issue of behavior and how we may contribute to our own allostatic load, inadvertently or otherwise. There's no question that an asthma attack is a stressor in itself. Patients who respond by crying or gasping for air may dry their throats, thus irritating the airways even further. The inability to breathe can cause hyperventilation or a full-blown anxiety or panic attack, which inevitably drives up stress levels. Because asthma attacks tend to come at night, they can disrupt sleep patterns, causing an imbalance in the daily rhythms of the cortisol cycle. Many asthmatics also avoid exercise, depriving themselves of an important coping tool. When examining the link between stressful events and asthma, all of these facts complicate the picture.

Cause and Effect in Inflammatory Disorders

Until now I have talked about how stress can exacerbate a condition that already exists. But it's also possible that stress causes asthma to develop in the first place. Some studies have shown that asthmatics of all ages report higher levels of negative emotion, such as fear and anger. But given the realities of life with asthma, this is hardly surprising. Few things are as terrifying as not being able to breathe. Particularly for children, the built-in limitations such as being left out of sports and having to keep away from animals can be heavy burdens. So it's possible that the asthma causes the negative emotions, not the other way around. One study, however, found that when children developed asthma between birth and one year of age, a substantial percentage of the parents reported high levels of perceived stress in their lives.

Studies are beginning to explore a causal role in other disorders of an inflammatory nature. One of them is a chronic pain condition called fibromyalgia. Pain, remember, is not just what happens when you put your hand on a hot stove; it's also a signature of the inflammatory response. Fibromyalgia and chronic fatigue syndrome, a condition believed to be closely related, are examples of the inflammatory response gone awry. They feature chronic pain, fatigue, poor sleep, and a multiplicity of sensitive muscular spots known as trigger points. Both conditions, which are more common in women, can appear after acute or chronic stress. And patients with both conditions show an under-responsive HPA axis—low levels of cortisol in general and a blunted cortisol response to increased adrenocorticotropic hormone and to exercise.

Stress, particularly traumatic stress, may combine with a blunted HPA axis to produce another chronic pain condition: chronic pelvic pain in women with no visible pelvic abnormalities. Christina Heim of the University of Trier studied 30 women with and without chronic pelvic pain, evaluating patients' history of stress, posttraumatic stress disorder, and depression and then measuring their cortisol levels. She found that women with chronic pelvic pain had a higher incidence of sexual and physical abuse as well as blunted cortisol responses. The study does not prove a direct cause-and-effect relationship between trauma and illness, but it is provocative nonetheless.

Another investigator at Trier, Angelika Buske-Kirschbaum, studied the inflammatory disorder known as atopic dermatitis, an itchy skin rash. A group of children ages 8 to 14 were asked to perform public speaking and mental arithmetic tasks. This stress caused a slight increase in cortisol levels in children without rashes, but those with dermatitis had a blunted cortisol response to the challenge. The authors noted that personality type did not appear to be a factor. It's even possible that the weak HPA response might have caused the stress as well as the dermatitis. Buske-Kirshbaum believes that a well-functioning HPA axis is necessary to keep the immune system working for the benefit of the individual but, once again, proof of a causative role for stress remains elusive.

The Immune System's Grievous Mistake

Autoimmune conditions can be thought of as allergic responses taken to the extreme. They occur when the white blood cells mistake a stretch of the body's own protein for an invader of some kind, destroying the erroneous target and forming an immunological memory. One example is juvenile-onset or insulin-dependent diabetes—now usually known as type I diabetes. In this condition the immune system destroys the islet cells of the pancreas, which produce insulin.

An under- or hyporesponsive HPA axis is thought to contribute to type I diabetes, rheumatoid arthritis, and MS. In one strain of rat, called the Lewis rat, the HPA response is genetically sluggish and not enough cortisol is released. These rats are susceptible to a variety of autoimmune and inflammatory conditions. Lewis rats are the workhorses of MS research, being prone to a disorder called experimental autoimmune encephalomyelitis that closely resembles the disease in humans. Normal rats, too, can react to certain stressful living conditions with the same weakened control of immunity.

Autoimmune responses aren't always due to a lack of cortisol; they can be triggered in several ways. Sometimes a natural body substance is altered, by a virus or by radiation. Sometimes the antigen presented by a virus or bacteria is structurally similar enough to a bodily self-protein that the immune system inadvertently goes after both. For example, certain types of the kidney condition known as nephritis are thought to occur when the immune system mistakes proteins in the surface of the kidney cells for proteins in bacterial cell walls.

But sometimes certain T cells simply fail to distinguish between self and nonself; low cortisol may contribute to the error. Normally T cells receive their "education" in the thymus gland, located at the base of the neck. Any T cells that attack an individual's own thymus cells are normally destroyed—by cortisol—before they have a chance to get into the bloodstream. So it's conceivable that chronically low cortisol levels allow autoreactive T cells to escape from the thymus when they ordinarily wouldn't. Cortisol also directly suppresses many of the substances that produce inflammation. Several studies do link a defective HPA axis, and decreased cortisol levels, to rheumatoid arthritis. Still, when it comes to autoimmune diseases, lack of cortisol is probably not the whole story. There may be a combination of genetic predisposition, disrupted HPA axis, and other unidentified environmental factors. Which brings us back, yet again, to the question: Is stress one of the factors?

Several studies have shown an association with childhood stress and insulin-dependent diabetes. Connie Lehman of Yale University, working with rats prone to autoimmune insulin-dependent diabetes, found that 70 to 80 percent of rats that were moderately stressed (by being periodically restrained, rotated, and mildly shaken) developed the disease, whereas only 50 percent of the others did. One of the best-known studies in humans is the Swedish Childhood Diabetes Study, a survey of over 800 children from newborns to age 14 who had recently been diagnosed with diabetes. Stressful life events, generally an actual or a threatened loss of a family member, conferred a higher risk of developing the disease. Some of the same authors studied a smaller group of children and found a link between onset of diabetes and negative life events before age 2, behavioral problems, and a chaotic family structure.

Evidence for a link between stress and MS is more sketchy. One survey of MS patients found that they reported higher levels of life stress than did patients without the disease, but a study of Israeli MS patients exposed to the threat of missile attacks during the Persian Gulf War showed that they actually had fewer relapses during the war and shortly before and after than in the preceding two-year period. One of the biggest problems in proving a link between stress and illness is that, in retrospect, people with a serious or chronic illness are more likely to interpret their past as stressful. The only real way to establish cause and effect is to do a prospective study—taking a group of people, inquiring as to the stressful events in their lives, and then following them over a period of time to see who gets sick and who doesn't.

As the connection between stress and the immune system becomes better understood, what to do about it becomes clearer. For autoimmune disorders and allergies where an overactive immune system is the culprit, glucocorticoids with their reining-in effect are an effective way to calm the abnormal immune response—although such treatment runs the risk of suppressing beneficial immune responses as well. In a sense, treatment with prednisone or other synthetic glucocorticoids mimics aspects of what chronic stress does: it suppresses inflammatory cytokines and reduces the cell trafficking response.

On the other hand, for fighting off viruses or cancer, the trick is to relieve the signs of chronic stress and take advantage of the immune system's ability to mobilize in response to acute stress. Scientific research will offer more insights into how to do this as more is learned about acute versus chronic stress.

For example, our work with the DTH response has some reassuring implications for people who may be facing chronic stress. Even ongoing stress can enhance the immune system's protective actions for a substantial period. In our studies, rats could withstand daily restraint sessions for three weeks, during which time their immune systems responded on the positive end of the allostasis/allostatic load spectrum. For a rat, which typically lives about two years, three weeks is a long time. Even after five weeks of daily stress, a weakened immune system, as measured by the DTH response, can still right itself if the rat is given some time to recover.

Our team and many other scientists are now asking what these time periods translate into in human terms. At what point does acute stress turn into chronic stress—when and how does allostasis slide into allostatic load? Maybe it's a simple matter of time or maybe there has to be a precipitating incident, such as hearing a discouraging prognosis. We need to know more about what happens in the body's environment to bring about this shift. It's a frontier area, but even to be in the position of asking the questions represents great progress in science. Meanwhile, it stands to reason that health-bolstering, stress-reducing precautions can help prolong the immune system's grace period.

Stress and the Brain

The Norse god Odin had two ravens that flew over the world and brought him news at the end of each day. Their names were Thought and Memory. In a saga known as the Grimnismal, Odin voices a concern very much present today:

> I fear for Thought, lest he come not back,
> But I fear yet more for Memory.

Thought and memory are the messengers of our humanity and of our very selves, through which we reason and analyze, contemplate and visualize, and weave the collected experiences of our lives into a coherent and individual whole. The pattern is based on, though not limited to, the physical structure of the brain, with all its biochemical and electrical activity. In an age when brain disorders such as Alzheimer's disease are becoming increasingly more common, we are more aware than ever that, as much as we depend on our thoughts and memories to tell us who we are, the brain that supports these qualities is fragile. Both thought and memory depend on the integrity of this 3-pound organ, and both are vulnerable to stress.

Taking an evolutionary view, it's easy to see why memory and stress are interrelated. Stressful events are arguably the most important ones to remember. An animal has to be able to tell immediately whether sounds, places, scents, and other animals are dangerous. An animal that has to mentally rehearse the sounds and smells of, say, a brushfire, is not likely to survive. Memories associated with stressful events can take shape instantaneously and can be retrieved just as fast. They are formed by a part of the brain called the amygdala working in close conjunction with the hippocampus, which is the keeper of the citadel of memory.

To make sure stressful events leave an imprint deep enough to produce a strong memory, the hippocampus is studded with receptors for the stress hormone cortisol, which is instrumental in memory formation. But this trait leaves the hippocampus vulnerable to high or chronically elevated levels of the hormone, and memory and other cognitive or "thinking" processes can suffer as a result.

The Hunt for Memory in the Brain

Scientists began looking for the brain's memory centers in the early 20th century. The first contributions were made by Karl Lashley of the University of Chicago, who focused on the cerebral cortex, the brain's outermost, thin, wrinkled layer. Though sensory input and motor input come together in the cortex, Lashley found that making selective scars or lesions in the cortex of rats' brains did not prevent the animals from learning to navigate mazes. Clearly, the memories must be stored more globally, and there is redundancy in the neural circuits that support memory. Nevertheless, specific brain areas are associated with specific functions. In the 1930s, neurosurgeon Wilder Penfield of the Montreal Neurological Institute used electrical stimulation to identify functional areas in the brains of human patients. Because the brain has no pain receptors, surgery and stimulation can be performed while patients are conscious (once the scalp is anesthetized), allowing the patients to describe their experiences. Penfield found that stimulating certain areas of the temporal lobe, deeper in the brain, caused a sensation of déjà vu. Though his experiments were not conclusive—for one thing, all of the patients were epileptic and thus had abnormal brains—his work did bring scientists one step closer to finding a brain area devoted to memory.

Brenda Milner, a student of Penfield's, delved into the temporal lobe and identified the hippocampus, located there, as the crux of memory formation. Working with neurosurgeon William Scoville, Milner reported in 1957 her initial studies of a patient known in the annals of science as H.M. This patient had had most of his hippocampus removed in an attempt to treat uncontrollable seizures that concentrated in that area. The surgery did relieve the seizures, but H.M. was left with a bizarre pattern of memory loss. Both his long-term memory and short-term memory functioned well; he could remember his childhood and learn new telephone numbers. His command of English stayed at the same level. Even more provocative, he could learn motor tasks, such as drawing, and even retain the ability to do the task. What he couldn't do was remember, the next day, that he had learned how to accomplish the task, even though he could still do it.

The specific type of memory that H.M. lost was declarative memory—the knowledge that we know something. Declarative memory is the ability to remember facts, names, places, and dates. On an even finer level, H.M. lost the ability to form new declarative memories. The deficit was due to the loss of his hippocampus. Forming declarative memories is the hippocampus's job.

Declarative memory is important in times of stress. The other brain structure I mentioned, the amygdala, is responsible for the emotional content of memory, chiefly fear. An animal that gets a whiff or glimpse of a predator will show all the signs of fear, and this is the amygdala's doing. But the animal has to remember more than the simple signal DANGER. He has to learn where he saw the animal, what time of day it was, what the animal looks like, and where the escape routes are—these and many other facts that we call *context*—so he can avoid the predator if possible and escape when necessary. This is the province of the hippocampus. An emotional memory is a joint product, with the amygdala packing the emotional wallop and the hippocampus providing the when, where, and how. These memories, called episodic memories, are an offshoot of declarative memory.

In an earlier chapter I retold Joseph LeDoux's account of a woman with hippocampal damage whose doctor concealed a pin in his palm when he shook her hand. The woman's declarative memory had been obliterated, and the next day she had no memory of having met the doctor before. But somehow she did know to withdraw her hand. This is because her amygdala still functioned, providing the fear of the pinprick. If the damage had been to the amygdala instead, she would have remembered the doctor and even the pin but would have extended her hand anyway, heedless of the pain. The importance of memory in stress, particularly the type of memory provided by the hippocampus, reveals the "protection versus damage" continuum starkly. Remembering and dealing with danger are some of our most vital means of protection. The hippocampus is the nexus of the process, helping us decide quickly whether something is a threat or not and helping us remember what to do about it. But this means that when stress levels are off the charts or when a stressful condition goes on for too long, the hippocampus and its role in forming memories are at risk.

How Stress Gets into the Brain: The Role of Cortisol

Our understanding of how stress wields its two-edged sword in the brain emerged from several lines of research, all going on at once. By the end of the 1960s, my Rockefeller colleague Jay Weiss and I had shown that cortisol gets into the rat brain through specialized receptors located in the hippocampus. Later, we found the same pattern of uptake in the brain of the rhesus monkey, indicating that the phenomenon was likely to occur in the human brain as well. Today, perched atop three decades' worth of research, I can account for both the cortisol uptake and its occurrence in diverse species: the hippocampus is rich in cortisol receptors because cortisol works in this part of the brain to consolidate some types of memory. But the road to this summit of understanding took many twists and turns, and the initial clues were somewhat alarming.

At about the same time we were doing our initial studies on cortisol and the hippocampus, a team of German scientists reported in 1969 that glucocorticoids, the class of fuel-replenishing hormones to which cortisol belongs, had a toxic effect on brain cells. In 1978, Phillip Landfield, then at the University of California at Irvine, found that as rats aged, their hippocampi began to be impaired. Landfield also observed increased activity of the glia, brain cells that play "supportive" roles like mopping up excess chemicals; this heightened activity suggested that some form of damage was taking place, to which the glia were responding. Some of the aging rats in Landfield's studies began to lose their memories, performing poorly in maze tests that involved memory functions of the hippocampus. Landfield found that he could slow down these changes by removing the rats' adrenal glands as the animals neared middle age. This was fairly convincing evidence that the stress hormones played a role in hippocampal demise.

Throughout the 1980s, Robert Sapolsky, then a student in my lab at Rockefeller University made a series of discoveries. I've mentioned Sapolsky several times already—his contributions to the field of stress research are difficult to overemphasize. First, he found that exposing young rats to high levels of corticosterone—their version of cortisol—accelerated aging of the hippocampus. He found that corticosterone increased the damage that occurred during cerebral ischemia, the blockage of oxygen to the brain that's associated with many types of strokes. This finding was of enormous importance because at the time neurologists were actually treating stroke patients with large doses of glucocorticoids, hoping to keep down the inflammation; now, thanks in part to Sapolsky's work, safer treatments have evolved.

Some of the most important studies to underline the concept of allostasis versus allostatic load came from Sapolsky. For example, his work with cerebral ischemia called attention to the importance of neurotransmitters called excitatory amino acids, chemical messengers by which neurons pass along the message to speed up their activity rate. Foremost of these is glutamate, which turns out to be the classic "Dr. Jekyll and Mr. Hyde" of the neurotransmitter world. Glutamate is prevalent in the hippocampus and is essential to many kinds of learning and memory at their most fundamental level, the level at which neurons change both their structure and their function in response to what is learned. At high doses, though, glutamate is toxic; it's responsible for the damage that occurs after stroke and injury to the brain and spinal cord.

Another key concept Sapolsky both confirmed and extended was that the hippocampus participates in shutting off the hormonal stress response, sending inhibitory signals to the hypothalamus where the hormonal stress response is governed. During stress, rats and monkeys with lesions to the hippocampus take longer to shut off their stress response; they also have higher levels of corticosterone. This brings us back to the dynamic of protection and damage. Stress hormones acting on the hippocampus can engrave important experiences into our long-term memory, but excessive or chronically elevated levels of these same hormones can damage the very part of the brain that shuts them off.

Sapolsky also found this vicious cycle to be more prevalent in older animals. This research led him to propose the so-called glucocorticoid cascade hypothesis for the aging of both brain and body. This gradual aging process in which the glucocorticoid, cortisol, plays a key role was perhaps the first way of formulating the concept now called allostatic load. In this scenario, glucocorticoid levels become higher during aging and damage the shutoff mechanism in the hippocampus, which leads to yet higher levels of stress hormones, which damage the hippocampus even further. Many problems associated with high cortisol levels do become more common in older people, such as diabetes, hypertension, and an immune system that functions less than optimally. Of course, many people sail into their nineties without having any of these problems and scoff at the whole concept of "stress," but the fact remains that older individuals are more vulnerable to conditions related, if not to external stressors in life, to elevated cortisol.

Mapping Stress and Memory Circuits in Humans

By the late 1980s and early 1990s, Sapolsky and other researchers had confirmed that stress-induced hippocampal damage is not just a peculiarity of rats. Sapolsky and Hideo Uno, who was then at the University of Wisconsin, found in 1989 that the stress of being subordinate in a social group caused damage to the hippocampi of vervet monkeys. (Curiously, this damage to the hippocampus happened only in males, although there were females who had undergone similar degrees of social subordination and had developed physical symptoms of chronic stress like stomach ulcers and immune suppression.) The next question to tackle was whether stress had the same deleterious effects on the brains of humans.

To make the jump from animal subjects to humans, two things had to happen. First, when studying stress in humans the emotions have to be taken into consideration, so the study of emotion had to become a part of science. Second, a way to study the living human brain had to be found.

Throughout the 1980s and 1990s, scientists like Joseph LeDoux of New York University, Mike Fanselow of the University of California, Los Angeles, and Mike Davis, then at Yale and now at Emory, brought the study of emotion into the realm of neuroscience. And the emotion that these scientists chose to investigate was the least controversial and easiest to study—fear. Working with rats and then primates, these researchers identified the amygdala as the cornerstone of the fear process. Using electrical pulses or injected chemicals to make lesions in various neural pathways, they found that animals with damage to the amygdala couldn't form ordinary conditioned reflexes in response to fear. For example, if healthy rats receive a shock and hear a tone at the same time, they will quickly learn to freeze when they hear the tone by itself. Rats with lesions to the amygdala fail to make this association, indicating that the amygdala is necessary to the process. This is a classic experiment known as fear conditioning.

The role of the hippocampus became clear in a related experiment known as contextual fear conditioning. This time the rat received a mild shock in a visually distinct type of cage. Thereafter the rat froze whenever it entered that cage, demonstrating its memory for context— the where and when. Hippocampal lesions interfered with this type of conditioning but not classic fear conditioning, thus establishing the role of the hippocampus in contextual memory. Lesions to the amygdala blocked both processes, meaning the amygdala is vital to both. Taken together, these studies were elegant proof that the amygdala provides the emotional component of memory and works with the hippocampus to provide the context, giving scientists an idea of what to look for in the human brain.

Scientists were also developing the means to find what they were looking for. The 1990s saw the advent of imaging techniques, such as positron emission tomography (PET) and functional magnetic resonance imaging (fMRI). These new techniques allowed researchers to watch the living human brain in action. With imaging technology, researchers can take pictures of the living brain, detecting specific processes, such as glucose or oxygen consumption, which indicate where most of the activity is taking place. The degree of activity shows up in color, providing a virtual snapshot of what's going on in the brain. It's true that scientists can't tell precisely what the brain is doing based on how much glucose it's using. But if certain areas use less glucose, say, in people with chronic depression compared to unafflicted people, it's reasonable to assume that those areas are somehow compromised in depression. Or other brain areas may show more activity in depression, indicating that they may be functioning at abnormally high levels.

MRI can provide highly sensitive structural information about the brain. These techniques allowed scientists to confirm the function of the hippocampus and amygdala in humans. Obviously researchers can't just damage someone's brain to observe the effect on fear-related memories, but they can study memory formation in patients who already have lesions in certain areas due to stroke, injury, or brain surgery, as detected by MRI.

By the 1990s the respective roles of the hippocampus and amygdala were clear in humans as well as laboratory animals. For example, in a 1994 study, Antonio Damasio of the University of Iowa showed photographs of faces with various emotional expressions to a patient with brain damage restricted to the amygdala. The patient correctly identified each facial expression except fear. The damage to her amygdala prevented her not only from experiencing fear but also recognizing it in others. Other studies have shown that the amygdala is a hub of pleasant emotions as well. A team from Emory University using PET scanning showed that pictures of cute animals, appetizing food, and sex scenes provoked activity in the amygdala similar to that caused by un-pleasant, grisly images, whereas neutral pictures, such as chess games, did not seem to involve the amygdala.

Cortisol Shows Its Worth

While Joe LeDoux and others were showing researchers where emo-tions could be found in the brain and imaging technology was provid-ing the window through which to look, a third line of research in the 1990s produced some of the first solid evidence for the role of stress hormones in memory. Initially these studies focused on the first-wave stress hormone, adrenaline, and they bucked tradition by beginning in humans and then moving into animal research. Jim McGaugh and Larry Cahill of the University of California, Irvine, asked healthy adult volunteers to watch two films of cars and pedestrians. One film was fairly innocuous; the other showed a gruesome accident.

The viewers were divided into two groups. One group was in-jected with propanolol, one of the so-called beta blockers used to treat heart disease by blocking the receptors for adrenaline. The other group received no treatment. Both groups viewed both films. When the propanolol group watched the grisly scene, the treatment decreased heart rate and blood pressure, as expected. It did not prevent the vol-unteers from experiencing emotional responses, which they described immediately after seeing the film. But a week later the viewers had trouble recalling details of the disturbing film, while their memories of the neutral film, in which no one was injured, were unimpaired. On the other hand, the volunteers who received no propranolol treat-ment—whose adrenaline was unimpeded—had much better memory for the grisly story than for the neutral one. This differential effect pro-vided clear evidence that adrenaline helps to develop memories of un-pleasant things. But the study didn't explain what went on in the brain, since adrenaline does not work in the brain but in the blood vessels that pass through the brain, transmitting signals to the brain by mecha-nisms that are not fully understood.

Cortisol, however, does enter the brain. So McGaugh teamed up with Benno Roozendahl, who had recently arrived from the Netherlands, to see if this hormone also played a role in memory formation. Working with rats, the researchers focused on a phenomenon known as passive avoidance. If a rat walks through a door into another part of its cage and receives a shock, the next time the door opens the rat won't go in. But if the shock is a mild one, curiosity will win out and the rat will soon venture into the new area. (Unlike the contextual conditioning that LeDoux used, in which the rat simply froze on hearing the tone, in these studies the rat had to choose to walk into the new place.) When McGaugh and Roozendahl added cortisol to the experiment, introducing the hormone directly into the amygdala and hippocampus, the rats wouldn't budge. This finding indicated that cortisol was helping not only to solidify the fear but to link the shock with the place where it occurred. This was another example of the contextual memory governed by the hippocampus—the when and where associated with the frightening event. It became clear that cortisol was a necessary ingredient.

Allostatic Load Takes Its Toll on the Hippocampus

Now the presence of cortisol receptors in the hippocampus made sense. So did the idea that cortisol could play a protective role in the brain

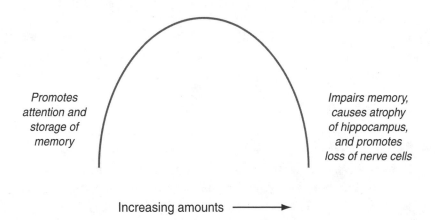

FIGURE 6   Protection versus damage: brain function and memory. Normal levels of stress hormones promote the storage of memory, but elevated levels over long periods can impair memory.

during an emergency; evolutionarily speaking, there's limited benefit in escaping from danger if you can't remember how to avoid it in the future. By now this explanation was sorely needed because imaging studies in humans were showing that cortisol could damage the brain and that this damage could be quite severe.

Some of the first clues came from Monica Starkman, a researcher and psychiatrist at the University of Michigan who studied patients with a condition called Cushing's syndrome. Cushing's is an intrinsic form of allostatic load in which noncancerous tumors in the pituitary gland cause massive glucocorticoid production. Though not related to external stressors of life, the condition leads to hypertension, diabetes, immune system troubles, and many other conditions associated with chronic stress. These patients also have memory troubles. Starkman and colleagues found that in Cushing's patients the hippocampus was smaller than normal; what's more, both the degree of shrinkage and the extent of memory loss were proportional to the elevation in cortisol. No other part of the brain was affected—only the hippocampus, where memory, cortisol, and stress all meet. Other studies showed that people who had suffered trauma earlier in life also had smaller hippocampi; these studies included people with posttraumatic stress disorder (PTSD) from combat in Vietnam and survivors of childhood sexual abuse. Then, in 1996, Yvette Sheline and colleagues at Washington University found the same pattern in people with chronic depression (many depressed people have elevated levels of glucocorticoids in their blood). A particularly intriguing aspect of Sheline's work is that the patients were not depressed at the time of the study; their bouts with depression had been years earlier. The extent of the hippocampal shrinkage, or atrophy, corresponded with how long the period of depression lasted at the time, even if that time was 10 years previously.

The studies unleashed a blizzard of questions with regard to mental illness. For one thing, there was no proof that emotional trauma or PTSD had *caused* the hippocampus to get smaller; it might have been smaller to begin with, a trait that might set the stage for the condition to develop. Assuming that cause and effect could be established, the elapsed time in Dr. Sheline's studies between onset of depression and discovery of the smaller hippocampus was also puzzling. It might mean, ominously, that a single trauma or depressive episode left trails of destruction and cognitive impairment that had not fully healed even years later. On the other hand, maybe some slower process was going on, which treatment might be able to head off. This possibility was tantalizing not only for therapists, for whom it underscored the importance of prompt intervention in mood disorders, but also for scientists like myself who were interested in allostasis and allostatic load. If some ongoing process was causing the hippocampus to get smaller, what was it? And could it conceivably be beneficial, at least in the short term? Finally, could the hippocampus be restored to its normal size?

Research answered the last question first. In the case of Cushing's disease, Starkman and colleagues found that when they corrected the elevated cortisol and imaged the brain again, the hippocampus began to resume its normal size. In other words, the effects of elevated cortisol on the volume of the hippocampus may not be permanent after all. Then, animal studies showed that some dramatic effects of psychological stress could indeed be reversed.

Dominance Has Its Price

In our lab, Randall Sakai, now at the University of Cincinnati, put together a team that included Caroline and Robert Blanchard of the University of Hawaii, who are experts in the study of defensive behavior of animals in social groups. We used the Blanchards' Visible Burrow System, a living environment with clear plastic walls that allowed us to watch the animals in a habitat more natural than a laboratory cage. Normally, groups of male rats will get along pretty well, but if you introduce females, the males will fight until they form a dominance hierarchy. The animal that emerges victorious controls access to the water and food—and to the females. The other males have to hide out in closed tunnels and chambers included in the burrow, sneaking out to get food and water when the top rat isn't looking. The subordinate rats can't even get near the females.

Being confined together is stressful for subordinates and dominants alike. Within 14 days of this type of life, some of the subordinates died—not from injuries inflicted by the other males but from severe disruption to their autonomic nervous system, possibly even the voodoo death that I talked about in Chapter 5. They simply died. Of the survivors, the most severely stressed ones had practically zero testosterone and showed other hormone changes that indicate allostatic load. In the brain, neurochemical changes reminiscent of depressive illness, including imbalances in the brain chemical serotonin, suggested that the subordinate animals probably had some degree of rat-type depression. The dominants' neurochemistry also changed but in slightly different ways.

In both the subordinates and the dominants, the neurons in the hippocampus became shorter and less branched—less dramatically in the subordinates, for some reason. We described this phenomenon as dendritic remodeling because it was clearly not atrophy, which the imaging studies showing smaller hippocampal volume had initially caused researchers to suspect.

Our studies showed that these dendritic changes are reversible. When the animals were put back in their home cages, the hormone and neurotransmitter levels also reversed themselves. So, clearly, more was going on than just a straightforward case of cortisol poisoning. The signs of stress observed in our rats represented not damage but a pause in some of the processes through which the brain recovers and renews itself. These processes are plasticity, through which the brain reconfigures itself in response to stimuli from the outside world, and neurogenesis, the birth of new neurons in the mature brain. We came to believe that in response to stress the brain puts both plasticity and neurogenesis on hold as a protective measure, and this, we suspected, explained the hippocampal shrinkage observed by so many researchers.

Regrowth and Renewal in the Brain

In the late 1980s, scientists began to realize that the brain is a plastic organ. For many people the word *plastic* conjures up an image of the brain as something cheap and brittle that dangles from a key ring and possibly even glows in the dark. Actually, the brain is plastic in the sense that it's malleable, resilient, and responsive. The brain changes in response to experience, not only modifying the way it works but also remolding and reconfiguring its very structure. This process of modification is how we learn and remember.

One brain cell sends a signal to another over a long projection, the axon. The message is picked up by a shorter projection called a dendrite; these structures extend from the receiving cell like tree branches. Between the axon and the receiving dendrite is a space, called a synaptic gap, and the connection as a whole is referred to as a synapse. Learning and memory are examples of plasticity that stimulate the brain to produce new synapses. The more synapses are dedicated to an experience, the more likely that experience is to become a permanent feature in the memory's landscape. Imagine a trail through the woods. The more hikers that walk on it, the more deeply it will be imprinted on the forest floor.

The brain contains a "map" in which every part of the body has a corresponding group of nerve cells. Through plasticity, learning and memory regroove the paths in this map quite literally. The principle plays out in the brain in a way that was first proved by Michael Merzenich of the University of California at San Francisco. Merzenich taught a monkey to tap a bar using only one finger. The "rehearsals" actually changed the monkey's brain in a way that reinforced the action. Although the explanation for these changes in not clear, it is possible that in the monkey's brain the cells that "mapped" to the tapping fingers may have grown more synapses, thus devoting more space and more wiring to support the new skill.

Such plasticity is at work behind everything we learn, all of our memories, declarative and otherwise. We remember facts and faces, we sing, we play musical instruments, we ride bicycles, and we hit tennis balls because experience rewires the brain to reinforce this knowledge in our lives. Memory is not the only thing that's due to plasticity. Drug addiction, for example, arises when exposure to a particular drug changes brain cells in a way that makes them function poorly without it. Although people may start using a substance of abuse to feel good, eventually they must continue taking it to avoid feeling miserable, because their brains have been altered and now need the drug to function normally.

But the brain can do more than rewire itself in response to simula-
tion from the outside world: it actually grows new cells throughout
life. This process, known as neurogenesis, was not accepted by scientists until the tail end of the 20th century, partly because the sophisticated technology needed to detect new brain cells wasn't available. In
the late 1990s a postdoctoral fellow in my laboratory, Elizabeth Gould
(now a professor at Princeton) showed that the adult rat hippocampus
continues to produce new cells in an area called the dentate gyrus. She
also found that increased cortisol and chronic stress could suppress
this production of new cells, working first with rats and then primates.
In the late 1990s, Fred Gage and colleagues at the Salk Institute provided evidence of neurogenesis in humans. Both researchers used a
chemical called bromodioxyuridine (BrdU), which is taken up into dividing cells and can be detected by specialized staining.

To establish neurogenesis in humans, Gage studied brain tissue
from five patients who had died of cancer and who had received BrdU
injections to check the progress of their tumors. Gage and colleagues
did find BrdU in the dentate gyrus of these patients, confirming that
there were dividing, and hence newborn, cells in this part of the brain.
Given what is known about the effects of stress on neurogenesis and
given that these individuals were undergoing one of the most severe
stressors imaginable, the presence of new brain cells in these patients is
remarkable. Perhaps the phenomenon is even more robust in healthy
people.

Neurogenesis is closely linked to learning and memory. For example, in 1997 Gage found that when rats were raised in an enriched
environment the dentate gyrus stepped up its production of new cells
by 15 percent. This augmented the work of William Greenough at the
University of Illinois in the 1980s, which showed that an enriched environment increased the number of synapses in parts of the brain.

So neuroscientists had proved the existence of plasticity and
neurogenesis; we had shown that stress can stifle and learning can
stimulate both processes and that the hippocampus was the hotbed of
all of this activity. With this new knowledge, we were finally glimpsing
the way in which the effects of stress on the brain could be considered
a good thing. We suspected that long before allostatic load caused

structural damage to the hippocampus, the protective hand of allostasis might ward off such damage by holding the brain's adaptive processes in temporary check. We believed that stress-induced hippocampal shrinkage resulted from the brain's attempts to put both plasticity and neurogenesis on the back burner.

How Shrews Tame Each Other

With our German colleagues Eberhard Fuchs and Gabrielle Flugge of the German Primate Center in Göttingen, we embarked on a series of experiments to confirm our suspicions. To come closer to understanding how stress affects plasticity and neurogenesis in humans, we worked with the tree shrew, an animal that looks like a squirrel but is thought to be a primitive primate. Through these experiments we established that when an animal experiences chronic psychological stress, nerve cells in the hippocampus shrink and change shape, and new brain cell formation in the dentate gyrus is suppressed. We also established that these effects are reversible.

The tree shrew is a loner, an animal that doesn't like company in its cage. If you put a naive tree shrew (one that has never been in an experiment before) into the cage of a proven dominant, a scuffle ensues; the intruder is made to feel under continual threat. The intruder is markedly stressed and produces both major stress hormones, adrenaline and cortisol. And you only have to do this for one hour to see striking changes on many levels.

Normally, in the tree shrew, as in the other animals that have been studied, neurogenesis goes on throughout adult life in dentate gyrus. In our tree shrew studies, a single hour of stress suppressed the formation of new nerve cells in the hippocampus, but this reduction reversed itself when the animal was put back into its own cage. When we kept the intruder living next door to the dominant for one month and opened the cage door between them for one hour a day, the body weight of the newcomer decreased. Levels of cortisol and adrenaline rose daily, indicating allostatic load. The dentate gyrus became smaller and showed a severe suppression of neurogenesis. We also found dendritic remodeling in other nerve cells in the hippocampus.

We understood this remodeling thanks to parallel studies by Ana Maria Magarinos in my laboratory. Working with rats, she showed that three weeks of repeated stress scaled back activity in the hippocampus in two ways. First, dendrites of the hippocampal neurons showed remodeling in the classic sense: they became shorter and less branched, which meant fewer synaptic connections and hence reduced opportunity for the flow of information. Second, in the nerve endings the vesicles, or small reservoirs of excitatory amino acid neurotransmitters, began to dry up—a phenomenon we dubbed synaptic remodeling, a sort of companion process to dendritic remodeling. Because neurons use excitatory neurotransmitters to tell each other to increase their level of activity, fewer of these vesicles meant that fewer signals could be passed. Both types of remodeling result in a mild-to-moderate impairment of those memories known to depend on the hippocampus. However, the hippocampus still functions and memory still occurs, so the hippocampus obviously hasn't been severely and permanently damaged.

In the repeatedly stressed rat we saw the same inhibition of neurogenesis in the dentate gyrus as in the stressed-out tree shrew. Kara Pham in my laboratory has found that prolonging daily stress for six weeks causes the number of certain hippocampal neurons to decrease. Thus, chronic stress in two different animal species has the same effect: to cause reorganization of nerve cell structure—that is, the dendrites—and to decrease the production of new dentate gyrus neurons.

What Is Protection and What Is Damage?

As lopsidedly negative as these findings sound, they fit neatly into the picture of protection versus damage. We interpret dendritic remodeling and the halt in neurogenesis to mean the hippocampus is bending but not breaking in response to stress—a compensatory effort to protect itself, like a turtle withdrawing its head and legs into its shell when it senses danger. This is the other side of the phenomenon that Dr. Greenough observed when rats in an enriched learning environment showed more dendritic branching and more synaptic connections. In that situation the new experiences and learning made the brain grow, getting larger and stronger. Here, under severe stress, the brain is quite literally withdrawing, showing a slight amount of cognitive impairment but protecting itself to fight another day. So even then we're still seeing the two-sided effects of stress in action.

What about the tendency of stress to interfere with neurogenesis? Studies now going on in our lab show an intriguing possibility. Earlier I mentioned fear conditioning in rats. If a rat is in a familiar cage environment and hears a loud sound followed by a mild shock, he learns to freeze as soon as he hears the tone. We're finding that rats in this situation, although they are learning quite quickly, actually produce fewer cells in the dentate gyrus than control rats that aren't receiving the passive avoidance conditioning. How can *fewer* cells result in learning? One possibility is that, although the stress of the conditioning affects the total number of cells produced, the cells that *are* produced are dedicated to one particular purpose—in this case, what to do when that noise is heard. Perhaps these fewer cells may live longer. This is something we are now testing.

It's possible that under conditions of prolonged or extreme stress the brain's resilience may give out, with the synaptic remodeling, the reduction of neurogenesis, or both becoming permanent, resulting in the hippocampus becoming smaller. This situation may explain the most extreme form in which allostatic load affects the brain: PTSD.

When Trauma Dominates the Brain

In PTSD the traumatic event engraves itself in the brain, often obliterating more recent, and less significant, memories. Combat veterans with PTSD may forget to show up for appointments with their psychiatrists—sometimes interpreted as a resistance to treatment—and many of them score lower on memory tests aimed specifically at testing the hippocampus, such as remembering whole paragraphs or lists of words. The trauma comes flooding back in nightmares or as a flashback in waking life. At such times the remembered scene can preempt reality, causing the sufferer to lose touch with what is actually going on. PTSD affects an estimated 15 percent of people who experience severe trauma, such as combat, rape, child abuse, or auto accidents.

Imaging studies of patients with PTSD show that about half have a smaller hippocampus than usual.

At first glance, it seems logical that people beseiged with horrific memories would have cortisol flooding their brains—shriveling dendrites, stifling neurogenesis, and destroying neurons—ultimately resulting in a smaller hippocampus. But this assumption leads the unwary scientist into a thicket of controversy. Some PTSD sufferers actually have low cortisol, at least at times. Several groups of researchers have obtained blood samples taken within hours after traumas such as rapes or auto accidents and found that the victims who went on to develop PTSD had lower than normal cortisol levels. Other studies show that, although some PTSD sufferers have low cortisol in the aftermath of the trauma and at times when they are reminded of it—during flashbacks, for example—they have higher levels of the hormone at other times, and in general the hypothalamic-pituitary-adrenal (HPA) axis of these patients is oversensitive to being activated. Normal daily fluctuations may be skewed as well. Researchers who studied United Nations soldiers after a mine accident in Lebanon reported that their daily cortisol rhythms were reversed. Five days after the accident, levels of the hormone were lower than usual in the morning and higher in the evening in subjects who reported posttraumatic distress, while nine months later this reversal was even more pronounced in those who continued to show PTSD. However, the normal daily rhythm righted itself in those soldiers who showed recovery from their traumatic distress.

Scientists are divided on how to interpret this conflicting evidence. It does appear that, regardless of the role of cortisol, reduced hippocampal volume and memory impairment are associated with PTSD, at least sometimes. Based on our tree shrew studies and Magarinos's work with rats, it is clear that chronic stress can shrink the hippocampus, remodeling dendrites and putting neurogenesis on hold. But we've also shown that these processes can be reversed. To know for sure whether trauma or severe depression doom sufferers to hippocampal atrophy and memory loss down the road—and to clarify the cortisol picture—studies are needed that follow such patients over many years, checking cortisol levels and imaging the hippocampi. Because trauma can't be foreseen, there will probably never be a way to find out exactly what cortisol levels were at the time the trauma occurred.

One thing that may be on the horizon, though, is a way of heading off hippocampal atrophy *before* the hippocampus begins to shrink. Working with tree shrews, Fuchs has used an imaging technique called magnetic resonance spectroscopy (MRS) to show that even in animals that don't have reduced hippocampal volume, chronic stress reduces levels of a chemical called N-acetylaspartate (NAA), which is found only in the axons of adult brains and is considered a chemical sign of brain cell health. Treating the animals with the antidepressant tianeptine corrected the levels of NAA and restored neurogenesis activity to normal.

In 2001 a team from the University of California, San Francisco, used MRS to detect levels of NAA in combat veterans with PTSD. It was found that NAA was reduced by about 23 percent compared to men without the disorder. The NAA levels showed that something was clearly amiss in the hippocampus. However, the PTSD sufferers showed no measurable reduction in the volume of the hippocampus. It is possible that the decreases in NAA reflected decreased volumes of nerve cells that were compensated for by increased amounts of the glia, or support cells. Clearly, findings like this cry out for studies of the same individuals over many years—would actual atrophy develop later in life?—but they also raise the possibility that treatments may be able to stop the progression of this terrible disorder. (Tianeptine, found effective in the animal studies, is one of the best-selling antidepressants in France but is not yet approved by the U.S. Food and Drug Administration, and only about half of PTSD patients respond to the antidepressants currently available in this country.) Taken together, I believe the available research is a powerful argument that the allostatic load represented by PTSD is years in the making and can be forestalled with the right kind of treatment.

One such treatment might be the use of cortisol therapy to fend off PTSD. In 1999 a German team of researchers studied patients who were in intensive care units due to septic shock, a massive overreaction of the immune system to bacterial infection. Noting that medical emergencies sometimes result in PTSD, the researchers treated half of the septic shock patients with high doses of hydrocortisone, while the other half received the standard treatment; there were 27 patients in each group. Only five of the subjects who received the hydrocortisone developed PTSD as a result of their medical trauma, whereas 16 of the others developed the condition.

Another approach already under investigation is the use of beta blockers to interfere with the action of adrenaline, the first and quickest acting of the stress hormones. Adrenaline helps to shore up memories that have a high "emotion index," as Jim McGaugh and Larry Cahill showed with their films of highway carnage. It is possible that beta blocker treatment could prevent the development of PTSD in trauma victims. The question is whether beta blockers would also calm down the intrusive memories in a brain already ridden with PTSD. By the same token, we need to find out if cortisol could calm the PTSD symptoms in people who already have the disorder. At the very least, cortisol levels in the aftermath of trauma seem to be a good way to judge who is most likely to develop PTSD, particularly if used along with psychological testing.

Genes and Stress

The dawn is only now starting to break on the questions that I came to Rockefeller University more than 30 years ago to investigate. Exactly how does the biochemistry of allostatic load damage and reshape brain cells, and specifically what genes bring this about? To really understand how chronic depression can leave someone with memory impairment or reduce the hippocampus, either permanently or as a short-term protective strategy, science has to start answering these questions, and some answers are beginning to emerge.

Based on animal studies, we know that cortisol is only part of the story when it comes to stress and the brain. Another key player is a neurotransmitter known as glutamate, the most "exciting" of the excitatory neurotransmitters, through which nerve cells tell each other to speed up. Glutamate is widely used in many processes related to learning and memory; it's responsible for virtually all of the synaptic transmission in the hippocampus. When a group of cells exchanges glutamate like runners passing the baton in a relay race, the result is a memory. At high doses, on the other hand, glutamate can be dangerous. The seizures of epilepsy, for example, occur when excess glutamate causes large masses of cells to increase their activity rate; at this point the neatly coordinated brain-cell relay begins instead to look like a large mob running around in a panic. High doses of glutamate can also be lethal to neurons. In fact, drugs that work against epilepsy, or by blocking certain glutamate receptors, can block stress-induced or even cortisol-induced atrophy of hippocampal neurons.

Glutamate is a key player in dendritic remodeling. Under conditions of chronic stress—and also in the aging brain—dendritic shrinkage at some point becomes irreversible. This may be because some routine process of clearing away excess glutamate, or shutting off its actions, is no longer operative. Earlier I said that one type of allostatic load involves a stress response that can't be shut off—for example, when people are still brimming with rage about an altercation that took place hours earlier. High levels of glutamate may well represent the same type of scenario on a cellular level, and we now know that cortisol can work in the brain to exaggerate the effects of glutamate.

Cortisol would earn its keep if all it did was replenish fuel stores and regulate allostasis, even with all the damage that's done when we're chronically stressed. But cortisol also has effects at the level of our genes—stepping up the activity of glutamate, for example, which can lead to either learning or allostatic load.

Cellular On/Off Switches

Major changes in our bodies, including the stress response itself, occur when genes are activated. Research to date hasn't turned up any genes specifically associated with a vulnerability to allostatic load—a hair-trigger HPA axis, for example, or a poorly regulated vagal brake. However, some studies do suggest that a less than ideal stress response may have at least a genetic component. For example, as I mentioned in connection with stress and the heart, one study showed that subjects whose blood pressure rose for longer than usual in response to a psychological stressor had two parents with hypertension. Unfortunately, we're far from identifying the gene and its protein product—information we might be able to use to design a medication that could nudge the blood pressure back to normal levels.

In only a few diseases does someone with a "bad" gene inevitably inherit the disease, as with Huntington's disease. Most genes confer *possibility* only; whether the disease, or trait, actually emerges depends on how and when the genes are activated. Think of DNA as a piano. A piano always has 88 keys and they're always the same 88 notes, but no music comes out until the keys are pressed. Then, there's virtually no limit to the music a piano can produce. It depends on which keys are pressed, in which combinations, at which times. In human life the musician is often the person's environment.

Eric Kandel of Columbia University won a Nobel Prize in 2000 for showing how signals from the environment activate genes that result in memory consolidation. Working with a marine snail called *Aplysia* and with mice, Kandel showed that the combination of a touch and a mild shock, repeated often enough, activated a protein in the nucleus of key hippocampal cells. This protein, the cyclic-AMP-responsive element binding protein—mercifully abbreviated CREB—attached itself to the DNA and turned on a series of genes that built new synapses dedicated to the memory of the shock. Then, Tim Tully and Jerry Yin at Cold Spring Harbor Laboratory showed that increasing or overexpressing CREB in fruit flies allowed the insects to learn a conditioned response—flying away from a sound that's coupled with a shock—after just one training trial, whereas normal flies required 10 sessions. Overexpressing CREB did not result in more memory or better memory. What it did was condense the time needed for a short-term memory to become a permanent feature in the landscape of the brain. The CREB research neatly shows how events in the outside world—the shocks—cause chemical changes that activate genes, playing the notes on the keyboard of DNA that result in long-term memory.

Nitty-Gritty Effects of Cortisol

Like CREB, cortisol also binds to DNA but through a different route. When the hormone comes in contact with its receptor, the receptor's structure changes, allowing cortisol to bind to specific sequences in the cell's DNA and induce changes in the cell's functioning by stimulating the readout of the genetic code. Through this action, cortisol appears to affect nerve cells in several ways that raise their activity level, helping them work better in the short term but perhaps exhausting them over long periods. For example, back when I talked about metabolism and diabetes, I said that all the food we eat must be metabolized into glucose before it can enter and fuel our cells. (This is easier for the body to do with food high in carbohydrates, like English muffins, because carbohydrates are essentially more complex versions of sugars such as glucose. Turning a hamburger and fries or a Thanksgiving dinner into simple glucose requires more steps, but the body does it.) The main hormone that ushers the glucose into the cells is insulin, which is insufficient in the case of diabetes, either because the body doesn't make enough or because the cells become insulin resistant. But because it's so important that glucose get into cells, particularly brain cells, other hormones can take on insulin's responsibility for glucose entry. One of them is cortisol.

The brain uses colossal amounts of glucose; though accounting for only about 3 percent of the body's weight, it uses about 20 percent of incoming energy. A decrease in blood sugar levels may mean a corresponding slump in mental acuity; indeed, most people will agree that they're not at their sharpest just before lunch, when they're hungry. In times of acute stress it's just as important for the brain to get its share of fuel as it is for the muscles of the arms and legs. Normally, cortisol is not the chief of supply; its humdrum everyday task is to pack fuel off into storage by stimulating enzymes in the liver. But in times of crisis, cortisol, with its special relationship to the brain, can bring in emergency provisions. When absolutely necessary, cortisol speeds the delivery of glucose into brain cells, and it does so by activating genes that increase the neuron's glucose uptake.

Cortisol also works through genes to increase what neuroscientists call their excitability (the genes' excitability, not the scientists'), and this has direct consequences for learning and memory and probably for allostatic load. Real learning doesn't happen until the cell's excitability increases. The process works like this: repetition of stimulus—the multiplication tables if you're a person, a shock to the tail if you're the marine snail *Aplysia*—sends a spurt of glutamate between brain cells, again and again until a certain threshold is crossed. Now it will take less glutamate each time to send the message. The receiving cell has become more sensitive to glutamate, or more excitable; the synaptic connection has been strengthened; something has been learned. The strengthening of the synapse is also called potentiation, and the whole process, because it can last for long periods and even permanently, is called long-term potentiation.

Cortisol appears to affect this process in two ways. First, it binds to genes that increase the neuron's level of excitability. Second, when we experiment in the laboratory on cells, glucocorticoids increase the levels of a specific type of glutamate receptor known as the n-methyl-D-aspartate (NMDA) receptor, although whether this happens in you or me under acute stress remains to be seen. But it's reasonable to assume that stress is working on the brain in these ways. More sensitivity to glutamate, and more receptors for the same, will mean that more glutamate-mediated messages will be received. This in turn means that the brain can learn and remember more quickly, which is enormously beneficial (up to a point) in conditions of acute stress. But because glutamate is toxic to nerve cells at high levels, it may also explain both the hippocampal atrophy and the memory impairment observed under conditions of chronic stress.

Stress and the Aging Brain

Stress is no respecter of age, and, inevitably, we will confront it with an aging brain. It would be nice to say that a lifetime of experiences gives us an advantage, but, alas, the brain, as it ages, becomes more vulnerable to the effects of stress. Much of the supporting research for this gloomy news comes from animal studies. In young rats, for instance, repeated stress causes down-regulation, or a decrease, in glucocorticoid receptors, meaning that fewer receptors are produced in the brain cells. This is a built-in neutralizer by which high levels of cortisol actually become less effective, because the hormones find fewer receptors to lock into. However, with increasing age, the rats tend to lose this safety catch; the receptors don't down-regulate as efficiently, leaving more of them when there should be fewer, thus giving stress-generated cortisol a broader target area. This decrease in down-regulation is particularly apparent in older rats that also happen to be cognitively impaired. When aging rats undergo restraint stress (kept for brief periods in a clear cylinder that restricts their movement), glutamate levels in the hippocampus are elevated and prolonged, increasing the potential for damage and allostatic load.

Again, not all older individuals, rats or humans, have these problems. Those that do, however, show cognitive impairments that seem to be related to high cortisol levels. Sonya Lupien, who did postdoctoral work in my laboratory and is a faculty member at McGill University, has done some studies of basically healthy people over a number of years, checking both cortisol levels and mental acuity as measured by psychological tests of explicit memory and selective attention. In the most extensive of these studies, Dr. Lupien and colleagues followed 11 healthy elderly subjects over a period of four years. In six subjects, cortisol levels climbed over the four years and peaked in year 4. The subjects had trouble with memory tasks such as navigating a maze designed for humans and remembering lists of words. The other five, whose cortisol levels went down or stayed the same at the end of the four years, marched through the maze and rattled off the lists of words with no problem. In a follow-up, MRI revealed that the subjects with higher cortisol and poorer memory also had hippocampi that were about 14 percent smaller than their more successfully aging counterparts.

I've said that cortisol works together with excitatory neurotransmitters, chiefly glutamate, to produce stress-related learning and memory as well as damage, but there is another consequence. One result of having excess excitatory neurotransmitters like glutamate is that destructive compounds known as free radicals begin to accumulate. When glutamate activates the NMDA receptor, it allows calcium to flow into the cell, and too much calcium generates free radicals. Hence, too much glutmate will lead to too many free radicals. These compounds are elements, like oxygen, that have one or more unpaired electrons. That means that they're ready to snatch electrons where they can to make a stable pair; the resulting "reactivity" makes them able to damage cells, proteins, and DNA. Free radicals are considered to be the culprits in many diseases, including cancer and neurodegenerative diseases of the brain, as well as in the normal wear and tear associated with aging. The interaction of neurons with cortisol facilitates this process, since cortisol makes neurons more sensitive to glutamate and increases the number of NMDA receptors.

The implications for the elderly are uncertain, but if cortisol enhances the effects of glutamate to produce free radical damage, this may be one way stress exerts its effects. Although the body has a host of antioxidants, which help to mop up free radicals (as do antioxidants such as vitamins C and E), older individuals tend to have less of one type, called magnesium-dependent SOD. If older people also have mounting cortisol levels and glutamate activity throughout the years, thus weakening their own ability to stave off free radical damage, it may partly explain the cognitive problems observed by Dr. Lupien and colleagues.

Another important consequence of elevated excitatory neurotransmitters and elevated glucocorticoids in the aging animal is suppression of the formation of new brain cells, or neurogenesis. Heather Cameron, a former student of Elizabeth Gould, now working at the National Institutes of Health, coauthored a paper showing that aging rats have very low levels of neurogenesis in the dentate gyrus; removing the adrenals from these aging animals restored the rate of neurogenesis to that found in younger rats—and it did so in only a few days. This result recalls Phil Landfield's work, which I mentioned before and which showed that age-related impairment of the rat's hippocampus could be prevented by removing the adrenal glands in midlife. These findings strongly suggest that some aspects of individual age-related decline of cognitive function may, in fact, be reversible. But no one should contemplate going out and having their adrenal glands removed, because these glands provide protection and promote the process of allostasis that lets us successfully adapt to changes in our lives. There are better ways of dealing with age-related changes in our stress hormones—the same steps that will help people of all ages prevent many kinds of stress-related disorders.

This brings us to the final chapters of this book. You've read, in possibly alarming detail, that allostatic load can affect the heart, brain, and immune system—in short, that it's bad for you to be stressed out. Keep in mind, though, that although everyone encounters stress, not everyone proceeds to allostatic load to the same degree. Now it's time to look at the questions: Who *doesn't* get stressed out, and what can you do to put yourself in that category?

How Not to Be
Stressed Out

Having read about hypertension, autoimmunity, and hippocampal atrophy in the last few chapters, you may be feeling as if the difficulties of life take us into a biological minefield and that somewhere in our bodies, at any moment, an explosion is imminent. So now it's time to turn to the other side of the story: the resilience that is intrinsic to the brain and other parts of the body. This is the essence of allostasis.

Throughout this book I've emphasized that allostasis works in a consistent "protection versus damage" pattern. Naturally, you're reading this book because you want to maximize the protection and avoid the damage. So let's start with the key truths. First, you don't need to be stressed out—meaning that you don't need to experience allostatic load. Second, stress in the sense of trying times and hectic schedules isn't the only source of allostatic load. Poor lifestyle choices can also tilt the hypothalamic-pituitary-adrenal (HPA) axis and increase levels of cortisol, even if you aren't consciously fretting about anything. And if you are in a state of crisis, the coping techniques you choose can have biological effects that are just as punishing as the consequences of chronic stress. This is particularly worrisome since many people who feel trapped in difficult situations turn for consolation to the very things that are bad for them—french fries and doughnuts, alcohol and cigarettes, pulling all-nighters at the office—piling on yet another layer of allostatic load to whatever is causing the stress in the first place.

To keep allostasis functioning on the protective end of the spectrum, the most effective steps you can take are the simplest: exercise, a healthy diet, regular sleep, moderate-to-minimal alcohol intake, and no smoking. If this sounds suspiciously like what your grandmother always told you, all I can say is that according to the most sophisticated, up-to-the-minute, cutting-edge science available, your grandmother was right.

Walking to Health

In early 2002 the National Institutes of Health (NIH) announced the results of the Diabetes Prevention Program, in which something called intensive lifestyle intervention dramatically reduced the risk of diabetes in over 3,000 people. Intensive lifestyle intervention sounds sinister, but what the participants actually did was follow a low-fat diet and engage in 150 minutes of moderate exercise—half an hour, five times a week. Most of them chose walking.

Type II diabetes is a form of allostatic load. In this disease, which usually goes hand in hand with obesity, heart disease, and high cortisol levels, the body becomes resistant to its own insulin. The NIH study focused on participants who were at risk for type II diabetes: all were overweight and had impaired glucose tolerance, a condition that usually precedes onset of the disease. In addition, many belonged to groups at higher than normal risk: African Americans, Hispanic Americans, Asian Americans and Pacific Islanders, and American Indians. Other high-risk participants were people with a first-degree relative with the disease, people age 60 and older, and women with a history of gestational diabetes (which occurs due to the increase of hormones, including cortisol, during pregnancy).

The results were nothing short of astonishing. Participants in the lifestyle intervention group reduced their risk of diabetes by 58 percent, whereas participants in another group who took the medication metformin reduced their risk by 31 percent. In other words, the combination of walking and a sensible diet was almost twice as effective as the front-line medical treatment. This study, exciting enough in itself, is a promise of even better things to come as more and more people take responsibility for their lifestyle habits, particularly in terms of fending off allostatic load.

Numerous studies have shown that simple walking is one of the best ways to prevent heart disease. In a study of more than 2,500 elderly men, the risk of heart disease went down in accordance with the distance walked. A huge study of more than 72,000 middle-aged women showed that walking significantly reduced their chances of developing heart disease—even if they only began walking later in life. Importantly, both of these studies were prospective studies, meaning that the researchers started by taking some measurements at the outset and then monitored the subjects of the experiments over long periods of time. These kinds of studies are considered more accurate than retrospective studies, which survey people who have already developed a given disease to look for the things they might have in common.

In the diabetes prevention study conducted by NIH, exercise probably staved off the disease by increasing the rate at which glucose gets taken up into muscle tissue, possibly overcoming insulin resistance. Exercise may also help us protect ourselves in ways that are more specific to the stress response. Take the immune system. In a study in which mice were allowed to run on an exercise wheel for eight weeks, the exercise boosted the activity of key white blood cells, such as macrophages and lymphocytes.

Exercise and the Brain

Some of the most promising research has to do with the way exercise affects the brain. Running appears to make humans smarter. Kisou Kubota of Nihon Fukushi University in Aichi, Japan, asked seven healthy adult volunteers to jog for 30 minutes three days a week. At the end of 12 weeks, the joggers scored 30 percent higher than their sedentary fellow subjects on tests of working memory—the ability to hold information transiently in the mind. Researchers hope to use MRI (magnetic resonance imaging) to pinpoint the changes in the brain. The study is particularly exciting since 30 minutes three times a week isn't exactly boot camp—it's something anyone should be able to manage.

Animal studies are providing some possible explanations. In studies that showed how an enriched environment can enlarge the brains of rats and mice (William Greenough's studies that showed increased synaptic connections and Fred Gage's work that found an increase in neurogenesis), physical exercise was one of the "upgrades." Others were social interaction with other animals, mental stimulation in the form of maze training, and extra treats like apples and cheese. All of these things could potentially have salutary effects on the animals' brains. So Gage and colleagues decided to break down the enriched environment into components. In a 1999 study they put some mice in cages with unrestricted access to an exercise wheel, whereas others were forced to swim for their exercise; some mice received training in an underwater maze, and some got the traditional enriched environment in which they did all of these things. A group of mice in standard laboratory cages served as controls.

The researchers found that the mice who ran on their wheels whenever they liked produced significantly more newborn cells in the hippocampus than did the mice in the other two groups. In both the runners and the "enriched" mice, more of these new cells ended up surviving into adulthood and becoming functional neurons, compared to the maze mice, the obligatory swimmers, and the controls. (The runners didn't get any apples or cheese, ruling out extra snacks as a possible explanation.)

From this study it wasn't clear whether there was any net benefit to the mice, whether the new cells made them any smarter. Research had already shown that both exercise and learning can contribute to neurogenesis, that enhanced neurogenesis leads to better performance on maze tests (in rodents), and that exercise may improve cognitive function. So in a follow-up study also published in 1999, Gage and coworkers decided to test whether the neurogenesis resulting from voluntary exercise had any effect on subsequent performance in memory tasks. They put mice into groups with free access to running wheels or standard lab cages and then tested their performance on water mazes. Once again, the runners showed greatly improved performance compared to the controls. By recording electrical activity in the brains of the mice, the investigators also found that the runners showed more long-term potentiation (the learning that takes place on the level of the individual neuron) in some parts of the hippocampus.

These experiments aren't rock-solid proof that exercise can stave off allostatic load, but the possibility is exciting. What is clear, though, is that stress can stifle neurogenesis in the hippocampus, that reduced hippocampal volume and poor memory have been found in people suffering from long-term stress and depression, and that aged rats with smaller hippocampi are less able to shut off the stress response at the appropriate time. It stands to reason that making a change in exercise habits should reduce the odds of developing allostatic load, especially when that change is relatively easy to make and has so many other health benefits.

Eating Our Way to Stress-Free Living

When someone has felt threatened or pressured for a while, the body assumes that energy supplies are being drained. The stress response kicks in automatically, not distinguishing between running away from a predator and getting ready for tomorrow's board meeting. The end result is the same: glucocorticoids go up, and before they cause any of the events more commonly associated with stress, they do the job from which their name is derived. They signal the liver to convert energy into long-term storage, as glycogen and fat. They also act on the brain to encourage what scientists call food-seeking behavior, making sure that the supplies are replenished. In one of biology's ironies, stress makes us hungry.

To make matters worse, stress may increase the rate at which what we eat is turned into body fat as well as determine where the fat goes. Too much fat around the midriff (the so-called spare tire) is a risk factor for both diabetes and heart disease, as opposed to flab around the hips and thighs, which doesn't seem to pose as much of a health threat. One explanation may be that abdominal fat, being closer to the pumping action of the heart, is more likely to get into the bloodstream and collect in the arteries. Another is that abdominal fat is a ready source of fatty acids that can increase the release of more cortisol and also make the body resistant to insulin. Abdominal fat accumulation is particularly sensitive to cortisol, and chronic stress causes more fat to accumulate in high-risk areas of the body, especially the abdomen. Jay Kaplan and colleagues at Bowman Gray University have found that in research monkeys the stress of a constantly shifting social environment can speed up the accumulation of abdominal fat. In humans the higher cortisol levels indicative of stress may affect body fat distribution the same way. One study showed that stress and elevated cortisol cause an increase in abdominal fat in women, who normally have a tendency to gain weight more safely, in the derriere.

The importance of making good food choices, in times of stress and in general, goes way beyond improving self-esteem by shedding those unsightly extra 10 pounds (though that may provide a significant boost in itself). It's vital to avoid adding poor food choices to the scales of allostatic load, and the best way to do so is to keep dietary fat to a minimum. Excess fat in the diet can obviously lead to excess fat on the body. Too much dietary fat also increases the production of cortisol, which can lead to still more accumulation of body fat, particularly around the midriff. This in turn contributes to atherosclerosis and insulin resistance, raising the risk of heart disease and diabetes, which are risk factors for each other. The result is not so much a vicious circle as a vicious cloverleaf, with each risk factor increasing the likelihood of the rest.

Research in rats shows that a high-fat diet doesn't just raise cortisol levels in general but also disrupts the workings of the HPA axis. Kalatu Kamara, Robert Eskay, and Thomas Castonguay of the University of Maryland fed rats a high-fat diet for 10 weeks, subjecting them periodically to restraint stress. Initially, the rats showed a greater increase in cortisol after the stress than rats kept on a normal diet. This surge subsided after the 10 weeks, but even at the end of that time the fat-fed rats took longer to recover from the stress (meaning that their hormonal changes took longer to return to baseline). Moreover, eating some types of fat also left the rats with impaired glucose tolerance.

So it's easy to see that a high-fat diet does more than just make us gain weight (in itself no minor stressor in today's image-conscious society). High-fat foods can also intensify our stress responses in ways that can very quickly spin out of control.

A Good Night's Sleep

Scientists know that sleep is a vitally important activity in the natural world, although they don't know why. All animals in whom sleep can be detected by electroencephalogram (EEG) are known to sleep, and even insects are observed to rest after periods of activity. What purpose sleep serves is still something of a mystery. In terms of conserving energy, sleep doesn't appear to be more beneficial than simply resting. Yet all animals spend time—sometimes quite a bit of time—not just in repose but completely insensible, during which they and their dependents are vulnerable to predators.

Animals not only need sleep but are willing to go to great lengths to get it. Large animals like elephants, giraffes, and horses lie down to sleep, even though their size makes it difficult to get up quickly in the event of an emergency. Marine mammals like dolphins, which must come to the surface periodically to breathe, can't afford to tune out from their environment for long periods, so they've evolved a way to rest one hemisphere of the brain at a time, while the other stays awake to keep them within spouting distance of the surface.

Studies have shown that sleep-deprived animals die fairly quickly. What's more, experimental animals die even if they're deprived only of the specific sleep stage known as rapid eye movement (REM) sleep. This stage of sleep has been observed in birds and in that bridge between reptiles and mammals, the duck-billed platypus. So whatever REM sleep does, it's important enough to have surfaced fairly early in the evolutionary scheme of things.

Humans have "evolved" far enough to use forcible sleep deprivation as torture for interrogation as well as, in measured doses, an accepted way for authorities to break down perpetrator resistance in hostage situations.

Some researchers believe that sleep is a way to expunge brain cells of memories that aren't needed; according to others, memories that *are* needed are reinforced during sleep. Sleep also promotes restorative processes throughout the body. But it's regulated by the brain, with the help of many sleep-promoting substances, including immune system chemicals known as cytokines, and hormones.

Sleep and Stress

The connection with the fight-or-flight response becomes clear when you consider that allostasis helps us cope with many changes in the environment, not just the ones we perceive as stressful. For daytime creatures the first major change is waking up in the morning. The process is quite involved—going from lying down to sitting and then standing, and if you're a human, getting into the shower, coping with morning traffic, meeting the challenges of school or the workplace. Even if none of these things are stressful in the sense of being upsetting, they all place certain demands on us. So the allostatic response prepares us to cope by increasing cortisol levels, beginning in the wee hours of the morning and tapering off during the evening.

The ebb and flow of stress hormones is tied into our daily, or circadian, rhythms; stress can result when these get out of whack. Elevated levels of cortisol in the evening are a sign of allostatic load. Changes in sleep patterns are one of the first things doctors look for (or should look for) in cases of depression; severely depressed people may have insomnia or may go to the other extreme, wanting to do nothing but sleep. People with bipolar disorder, also known as manic-depressive illness, have severely disrupted sleep-wake cycles; during their "highs" they may get so wired that they go without sleeping for days. In fact, the role of circadian rhythms in bipolar disorder is becoming more appreciated. So is their role in another condition, the wintry depression known as seasonal affective disorder.

Of course, these types of mood disorders are not synonymous with allostatic load. High levels of stress hormones are seen in many cases of depression but not all. Sleep and stress are intricately linked, however, because the intense activity of the fight-or-flight systems leads to fatigue and, eventually, sleep. Both the HPA axis and the immune system are key players in sleep, presumably because during times of threat to the body, such as injury or bacterial infection, the restorative powers of sleep are most urgently needed. Sleeping is perhaps the thing we want to do most when we're sick.

Sleep deprivation qualifies as a stressor in the sense of making life miserable and in the sense of producing allostatic load. Eve Van Cauter of the University of Chicago has shown that in subjects who get only four hours of sleep per night for several nights, the activity of the sympathetic nervous system is increased and the vagal tone—that index of a healthy response to a stressor—goes down. In addition, evening cortisol levels and evening blood glucose levels are elevated in the sleep deprived—all of which indicate allostatic load. When the subjects are allowed to get 10 to 12 hours of sleep a night, however, the signs of allostatic load disappear.

While sleep is a response to stress as long as the allostatic systems are functioning on the "protection" end of the continuum, poor sleep is a characteristic of allostatic load. A good example is a disorder often considered psychosomatic or stress related—the inflammatory condition of chronic pain, fibromyalgia, and its counterpart, chronic fatigue syndrome. In the medical community, fibromyalgia is often dismissed as a nondisease because of its indefinite and psychosomatic nature. Beginning in the mid-1970s, however, Harvey Moldofsky of the Toronto Hospital drew up a set of objective criteria for diagnosing the disorder. These include diffuse musculoskeletal pain, tender spots (often called trigger points) in key areas, chronic fatigue, and brain wave changes in EEG recordings that show poor sleep.

The poor sleep in question is a problem with non-REM sleep, the sleep stage in which muscle and tissue restoration is thought to occur. People with fibromyalgia don't feel restored after a night's sleep and instead feel tired and achy, whereas normally people have the least pain sensitivity in the morning and wake up feeling less tired than when they went to bed. Moldofsky and co-workers found that fibromyalgia patients have an abnormal EEG pattern in non-REM sleep and that disrupting a particular stage of non-REM sleep brought on fibromyalgia symptoms in normal sedentary subjects but not in physically fit long-distance runners. The researchers also found that the abnormal EEG pattern, the sleep disruption, and the symptoms could be provoked by both stress and viral illness. Finally, fibromyalgia patients have an underresponsive HPA axis and an altered cytokine profile, indicating that the stress response and the immune system are not functioning well.

Scientists are unsure how to interpret these findings, particularly in the area of prevention. If someone has disrupted sleep patterns, it won't help to tell them to try to get a good night's rest; they simply can't. Much research is going on in the area of fibromyalgia, which Moldofsky estimates affects 2 to 4 percent of the population (with over 90 percent of these being women). For the rest of us, however, it's safe to assume that throwing our sleep patterns out of balance—by staying up late and napping during the day, for example—may be adding another level of allostatic load to already existing stress levels.

Avoiding the "Demon Rum"

Drinking alcohol is one of the most common coping tools of all, but it's actually a bad choice, particularly when it becomes chronic. Most people feel stimulated and revved up after a drink or two. That is because ethanol, the type of alcohol found in beer, wine, and liquor, has a stimulatory effect on the HPA axis—at first. But alcohol can also throw off the HPA axis, leaving the drinker more vulnerable to stress than ever.

In a prospective study, one of the foremost researchers into alcoholism, Mark Schuckit of the University of California, San Diego, found that an exaggerated cortisol response to alcohol could predict whether someone would become an alcoholic later in life. At the Johns Hopkins University School of Medicine, Gary Wand and co-workers found a similar alcohol-induced rise in cortisol in subjects with a family history of alcoholism.

The initial "rush" doesn't last, however. Being on overly familiar terms with alcohol may actually produce a blunted response of the HPA axis to alcohol. In a study of rats, though an initial treatment with alcohol was a powerful stimulant, subsequent doses left the rats less able to mount an allostatic response. Alcohol is a stressor in its own right, to which the production of cortisol is a protective response. In fact, cortisol is so protective that in animals lacking adrenal glands a normally innocuous dose of alcohol is lethal.

In human beings, alcoholism may interfere with the normal process of allostasis. In a study conducted by Gary Wand and Adrian Dobs at Johns Hopkins University, about 50 percent of alcoholics tested had a significantly blunted stress response. For one thing, allostasis took longer. When given an injection of corticotropin-releasing hormone (which triggers the hormonal stress response), about half of the subjects took 60 minutes to show a corresponding rise in the hormone that signals the adrenals to produce cortisol, whereas 30 minutes is normal. The same group showed elevations in blood cortisol levels in the afternoon, suggesting that the circadian rhythms of the stress hormones had been thrown off. At first glance, this may sound as if alcoholics are less subject to stress than nonalcoholics. But the alcoholics were taking longer to mount the protective phase of allostatic response, not to show signs of allostatic load. And a sluggish, underactive HPA response is itself a type of allostatic load, likely to put a person at risk for inflammations, to say nothing of the toxic effects of alcohol.

Of course, most people who drink are not alcoholics, and alcohol in moderation has its place in life. Some research shows that a glass of red wine with dinner may even protect against heart disease. The key though is moderation. Overuse of alcohol is a stressor, not a coping mechanism.

A Little Help from Our Friends

People don't resort to alcohol solely for its mood-altering effects; drinking is often a pretext to socializing. For one of the best coping tools of all, try the conviviality without the booze. Social support is a powerful talisman against allostatic load. Again and again, with respect to cardiovascular disease, immunity, and brain function, people who have strong support networks fare better than those who are trying to go it alone.

In primates the most widely used model of psychological stress is social disruption—taking animals out of their customary groups and mixing them up. A rhubarb ensues, and until a dominance hierarchy establishes itself, things are very stressful. Young monkeys in this situation show fewer signs of stress if a few of them are put in the new situation together. Robert Sapolsky, who studies wild baboons in Kenya when he isn't in his lab at Stanford University, has reported that male baboons with more playmates and grooming buddies have lower cortisol levels than males with fewer attachments.

The buddy system is equally important when it comes to stress in humans. Those fiendish scientists who made their subjects do mental arithmetic and public speaking—William Gerin and Tom Pickering, then at Cornell University Medical School and now at Mount Sinai Medical Center—found that the people in the hot seat showed a less dramatic cardiovascular response to the challenge if they had a supportive friend in the audience.

Social support can do more than hold down the pulse rate during a stressful experience. Over time it may reduce your chances of having a heart attack. Several prospective studies show that psychological disorders such as anxiety, depression, and hostility can make heart disease worse. People with these conditions are more likely to develop heart disease in the first place; in the aftermath of a heart attack, those with clinical anxiety or depression are three to four times more likely to die from a subsequent attack. But at McGill University in Montreal, Nancy Frasure-Smith and colleagues found that even in heart attack victims with depression the three- to fourfold increase in risk occurred only in those patients with no social support.

When it comes to social support and the immune system, the literature is impressive. The evidence for the value of social support ranges from Ron Glaser and Janice Kiecolt-Glaser's demonstrations of the link between chronic stress, social support, and immune system activity in Alzheimer's caregivers to studies finding that married people tend to live longer than singles.

Social support even seems to benefit people undergoing another cruel stressor—coping with a fatal disease. In a prospective study of men who were infected with HIV (human immunodeficiency virus) but did not have symptoms of AIDS (acquired immune deficiency syndrome), the infection progressed more quickly in those who reported more stressful events and less satisfaction with social support and whose chief means of coping was denial. Social support can also ease the excruciating neuropathic pain (pain resulting from nerve damage) often seen in AIDS and other conditions, such as cancer and spinal cord injury.

Even when death is a certainty, support from doctors, family, and friends makes a patient's final days easier. Many hospitals and hospices now provide palliative care, treating the patient's symptoms and trying to improve the overall quality of life, rather than aggressively fighting the disease when the prognosis is grim. Improving the quality of life for the dying—which palliative care specialists don't consider to be a contradiction in terms—is a particular concern now that physician-assisted suicide is such a widely discussed topic. According to William Breitbart at Memorial Sloan Kettering Cancer Center in New York, terminally ill patients are more likely to consider assisted suicide if they have few "psychosocial" defenses like social support. Kathleen Foley, director of palliative care at Sloan Kettering, believes that a terminally ill patient's right to the best possible quality of life should be firmly established before the right to die is discussed.

Social Support and Cancer

Earlier I mentioned the much-debated question of whether people with cancer can extend their life expectancy by participating in support groups and that five studies had shown that participation in such groups extended survival moderately while five others found no increase in survival. All of the studies, however, pointed to an improvement in the patients' quality of life, and none showed that the patients' lives were shortened. This is an important point for patients who fear that confronting their emotions might be a stressor in itself.

Whether support groups help patients live longer or not, they do provide a positive way to explore emotions that, given the situation, can't always be positive. Stanford University psychiatrist David Spiegel, who led the first study to show a survival benefit of group therapy, explains that support groups don't merely stir up the emotions. Rather, emotions regarding illness and possible death are viewed as signposts to action that can be taken. For example, if patients react with anger to the many things they may leave undone, therapy can help them find ways to finish the projects they can finish. If personal relationships are problematic, this is something that can be resolved with the help of a support group and a therapist. Dealing with a serious illness, such as cancer, can follow the pattern of allostasis on a personal level. Human beings may not be able to maintain emotional homeostasis, meaning that things can't always stay the same. But with the help of a supportive group, the patients can tap unsuspected resources to cope with the change.

Mind Over Matter?

The role of social support in cancer treatment highlights another dispute: the whole question of mind over matter. The issue is a tantalizing one; solid evidence suggests that the power of thought and mind can lead to real biological changes in the brain and body. But it's also dangerous, leading the unwary to conclude that overcoming trouble and illness is a matter of maintaining the appropriate attitude.

All the research I've described so far suggests that the brain's perception of stress brings about changes in the body that are inarguably real. It's been one of the main points I've sought to convince you about. From sudden terror to chronic anxiety to anticipatory angst, the brain determines what is stressful and what isn't, and the results leave their mark on the cardiovascular system, immunity to disease, and mental functioning. Thus, it's logical to wonder if it's *only* in stressful situations that the brain can influence the body. Theoretically it should be possible to turn the tables and use our perceptions to calm the stress response and shore up our health instead.

The trouble is that because allostasis is geared toward protecting us from danger, the bad stuff has priority. Fear and pain blaze a trail through the brain and straight to the physiological systems that coordinate the best response. It is telling that more neural pathways go from the fear and emotional centers to the "higher up" regions, like the cortex, than come back down from the lofty heights into the stress response's engine room. Messages of love, reassurance, courage, and hope can almost certainly influence the body as well but not with the same galvanic effect. As animals navigate the perils of evolution, the positive emotions tend to take a backseat.

Nevertheless, remember the evidence that by repeated thoughts and actions we can alter not only the functioning but also the structure of the neural networks in our brains: Michael Merzenich teaching a monkey to tap a bar using three fingers and showing a rewiring of the brain; the enriched-environment studies in which exercise, social stimulation, and opportunities to explore made the rats' brains burgeon with new synaptic connections and cells; and, of course, Eric Kandel's Nobel Prize-winning studies, showing that repetition activates a protein that directs the construction of new synapses, which is the molecular basis for long-term memory and happens not only after endless repetition but during moments of powerful emotion. Although in Kandel's experiments the "stimuli" were coming from the environment, it's probably safe to assume that humans can activate the same process voluntarily. Memorization is simply repeating a thought until we remember it—as, for example, when we learn that William the Conqueror invaded England in 1066. We don't use any more direct means of stimulating the brain; we just memorize. Yet when we've done so, we've made a minute but long-term, possibly permanent, change in our brains.

Control: The Pros and Cons

Based on these findings, it's irresistible to ask whether we can change our stress response or our HPA axis by affirming positive thoughts to ourselves. It is possible to retool certain maladaptive processes in the brain to our advantage. A fascinating example is a 1996 study by Michael Phelps of the University of California at Los Angeles, who developed the first positron emission tomography (PET) scanner. He used the equipment to scan the brains of patients with obsessive-compulsive disorder (OCD), before and after 10 weeks of behavioral and cognitive therapy. Before the therapy, the scans revealed an anomaly in the brain's use of glucose in a key area related to movement regulation.

Since patients with OCD get locked into intricate, uncontrollable patterns of repetitive movement, it's likely that this abnormal activity is a marker for the disorder. After the therapy, follow-up PET scans showed that the abnormal activity in the brain was visibly and significantly decreased—correlating with an improvement in the patient's OCD symptoms. The study is exciting because the patients took no medication; there was no intervention that could have targeted this brain area directly—only 10 weeks of thought and behavior modification. So maybe we have more control over our brains than we think.

At best, our notions of control empower us in times of illness, helping us to stick to our treatment plans, get what exercise we can, and explore techniques like affirmation and visualization to help create an environment for healing. We Americans take responsibility for our own health. Instead of meekly obeying our white-coated, stethoscoped doctors, we read books, we look on the Internet, we investigate the things that we can do besides just getting prescriptions filled.

The idea of control has a downside, though. The danger lies in assuming that we have more control than we actually do. Sometimes the biochemical imbalances that result in disease prove resistant to our envisionings, and when this happens we may feel guilty and discouraged, concluding that we're still sick because we failed to sustain a sufficiently positive attitude. The worst-case scenario is when we abandon our medical protocols in favor of unproven fad remedies.

We should understand as much as we possibly can about our health and health problems—stress-related and otherwise—and take whatever measures we can to bolster our own well-being while working with our doctors and following approved treatment regimens. The idea is summed up best in the famous prayer by theologian Reinhold Niebuhr, adopted 60 years ago as the mantra of Alcoholics Anonymous: "God grant me the serenity to accept the things I cannot change, the courage to change the things I can, and the wisdom to know the difference." Taking charge of those parts of our lives that we can control means that we'll be better able to deal with the unforeseeable and inevitable.

In all of the research into stress, the concept of control appears again and again, the way a musical theme weaves in and out of the movements of a symphony. When stress is coupled with a lack of control, the music goes from major to minor: allostasis shifts into allostatic load. For example, if a rat has learned to push a lever to avoid receiving a mild shock and then the lever is taken away, the rat shows an exaggerated stress response—the sense of control is gone. A rat that still has a lever won't show as much of a stress response, even if the lever is disconnected from the shock mechanism and doesn't have any effect. Studies in primates show that social upheaval, unpredictability, and lack of control can set the stage for upper respiratory illness, atherosclerosis, reduced hippocampal volume, and even death. In this context, control doesn't mean controlling others, telling people what to do, and generally being the top dog in the outfit; in an unstable environment the top dogs are likely to be the ones with the psychosomatic illness. Rather, it means control over one's own life.

At the human level, control is just as important. For example, as described in Chapter 4, take the dramatic increase in the death rates among males after the breakup of the former Soviet Union from cardiovascular disease, alcoholism, suicide, violence, and other causes. Of course, as part of the widespread chaos in that area, medical services were disrupted as well; it's possible that more people died simply because ambulances didn't get them to the hospital soon enough or that the hospitals weren't well enough equipped to treat them. But given the social instability studies in primates, it's also possible that having their lives and identities completely uprooted resulted in more illness among these men. Also, the Whitehall studies showed that lack of control in the workplace tracks closely with cardiovascular disease.

A sense of control in the workplace is a dominant theme in stress research. Probably the most interesting and optimistic study took place in a Volvo automobile factory in Sweden. It was a traditional production line—workers had to do a specific job over and over again, always having to keep up with what came down the line. It was stressful and boring at the same time, and the high levels of job dissatisfaction often showed up as absenteeism. Many employees had elevated blood pressure.

So the Volvo management, working in conjunction with scientists, reorganized the workers into teams, with interchangeable jobs and more input into how things were done. The quality of the workers' health improved and their blood pressure went back to a normal range. Thus it is possible to influence physical health by changing the working environment.

When we can't change our environment—when we need the job or when the seriously ill family member needs us—this is the time to change the things we can. The advantages of good diet, regular exercise, and enlisting the support of family and friends extend beyond the intrinsic benefits of these actions. They also give us a much-needed sense of control.

On Behalf of the Medical Community

One final note when it comes to taking charge of our health and of the things in life that we can control: don't throw the doctor out with the bath water. Certainly some of our most powerful weapons against allostatic load are within our own reach, but help is also available from medicine. In fact, of the people who cope with stress successfully and avoid allostatic load, the chief common denominator may be that they listen to their doctors and cooperate with treatment plans when they do get sick.

Medical lore is peppered with stories about hard-driven type A's who deny they have an illness and in fact recover more quickly—an attitude along the lines of "I can't have a heart condition; I have a lunch meeting." There are also stories of people who accept themselves as they are, malignant tumor and all, and live to a ripe old age without following any treatment plan. But these are stories—anecdotal evidence, as scientists say. Even with the most positive attitude in the world, we are courting disaster if we let serious health conditions go untreated.

Medical treatment is particularly important in the case of mood disorders and mental illness. It's hard to make changes in our lives if we're stuck in negative, maladaptive thought patterns. Professional counseling, such as cognitive therapy, is extremely helpful in changing our ways of thinking for the better. Even with help from a professional, a change in attitude or a commitment to exercise may not be enough if we're also besieged from the inside by anxiety or depression. A clinical mood disorder can knock us adrift from our mental moorings, making it impossible to control our thoughts, however clearly we perceive the need to do so. In these cases, medications can ease some of the terrible psychological burdens of brain chemistry gone awry. The treatments already available can help keep us on an even keel while we're grappling with the issues that threaten to overwhelm us.

New understanding of the biochemistry of allostatic load is suggesting new and more effective types of treatment. In the case of depression, highly successful antidepressant drugs such as Prozac and its heirs resulted from a better understanding of the receptors for the neurotransmitter serotonin. Since antidepressants have benefits that range beyond treating depression—they are also used to treat conditions as diverse as anorexia, chronic pain, and bedwetting—this research may lead to a more nuanced understanding of the role neurotransmitters play in many conditions, including allostatic load. Drugs of the Prozac generation work more cleanly than their predecessors, meaning with fewer side effects. The near future may see drugs that work against anxiety by targeting more specifically the receptors for gamma-aminobutyric acid, one of the neurotransmitters that slow down nerve cell activity. We may even see some medications that impede the process of allostatic load. Now in clinical trials are drugs known as CRF (corticotropin-releasing factor) blockers. These slow the production of corticotropin-releasing factor, which sets the entire HPA axis in motion.

Also on the horizon, in addition to measures for avoiding allostatic load and medications to augment our own efforts when needed, are new insights into the body's ability to heal and bolster itself, which is what I'll explore in the next chapter.

Positive Health

My favorite thing about the concept of allostasis is that it helps move us away from a siege mentality when we confront life's challenges. Medical science tends to equate health with the mere absence of illness; even someone who acknowledges the adaptive, energizing systems at the brain's command may still be thinking in defensive terms. But allostasis in its truest sense does much more than stave off disease-producing onslaughts; by changing your life in ways that help keep allostasis on track—by exercising, following a healthy diet, and cherishing your friends and family—you do more than just keep yourself out of trouble. You actively enhance the body and brain's own properties that strengthen, nourish, build up, calm, and protect. Scientists are on the threshhold of understanding these processes, which are technically (and unromantically) known as anabolic factors. The term I prefer is *positive health.*

Positive health refers to the repetoire of systems and substances that confer the body's innate ability to keep allostasis from descending into allostatic load and to bounce back after the system has become temporarily overwhelmed. Some of the players in positive health fall within the domain of allostasis proper, such as restorative effects of the parasympathetic nervous system and the checks-and-balances system of cortisol. Other built-in positive health factors provide for resilience and recovery even after a brief descent into allostatic load; these are just beginning to reveal their possibilities, and many are best studied in the brain.

For starters the brain manufactures the body's own painkillers, the endorphins. "Bonding" hormones, which may explain the benefits of strong social support, are produced in the brain, as are substances that nourish and protect brain cells. New brain cells are produced through-out life, particularly in that all-important region, the hippocampus. And the multifaceted hormone estrogen is revealing itself as a power-ful protector of the brain and the memory.

Overriding the Pain Signal

Endorphins, or enkephalins, were discovered in the 1970s; they are the human body's version of opium. Their best-understood job is to sup-port the fight-or-flight response by bringing about a phenomenon known as stress-induced pain relief. This usually happens in a state of extreme emergency, however. In general, having one's pain sensitivity shut off is a dangerous thing, so I don't consider the endorphins per se to be positive health players. But their discovery was the prelude to further research that did heighten understanding of positive health.

When an animal is in the throes of allostasis it doesn't feel pain very keenly, for the simple reason that it can't afford to. To ensure sur-vival, the most important thing is to either win the battle or make the escape. Sitting down and howling with pain isn't part of the scenario; that can come later. So the brain steps in with a temporary override to the pain signal. Studies have shown that animals under stress really are less sensitive to pain; they aren't just valiantly ignoring it. Among hu-mans there are legends about Viking warriors called berserkers who in the heat of battle were oblivious to pain and injury. In modern times we hear anecdotes about people walking away from car wrecks on two broken legs and professional athletes notoriously "playing through the pain." This altered state of perception is made possible by the activity of endorphins in the brain. Endorphins also explain, in a roundabout way, how the best painkillers of all—the derivatives of the product of the poppy plant, opium—have such dramatic effects on the human brain and body.

The ancient Greeks and Romans were familiar with opium's ability to ease pain, promote sleep, and produce a calm and quiet sense of euphoria. In 1805 a German chemist named Friedrich Serturner isolated opium's active ingredient, pure morphine, from the poppy—a breakthrough discovery. Medicines obtained directly from plants can only be taken orally because they are impure. Many of their components are foreign to the human body and could be irritants when injected. And because drugs taken by mouth must make their way through the digestive system, they are slower to act and less effective. But the effects of pure injectable morphine are consistent and quick, making it the first of the opiate drugs to be widely used for pain relief, particularly in the Civil War (from which many soldiers returned as addicts). Even quicker are the effects of another purified version of opium: heroin, which has become a devastating drug of abuse.

Despite their dangers, the opiate drugs are unsurpassed even today as far as their ability to relieve pain is concerned. The powerful effects of these drugs, good and bad, led scientists seeking effective painkillers to wonder just how the opiates worked. In the early 1970s, Solomon Snyder and Candace Pert of Johns Hopkins University found strong evidence of opiate receptors in cultured brain tissue using an opiate blocker, naloxone, that was radioactively labeled to make it visible when it bound to the receptor. A few years later these scientists teamed up with Michael Kuhar, then at Johns Hopkins and now at Emory University, to pinpoint the location of these receptors using a technique that Kuhar had developed for viewing microscopically thin layers of brain tissue. The researchers injected radioactive opiates into rats; examination of tissue from the animals' nervous systems showed that receptors were located in the spinal cord, where opiates work by raising the pain threshold; in the thalamus, which is involved in perception; the amygdala, the cornerstone of the fear response; and several other sites—thus serving to explain the many levels at which opiate drugs help people feel better. Opiate receptors are also found in the brain stem, where breathing is regulated, which explains why large doses can kill by bringing breathing to a halt.

Having established the presence of opiate receptors in the human brain, the next logical question was: What were they doing there? Why should the human brain have evolved receptors for a chemical that doesn't exist in the body—a chemical that's produced by only one type of plant? It turns out that the efficacy of opiate drugs is an accident. The receptors found by Snyder and Kuhar are receptors for the endorphins, the brain's own kinds of opium, which the poppy's version resembles closely enough to affect the brain by working at the same site.

The Brain's Own Pharmacopeia

The connection between endorphins, stress, and pain relief surfaced in 1977, when Roger Guillemin showed that stress triggers the pituitary gland to produce one type of endorphin. (Guillemin was the scientist whose 14-year feud with Andrew Schally culminated in both scientists publishing, about three weeks apart in 1971, the structure of the first neurohormone, thyrotropin-releasing factor. At the time of his endorphin discovery, he had won a Nobel Prize for his previous work.)

The role of endorphins in stress-induced pain relief represents a turning point in the story of positive health, but let me explain why I consider them only a prelude to the main story and not positive health players in their own right. In general, it's dangerous to ignore pain, intentionally or otherwise. Pain alerts us to injuries and illnesses that need to be attended to, encouraging us to stay quiet in the meantime and leave the affected area alone. People with abnormal conditions that leave them unable to feel pain live in constant danger of receiving unnoticed injuries. So endorphin-induced pain insensitivity should be considered an attempt by the brain to deal with emergency and not a sign of resilience.

Even the famed runner's high, thought to result from endorphins, may be the brain's last-ditch attempt to keep the body going in what it perceives to be a life-threatening situation. Exercise is a stressor when taken to the extreme. Fanatical runners suffer from cardiovascular disease, and though they tend to be trim, the little body fat they do have is concentrated in the abdomen—a sign of allostatic load. When a person runs for prolonged periods, the body assumes that some grave danger exists and cranks up the endorphins to facilitate escape, causing a euphoria that's actually the advent of allostatic load.

It may be that endorphins exert their painkilling, calming effects in nonemergencies, but the hard evidence is lacking. Some studies show that acupuncture triggers their production. What can be said about the endorphins, though, is that their discovery paved the way to identifying other chemicals that do seem to be involved in positive health. These include oxytocin, a hormone produced during social interaction and bonding, and prolactin, a hormone released during breastfeeding that appears to have calming effects on the brain. To identify these neurohormones, scientists had to look beyond the traditional neurotransmitters as they were understood in the 1950s and 1960s, and endorphins were like a stepping stone.

Beyond Endorphins

Earlier I talked about acetylcholine, the first of the brain's chemical messengers to be identified. Acetylcholine was discovered in the 1930s as the chemical that the vagus nerve uses to slow down the beating of the heart. Later it proved to be one of the key neurotransmitters in the brain as well. By the late 1960s, many of the best-known neurotransmitters had been identified, including noradrenaline; serotonin; dopamine; glutamate, which tells brain cells to speed up their rate of activity; and gamma-aminobutyric acid, which sends the signal to slow down. Some scientists thought the brain's cast of characters was now complete.

Around the same time, suspicion was dawning that there might be more players in the signal-sending game. Sir Geoffrey Harris predicted that the brain influences the endocrine system through specialized hormones, the first of which was discovered by the rancorous Guillemin and Schally. The neurohormone that sets off the fight-or-flight response, corticotropin-releasing factor, was identified as recently as 1983 by Wylie Vale of the Salk Institute, one of Guillemin's former students.

In the meantime the hunt for these and other releasing factors provided evidence that other types of neurotransmitters besides the basic ones did in fact exist. It also provided the technology to identify substances that the brain produces in minuscule amounts. In the mid-1970s two teams—John Hughes and Hans Kosterlitz of the University of Aberdeen, Scotland, and Solomon Snyder and colleagues at Hopkins—used this technology to work out the chemical structure of the endorphins (which the Scottish team called enkephalins, from the Greek for "in the head"). Both the endorphins and the releasing factors fit into a class of neurotransmitters known as neuropeptides—very short chains of amino acids, which are the building blocks of proteins. Now it's becoming clear that some neuropeptides are clues to positive health.

One likely candidate is oxytocin, a neuropeptide that may explain the phenomenon that social support improves the outlook for people with cancer, AIDS, and heart disease. Oxytocin may be a bonding hormone. Larry Young and Thomas Insel at Emory University have shown that a typical female rat avoids baby rats until she has some of her own. Then surges in oxytocin help to rank her among the best of mothers. Oxytocin "knockout" mice, which are bred missing the gene that encodes for the hormone, fail to recognize cage mates with whom they've been raised. In humans, oxytocin is triggered by pleasant stimuli such as touch and warm temperatures and in the brain of mother and child during breastfeeding. Oxytocin's effects aren't limited to the psychological. In both male and female rats, injected oxytocin lowers blood pressure, heart rate, and cortisol levels for up to several weeks. So it's possible that, when social interactions ward off some of the physical as well as the psychological ill effects of stress, oxytocin is what makes this happen.

Another potential bestower of positive health is prolactin. In women this hormone is released by the pituitary gland to trigger lactation, but in both sexes it may be an inherent remedy against anxiety and stress. In 2001, Luz Torner and colleagues at the Max Planck Institute in Munich infused prolactin directly into the brains of rats. The rats were then put in mildly stressful situations, such as being placed on an elevated, exposed platform, which rats find disconcerting due to their preference for cover. Observations of the rats' behavior indicated that the prolactin dramatically reduced anxiety in a dose-dependent way, meaning the more prolactin the animals got, the less anxious they appeared to be. Prolactin also reduced levels of stress hormones and hypothalamic-pituitary-adrenal axis activity. Because levels of prolactin in the blood increase during times of stress, and studies show evidence of both prolactin and its receptors in the hypothalamus and amygdala, it's possible that Torner and colleagues mimicked a process that goes on all the time—that prolactin is one of the natural compounds that help keep allostasis functional.

Exercise is known to increase circulating levels of prolactin, although it isn't yet clear how this elevation affects the nervous system. However, there is increasing evidence that prolactin in the blood gains access to some parts of the brain that contain prolactin receptors and that the peptide may protect against specific forms of allostatic load. It is known to prevent stress-induced stomach ulcers in animals! In the future, both oxytocin and prolactin may be boosted by medications that could work more specifically against allostatic load than could antidepressants or sedatives. A drug that increases levels of oxytocin in the brain—an oxytocin agonist, as pharamacologists call it—is under development. A similar approach could be used for prolactin.

If the endorphins and neuropeptides help us to withstand stress and avoid going into allostatic load, other aspects of positive health help us pull out of it. These include growth factors or "neurotrophins," neurogenesis, and the hormone estrogen.

Helping Nerve Cells Grow

The growth factors or neurotrophins nourish and protect growing neurons, encouraging them to repair themselves and proliferate. Much attention is being paid to growth factors as possible treatments for spinal cord injury and neurodegenerative disorders, but researchers are also beginning to explore the role of these compounds under ordinary circumstances. Growth factors may be important players in the brain's defenses against many kinds of stress, providing benefits that scientists may one day be able to augment.

The first to be discovered was called, simply, nerve growth factor, or NGF. NGF had been known to exist in the peripheral nervous system—the nerves outside the brain and spinal cord that run throughout the body—where it encourages growth and proliferation. In the 1970s Hans Thoenen of the Max Planck Institute found that NGF also exists in the brain. As to its exact job, scientists were not certain, but the discovery dovetailed another line of research: the fact that in Alzheimer's disease, cells that produce the neurotransmitter acetylcholine die off in an area called the basal forebrain. Loss of this neurotransmitter, widely used in parts of the brain associated with memory, is a major cause of Alzheimer's symptoms. In the 1980s several groups working with animals found that NGF injected directly into the damaged brain could improve the survival rate of these acetylcholine-producing or "cholinergic" cells. Some researchers, including Fred Gage at the Salk Institute, have found that when skin cells genetically modified to produce large amounts of NGF are transplanted into the brains of experimental animals, the transplants prevent cholinergic cells from dying and form a sort of bridge across which damaged neurons can regrow. Other teams have found that, when transplanted into the brains of rats, NGF-secreting cells can prevent and even reverse age-related memory loss.

Scientists are using a similar treatment approach to help axons regrow through the site of a spinal cord injury in rats, with skin cells engineered to produce both NGF and a neurotrophin called NT-3. Another neurotrophin, called glial cell-derived neurotrophic factor, shows promise in helping dopamine-producing cells survive when transplanted into the brains of patients with Parkinson's disease, another neurological disorder that involves the death of brain cells. Much research is under way to study the ordinary, everyday effects of growth factors.

A relative newcomer is insulin-like growth factor, or IGF, which the brain actively takes up from the blood during exercise. IGF lowers elevated blood glucose levels and has been shown to help experimental animals recover their ability to function after lesion-induced damage to the spinal cord. IGF may explain how walkers in a diabetes study by the National Institutes of Health were able to reduce their risk of the disease so drastically. But by far the best-understood neurotrophin as far as allostatic load is concerned is brain-derived neurotrophic factor, or BDNF.

BDNF and Positive Health

BDNF's beneficial effects on the brain are legion. In particular, it may be the biological go-between that brings about the spectacular results of exercise on the brain. BDNF also protects the brain against ischemia (damage that results from lack of oxygen, such as might occur during a stroke) and against other types of neurodegenerative damage. It is also involved in memory.

Several labs have shown that, at the level of the synapse, BDNF and other neurotrophins play a role in the learning process known as long-term potentiation. BDNF is involved with higher levels of memory as well. Yasushi Miyashita of the University of Tokyo School of Medicine investigated whether BDNF was increased or "up-regulated" when monkeys were trained to form associations between pairs of visual stimuli. Intriguingly, the tests were performed on "split-brain" monkeys in which the corpus callosum, which connects the two hemispheres of the brain, had been severed. This procedure is sometimes performed on humans to treat otherwise incurable epilepsy, but the result is that the right side of the brain literally doesn't know what the left side is doing. The researchers trained the monkeys to form memories of paired shapes that were shown to one side of each monkey's brain, while the other side of the brain merely had to distinguish the shapes, not remember them. On the memory task side of the brain, BDNF was increased in a part of the cortex known to be involved in long-term memory of objects. But on the object recognition side, no increase in BDNF was seen, indicating that the memory, not visual processing, requires BDNF.

Many clues suggest that BDNF protects against allostatic load and possibly even the stress on the brain associated with aging. In particular, it may explain why exercise is helpful in so many situations. Research with rats conducted by Carl Cotman of the University of California at Irvine has shown that exercise significantly increases levels of both BDNF and NGF in the brains of rats that are allowed free access to running wheels for two nights (when rats, being nocturnal animals, are most likely to use them). The increase is most dramatic in the hippocampus. Cotman has also shown that the benefits of exercise make themselves apparent shortly after the exercise period begins— perhaps implying that one doesn't have to jog miles a day for years to protect the brain.

Studies presented at the 2001 annual meeting of the Society for Neuroscience extend Cotman's work. For example, Fernando Gomez-Pinilla and colleagues confirmed that voluntary exercises increased BDNF levels in the brains of rats and that the rats scored higher on maze tests than their sedentary cage mates. In a follow-up the researchers showed that exercise and BDNF can work together to counteract a known trigger of allostatic load—poor diet. Rats fed a typical American diet, high in fat and refined carbohydrates, showed a decrease in BDNF. But when the rats were allowed onto their running wheels, levels of BDNF began to climb again.

David Albeck and colleagues at the University of Colorado have shown that rats forced to exercise for 20 minutes showed even more of an increase in BDNF levels than rats that exercised voluntarily. Since rats consider forced exercise to be a stressor, the message for humans seems to be that, by undertaking moderate exercise in times of stress, we can make positive health factors like BDNF work overtime.

Doctors and advocacy groups emphasize the importance of exercise in keeping one's memory sharp as the years go by. Exercise is also one of the best things that people suffering from depression can do for themselves. Because exercise increases BDNF, which is known to protect neurons, it's likely that the growth factor is the intermediary through which exercise benefits the aging brain.

Upping the "Anti" in Antidepressants

According to Eric Nestler of Yale University, antidepressants may work by increasing the levels of BDNF in the brain. All of the antidepressants now on the market act at the level of the neurotransmitter and receptor. They work by interfering with neuronal "housekeeping"— methods that brain cells use to clear excess amounts of neurotransmitter out of the synapse, so that the space will be clear for the next message, which might come from a different messenger chemical. Prozac and its progeny are the latest antidepressants. Known as selective serotonin reuptake inhibitors, they attach to sites called transporters on the "sending" neuron, thereby preventing that neuron from sucking back the excess serotonin. In both cases, the result is that the neurotransmitter remains in the synapse for longer periods, so that more of it can reach the next cell in line and exert its positive effects.

What those effects are is anybody's guess, according to Nestler. The fact is that scientists don't know what antidepressants do that helps depressed people feel better. It's true that Prozac, for example, inhibits serotonin reuptake, but what does that accomplish? Many researchers believe that it's only the first step in a much more complex process. They argue that Prozac and related drugs begin inhibiting reuptake within 24 hours, yet people who take the drug for depression don't start feeling better for three to four weeks. It's logical to assume that something else is going on during those weeks, and if scientists were to identify and unravel the process, they might be able to design more effective antidepressants. Prozac and its progeny aren't any better than the older drugs at relieving the symptoms of depression; they just work more cleanly, with fewer undesirable side effects. A true breakthrough in treatment awaits a better understanding of how the drugs actually work. Nestler believes that by prolonging the presence of neurotransmitters, such as serotonin and noradrenaline, in the synapse, antidepressants let loose a cascade of events that ultimately raise the levels of BDNF in the hippocampus.

Although today's drugs have fewer side effects than earlier ones, there has yet to be a qualitative improvement in the treatment of depression. Antidepressants fail to relieve symptoms in about a third of patients. There may be explanations other than the BDNF story; some researchers believe, for example, that serotonin itself holds the key to why antidepressants work. But it will be interesting to see what happens once we go beyond the level of neurotransmitters and their receptors. The notion that BDNF or other neurotrophins may be involved takes us in that direction—and, perhaps, a step closer to understanding the pathways of positive health.

Neurogenesis and Positive Health

A continually replenished supply of nerve cells, especially in key areas like the hippocampus, may be the brain's built-in buffer against wear and tear. It also looks as if neurogenesis may play a role in memory formation in times of stress.

Researchers sometimes set themselves up in opposition to prevailing medical wisdom. Hans Selye shocked his professors by studying the supposedly miscellaneous symptoms of illness; John Mason wanted to investigate psychosomatic illness. Even the concept of allostasis—that stress can be healthy and protective up to a point—has met with some resistance in the scientific community. But no medical dogma has been so firmly entrenched as the assumption that new cells don't grow in the adult brain.

As early as the mid-1960s, Joseph Altman, a researcher at the Massachusetts Institute of Technology found evidence of neurogenesis in various parts of the mouse brain. But his work went largely unnoticed by the scientific community. A big reason was that the findings flew in the face of clinical observation. It's undeniable that, while people grow taller and their bodies grow larger, their brains stay the same size. And neurons lost due to injury or neurodegenerative disease aren't replaced the way old skin cells are. Miraculous tales are told of children as old as 9 who have entire hemispheres removed to treat epilepsy and grow up absolutely fine. But this is due to the remarkable plasticity of the surviving hemisphere, not to the brain's having sprouted a new one.

Another stumbling block to the acceptance of neurogenesis is that only recently has equipment sophisticated enough to label and count neurons become available. Altman, for example, used radioactive "tags" to identify dividing cells, but these could only be seen in the top few microns of brain tissue. Since the available slices were usually thicker than that, there was no way to tell for sure how many new neurons were present. It wasn't until the 1980s that the stain called bromodioxiuridine came into widespread use. A side-by-side development, confocal microscopy, has made it possible to see these markers in their three dimensions and to visualize the totality of a nerve cell that could never be seen with the conventional two-dimensional microscope.

These are the techniques that Elizabeth Gould, now at Princeton University, used to prove neurogenesis in the brains of primates. Fred Gage and co-workers at the Salk Institute used the same methods to study neurogenesis in the brains of adult human volunteers who had died of cancer (although not cancer of the brain).

Neurogenesis most likely contributes to positive health by acting as a built-in buffer against allostatic load. It's no coincidence that studies confirming the existence of neurogenesis found it in the hippocampus, the region most vulnerable to stress-induced wear and tear. Neurogenesis in the hippocampus is an exemplar of the protection versus damage theory. Gould, for example, showed that the production of new neurons in adult life is suppressed by excitatory neurotransmitters and by stress, while Gage and colleagues showed that an enriched environment and exercise cause an increase in neurogenesis.

In addition to compensating for wear and tear, neurogenesis in the hippocampus may help form stress-induced memories. A 1999 study by Elizabeth Gould and Tracy Shors, now at Rutgers University, suggested that a stressful event may earmark new hippocampal cells born around the same time, dedicating them to the memory of that event. The team used a procedure called trace conditioning in which rats hear a tone that is followed a second or so later by a puff of air that causes the eye to blink (an unpleasant stimulus for the rat). Gradually the rat begins to blink its eye when it hears the tone; the time lag between the tone and the puff brings the hippocampus into play for this type of learning. During trace conditioning, the newborn hippocampal neurons survived for much longer than in the so-called classical conditioning experiment, when the tone and the puff come simultaneously—a form of learning that does not involve the hippocampus. So when the hippocampus participates in learning, newly formed dentate gyrus nerve cells seem to live longer. The life span of these kinds of nerve cells may be connected in some way to the durability of certain types of memory.

Evidence of neurogenesis is exciting for another reason: it suggests another way of looking at brain damage and neurodegenerative disease. Both are currently viewed in terms of the cells that die, and certainly, the fact that cells die in Alzheimer's disease or spinal cord injury is beyond dispute. But what if such conditions are also due to a failure of neurogenesis? This might extend future treatment options beyond protecting and replacing the dying cells; therapies (still to be invented) that restore neurogenesis might come into the picture as well. Other parts of the brain besides the hippocampus show signs of neurogenesis. Working with primates, Gould has found new cells in the prefrontal cortex, a nexus of another type of memory—working memory, the ability to hold information transiently in mind while completing a task or solving a problem. Jeffrey Macklis and colleagues at Harvard Medical School and Children's Hospital have shown neurogenesis to occur in the mouse cortex. An intriguing aspect of this study is that the team stimulated neurogenesis in a roundabout way—by inducing apoptosis, or encouraging the neurons to self-destruct. In other words, cell death stimulated cell birth. An obvious question is: Why aren't similar repair mechanisms triggered in other instances of cell death, in neurodegenerative disease, for example, or brain or spinal cord injury or chronic stress? Perhaps these situations generate an environment full of obstacles to regrowth. Once scientists figure out what these obstacles are and how to overcome them, we might usher in a whole new school of thought—not only for treating brain disease but also regarding positive health and the brain—and neurogenesis may play a role.

Neurogenesis and Depression

As our work with the tree shrews demonstrated, a breakdown of neurogenesis as usual may at least partly explain the hippocampal atrophy detected long after depression and trauma. The news is encouraging because it shows that hippocampal shrinkage isn't just a matter of cortisol corroding the neurons like battery acid; the reduction is a long time in the making, and scientists hope it can be prevented. Since both stress and cortisol are shown to block neurogenesis, it stands to reason that recruiting the agents of positive health, such as exercise-induced BDNF, can get it going again. Interventions that are successful in treating depression, such as antidepressants and physical exercise, have also been found to trigger neurogenesis. Ronald Duman of Yale University has found that rats given antidepressants have significantly more dividing cells in the hippocampus. Eberhard Fuchs of the German Primate Center in Göttingen has shown that an antidepressant reverses the effects of a form of animal-to-animal stress in tree shrews that causes symptoms of depression and suppresses the formation of new nerve cells in the hippocampus.

Scientists would love to know if, in addition to being vulnerable to trauma and long-term depression, the hippocampus plays a role in everyday mood. It is linked to two structures that do play such a role—the amygdala and the prefrontal cortex. It's possible that the loss of cells at this site, plus the dysregulation of neurotransmitters and hormones in a larger network, contributes to depression. And it's conceivable that medications designed to boost neurogenesis—or other measures, such as exercise—might add to our arsenal of weapons against both depression and allostatic load.

The Estrogen Story

For many of us at Rockefeller University, the discovery that there are estrogen receptors in the brain was the beginning of our research into allostasis. At the time, we thought the finding was just a signpost pointing us toward the discoveries regarding cortisol. We still viewed estrogen in terms of its effect on sexual behavior; we didn't think that this sex hormone would itself turn out to be a key player in allostasis. Yet that's just what estrogen proved to be. In addition to its role in reproduction, estrogen has a plethora of effects on the brain. Many are interrelated, and many seem to be pathways through which the brain achieves positive health. Estrogen stimulates neurons to form new synapses and synapses to form new branches; it encourages the growth of new neurons and protects against the destructive effects of free radicals. Of all the potential benefits to the brain, the most striking is estrogen's ability to protect memory.

This possibility first surfaced in the late 1970s, when endocrinologist Victoria Luine and I gave estrogen to rats whose ovaries had been removed. We found that the treatment raised levels of an enzyme that increased levels of acetylcholine in the basal forebrain. The significance—and the memory connection—didn't dawn on us until a few years later when researchers began to find that Alzheimer's patients showed a massive die-off of acetylcholine-producing neurons in the same part of the brain. Around the same time another link emerged on the opposite end of the research spectrum. Barbara Sherwin at Concordia University in Canada found that women whose ovaries had been removed (and who thus could not produce estrogen) complained of changes in their memory. Apparently, estrogen, acetylcholine, and memory are connected.

Until then most of the estrogen research had zeroed in on the hypothalamus and pituitary gland—the areas most likely to be involved in reproduction. But when the memory connection surfaced, researchers began to find estrogen receptors in many parts of the brain associated with memory, such as the hippocampus and cerebral cortex. We now know that estrogen and related hormones have several actions related to memory in these brain structures.

Estrogen working together with progesterone, another ovarian hormone, may play a role in the adaptive plasticity called synaptic remodeling. In a checks-and-balances relationship, these hormones regulate the formation of new connections between nerve cells in the hippocampus. In particular, the formation of new "excitatory" synapses—ones that receive "speeding up" messages—is influenced by the estrogen-like hormone estradiol. Glutamate is involved in this process, working through specialized receptors called NMDA receptors, after N-methyl-D-asparate, a chemical used to identify them. (Estrogens actually induce the formation of NMDA receptors on certain key neurons in the hippocampus. Progesterone, on the other hand, down-regulates or inhibits these synapses. This push-and-pull effect of the two hormones may be the intermediary through which synaptic remodeling protects, in the short term, against the effects of stress.)

As an irresistible digression, the sex hormones also underlie the basic differences in hippocampal structure between males and females, possibly explaining the differences in spatial navigation strategies used by the two sexes (in rats at least). Male rats are more efficient than females at finding their way around mazes. When it comes to homo-sapiens, men are more likely to use global spatial cues and know approximately in which direction something is relative to where they are, whereas women tend to use "local" cues or landmarks, remembering to turn right at the church and left at the gas station, for example. In rats these distinctions take shape in utero. During a key period of embryonic development, when the sex hormone testosterone is elevated in the male, a group of enzymes actually convert testosterone to estradiol; more estrogen receptors are expressed at the same time. There's evidence that this pathway is behind the "masculinization" of both the structure and the function of the hippocampus, though it doesn't explain why men will do seemingly anything rather than ask directions.

Protective Effects of Estrogen

Many of the actions of estrogen seem to have a protective effect on the brain. Patima Tanapat and Elizabeth Gould of Princeton have shown that estrogen stimulates neurogenesis in the dentate gyrus of the female hippocampus in rats. Female rats also seem to be resistant to the stress-induced atrophy of hippocampal dendrites seen in males. In Alzheimer's disease, estrogen appears to protect against the rapid-fire cell death known as excitotoxicity. Another feature of Alzheimer's disease, in addition to the death of cholinergic cells in the basal forebrain, is the buildup in the brain of a toxic protein known as beta-amyloid. Estrogen appears to protect against the destructive effects of this protein as well.

One of the most impressive studies in humans was conducted by Victor Henderson, a neurologist at the University of Southern California School of Medicine, and his colleague Annlia Paganini Hill. These scientists analyzed a group of over 8,000 older women and found that the risk of developing Alzheimer's was sharply reduced in women who took estrogen replacement therapy. Their study also showed that the higher the dose and the longer the duration of the therapy, the lower the risk of the disease. Richard Mayeux and colleagues at Columbia University also found that elderly women who took estrogen after menopause had a significantly reduced risk of developing Alzheimer's disease and that those who developed the disease did so much later. Another striking finding is from the Baltimore Longitudinal Study of

Aging, in which Claudia Kawas and colleagues at Johns Hopkins University studied over 450 older women who had been followed for up to 16 years. This team also found a similar reduction in risk of Alzheimer's disease in women taking estrogen replacement therapy.

Operating on the Edge of the Neuron

By stimulating neurogenesis and protecting against hippocampal atrophy, estrogen takes its place as a contributor to positive health. To learn more about these processes and the neuroprotective effects of estrogen in Alzheimer's disease, many scientists are studying estrogen's effects in and about the neuron. Part of this research involves understanding in more detail how brain cells are affected by their environment.

An intriguing finding is another type of estrogen receptor that differs from the ones discovered in the 1960s and 1970s. The estrogen receptors discovered first actually reside in the cell nucleus, close to the DNA, where they regulate the way the genetic code is turned into reality. This is how sex differences emerge in the hippocampus, for example.

Many of estrogen's actions, however, take place so quickly that the hormone probably doesn't have time to affect gene expression. Dendritic remodeling may be due to these quick actions. A better-studied example is the way estrogens protect the smooth muscle cells of cardiac tissue—an effect that may explain the dramatic increase in heart attacks in postmenopausal women. Estrogen's "nongenomic" actions operate through receptors located not inside the cell nucleus but on the cell surface, which takes researchers into uncharted waters.

James Eberwine of the University of Pennsylvania School of Medicine believes that messenger RNA, which turns the genetic code of DNA into usable proteins, might be found not only in the nucleus of neurons but also in the axons and dendrites, where it may be activated by purely local signals that don't have to travel all the way to the cell's nucleus. Eberwine has also found that the transcription factor CREB is present in the cell's extremities, where it may be activated by new events in the cell's environment. Axons and dendrites are both sites of the plasticity that occurs in response to stress. The presence of genetic players in these structures might mean that neurons can respond to stress by making changes only in the parts of the cell involved in the particular connection related to the event—without having to invoke the command center in the nucleus and make changes that affect the entire cell. Since estrogen receptors are also found on the cellular outposts, our group at Rockefeller University is investigating a possible connection. This type of autonomy in the axons and dendrites may be one way through which estrogen exerts its protective effects.

Endorphins, growth factors, neurogenesis, and estrogens are the vanguard of positive health factors. This research will give rise to a newer understanding of how our brains take care of us, and the implications will be discussed in the next and final chapter.

CHAPTER 10

Where We Could Go from Here

T he study of the brain and the process we now call allostasis has been a source of endless fascination to me throughout my decades as a research scientist, and I hope that having journeyed with me this far you will feel the same way.

I hope I have convinced you of your inherent ability to cope with the slings and arrows of outrageous fortune. I've tried to limit the idea of stress to the slings and arrows themselves, bringing in the word *allostasis* to refer to the resilience, the power, the seeming intelligence of our bodies' responses to an ever-changing world. The physiological systems that support allostasis follow a basic pattern that's been used, quite successfully, for about 400 million years. Surely these provisions did not evolve for the purpose of causing illness. Although they can and do threaten our health when thrown out of balance, as many of the preceding chapters have shown, keeping the allostatic systems *in* balance—and thereby optimizing our ability to handle life's vagaries while remaining in good health—is something that almost all of us can achieve.

The fact that you've picked up and read a book about the science of stress already demonstrates optimism and energy, and I'm confident that you'll make at least a few lifestyle modifications. I am concerned, though, about the people who don't read popular science books and whose knowledge of their own health, and bodies, is limited. To reach those people and to bring the concepts of allostasis and positive health as far into the community as possible, stress management needs to mature beyond the popular commonsense fitness canon into something more sophisticated and more widespread. For this to happen several changes will need to be made—or at least many could be made. So let me share a few more hopes regarding the future of allostasis.

Allostasis and Preventive Medicine

I hope doctors will begin to screen their patients for signs of allostatic load.

Many doctors still disregard the very real consequences that our emotions can have on our health. But accepting the idea of allostasis and allostatic load means accepting the fact that our psychological state affects our bodies in very precise ways, operating through well-mapped routes. This, in turn, means taking a new look at many of the conditions discussed in these pages, most of which have traditionally been considered, sometimes dismissed as, psychosomatic.

Stress-related conditions *are* psychosomatic. The word derives from the Greek words *psyche*, meaning soul or mind, and *soma*, meaning body; it simply means that the mind and body work together to produce health or illness. But, unfortunately, the word *psychosomatic* as applied to physical symptoms often carries a connotation of "It's all in your head," which carries a further implication—"Snap out of it!" These shades of meaning, thankfully, are beginning to vanish. An example of how the mind and body work together, which also illustrates how the concept of allostasis can be applied to illness, is the discovery, a few years back, of a type of bacteria found in ulcers, called *helicobacter*. Some scientists who adhered to the hard-line biological model of disease considered this discovery a direct hit to the mind-body movement. But finding a biological mechanism does not negate the possibility that ulcers can be stress related. Instead, it raises the question of what made these people suddenly susceptible to this particular infection. Most of us probably have the odd *helicobacter* floating around in our systems. If there's a direct causal relationship between the organism and the ulcer and no other factors are relevant, why don't most of us have ulcers? Other factors also must be responsible, and it's entirely likely that the point at which the bacteria gain the upper hand and begin to cause disease is the breakpoint of allostatic load.

One way that doctors could determine which of their patients are susceptible to allostatic load-type illnesses is by running a comprehensive check for the known physiological risk factors. A typical allostatic load profile could include blood pressure, waist-to-hip ratio, blood cholesterol, glycosylated hemoglobin (which measures glucose metabolism over a period of days), and levels of the stress hormones cortisol and norepinephrine in overnight urine. With our collaborators at the MacArthur Foundation Health Program, some of us at Rockefeller University have used just such a scale to show that higher allostatic load scores predicted a decline, two and a half years later, in cognitive function and memory, as well as cardiovascular disease, in people with no observable symptoms of disease or disorder at the time of the study. Such a profile might be a more efficient way to head off disease than checking individual people for signs of heart disease, diabetes, and so forth, especially people with no symptoms or family history of those disorders.

Widespread use of the allostatic load profile poses a few problems, however. For one thing, physicians would have to be able to identify the patients most in need of the test. And as medicine is practiced today, with insurance companies second-guessing doctors' decisions and the average office visit lasting about as long as it takes to say "allostatic load," many primary care providers might not know their patients well enough to spot the best candidates for the profile.

An even thornier problem is what to tell the patient who has a high allostatic load index. A doctor can't very well say, "Mellow out or you might get brain damage." He or she could, of course, suggest many of the lifestyle modifications discussed here. Indeed, everyone should understand the importance of restful sleep, a balanced diet, and regular exercise. But, again, the patients who are most willing to make fundamental and often difficult changes in their lives probably have healthy, realistic outlooks in the first place, plus a sense of optimism that they can control the things that influence their health. What is a doctor to tell the other patients—the ones whose coping styles amount to a bag of potato chips and several cocktails, who don't think they have time to exercise, and who doubt that any change they make will do any good anyway—in short, the ones most susceptible to the evils of allostatic load? As medicine is practiced today, a physician may not be equipped to provide the ongoing support such patients need to change their approach to life. Many medical groups and hospitals are tackling this problem by establishing stress reduction and wellness programs, which are an excellent start and may result in real transformations in physical and mental health.

The fact remains, though, that the people most threatened by allostatic load are often the ones least able to protect themselves from its perils. Type II diabetes, now epidemic in the United States, is a good example. These groups include children, the elderly, people of low socioeconomic status, and ethnic minority groups. And their vulnerability to stress-related conditions nudges the allostasis philosophy toward being a major public health concern.

Stress and the Developing Brain

I hope that pediatricians, social workers, and counselors who deal with children will learn to appreciate the dangers of allostatic load.

Traumatic stress in the early years can influence the development of the brain, including the reactivity of the stress response itself. In the late 1980s, Michael Meaney of McGill University and Robert Sapolsky of Stanford University showed that when newborn rats are "handled," or separated from their mothers for about 10 minutes a day for two weeks, they have less reactive stress hormones and slower rates of brain aging when they grow up. On the other hand, stress in early life—even in the period before birth—seems to make the hypothalamic-pituitary-adrenal (HPA) axis more reactive and to speed up brain aging.

Most scientists are unwilling to make assumptions about humans based on studies conducted in rats. But research in rhesus monkeys—considered a much closer parallel—suggests that trauma in infancy can affect the stress response by fairly specific pathways. Separation from the mother can reduce levels of serotonin in the brain, decrease affiliative or friendly behavior to other primates, and increase both aggression and alcohol consumption. As with humans, these are warning signs for susceptibility to allostatic load. There are some disturbing reports based on research in humans as well. For example, a history of sexual and physical abuse in childhood is a risk factor not only for posttraumatic stress disorder and depression but also hippocampal atrophy and cognitive impairment in adulthood.

The consequences of severe stress, such as child abuse and family dysfunction in early life, go far beyond serotonin pathways and dysregulation of the HPA axis. One of the largest investigations in this area is the 1998 Adverse Childhood Experiences study, conducted by a group of researchers at Southern California Permanente Medical Group (part of Kaiser Permanente) in San Diego. The researchers mailed questionnaires to over 13,000 people who had recently had medical work-ups, asking about experience with any of seven categories of childhood trauma: psychological, physical, or sexual abuse; violence against the mother; or living with household members who were substance abusers, mentally ill, or suicidal or were ever imprisoned. Over 9,000 patients responded. Among those who reported even one such exposure, there were substantial increases in a startling array of disorders, including substance abuse, depression, suicide, and sexual promiscuity, as well as increased incidences of heart disease, cancer, chronic lung disease, extreme obesity, skeletal fractures, and liver disease.

It should be remembered that we're talking about fairly severe levels of trauma here, not just garden-variety stress, and that the brain is resilient—the brains of children most of all. It may be that rather simple interventions early in a child's life, such as home visits by nurses, can head off later illness and even antisocial behavior. But the risks of allostatic load are becoming ominously clear. This is an area where many more studies and large-scale interventions need to be carried out.

I hope that *all* children will be raised in an environment that supports and enhances allostasis. Where children are concerned, I want to reemphasize a point that I've mentioned several times. Stress in the sense of chaotic life events is not the only source of allostatic load. A sedentary lifestyle and poor diet can predispose a child to stress-related illness, even in the happiest and most stable of families. The lifestyle changes that foster a healthy allostatic response need to be made right from the beginning—and right now! Thirteen percent of American children and adolescents are overweight, according to the Surgeon General's 2001 report *Call to Action to Prevent and Decrease Overweight and Obesity*; in 1999, 43 percent of high school students watched two or more hours of television a day. As of this writing only one state, Illinois, required physical education for grades K–12. In recent years, type II diabetes (formerly called "mature-onset" diabetes and considered a disease of adults) has increased dramatically in children.

The *Call to Action* report advocates quality physical education for children in all grades and meals that are low in fat and calories and high in fruits, vegetables, and whole grains. Current U.S. Department of Agriculture regulations prohibit serving foods of minimal nutritional value during mealtimes in school food service areas, including vending machines. The Surgeon General also advises that children get 60 minutes of moderate exercise four or five days a week.

Allostatic Load and the Elderly

I hope that protection against allostatic load and treatment for the conditions that contribute to it, such as depression and alcoholism, will become increasingly available to older individuals.

Because of the intricate connections between allostatic load and brain aging, older people may be uniquely vulnerable to stress, particularly where depression is concerned. Stress and depression are not synonymous, but imaging studies of women over 60 show that major depression in the past is often linked with atrophy in the hippocampus, which, of course, is a nexus of the stress response. Chronically elevated cortisol levels (a major indicator of allostatic load), which can damage the hippocampus, are also found in depression, although not always. And as Robert Sapolsky has shown, the "feed-forward" cascade, in which aging of the hippocampus undermines that area's ability to shut off the stress response—producing more cortisol and thus further damage—can further predispose older people to allostatic load as it affects the brain.

Whether or not allostatic load and hippocampal wear and tear are to blame, depression is a problem for the elderly. According to the National Institutes of Mental Health, more than 2 million of the 34 million Americans age 65 and older suffer from some form of depression. Older people are also disproportionately more likely to commit suicide. Individuals ages 65 and older account for 20 percent of all suicide deaths, though they make up only 13 percent of the population. The highest rate is for white men age 85 and older (65 deaths per 100,000 persons in 1996, or about six times the national rate).

Our society's attitude toward aging may be partly to blame for this problem. Depression tends to be underreported and underdiagnosed in general, so it's not surprising that it should go unremarked in the elderly. A youth-worshipping culture may assume that anyone over 65 is bound to be depressed, not recognizing the condition as abnormal in this age group. We need to make the distinction between clinical depression—a treatable condition even in the elderly—versus feelings of disillusionment and low mood. It's true that the elderly struggle with many circumstances that most people would consider "depressing," including isolation, poor health, reduced income, and loss of occupation, activities, and control. But not everyone who faces these situations develops clinical depression. It's important to remember that real depression is rooted not in the external world but in a chemical imbalance in the brain, to which some elderly people may be particularly susceptible.

Although the difficulties associated with advanced age do not cause depression—there are many elderly people who deal with them without developing a mood disorder—they can certainly be contributors and must be addressed. To make things even more complicated, older people are exposed to influences that can aggravate depression in both a biochemical sense and a perceptual sense, such as alcoholism, some prescription drugs, many medical conditions, and other mental disorders, particularly anxiety. So how does one separate these overlapping factors? The allostasis philosophy can help clarify the picture. First, the biochemical realities should be acknowledged; if depression is at the heart of allostatic load, it should be treated. Then, adverse circumstances should be recognized not as logical and obvious reasons for depression but as opportunities to make changes that can restore allostatic balance.

Can such changes be made given the rapid aging of the population and so many elderly Americans living in nursing homes, many of whom have significant health problems and limited control over their lives? This is another question entirely and one reason that the vulnerability of specific groups, such as the elderly, will inevitably make allostasis a public health concern, if it hasn't done so already.

Allostatic Load as More Than the White Man's Burden

I hope that the allostatic load gap between whites and other ethnic groups will narrow and ultimately vanish.

Ethnic minorities are more vulnerable to the illnesses associated with allostatic load. For example, African Americans have higher rates of heart disease, obesity, diabetes, and stroke and are also more likely than whites to die of these illnesses. Infant mortality is higher among African American women than white, Hispanic, Native American, or Asian American women. At first glance this elevation would seem to be due to the fact that blacks are more likely to live in impoverished areas, to have poor diets and limited access to health care, to be exposed to violence, and to grow up in unstable families. But the rate of infant mortality is increased even after correcting for education. Among African American women with graduate or professional degrees, the rate of infant mortality is still higher than among white, Hispanic, Native American, and Asian American women with comparable levels of education.

Attention must be paid to the daily presence of allostatic load in the lives of many minorities. In an article on health inequalities among the races, Burton Singer of Princeton University's Office of Population Research and Carol Ryff of the University of Wisconsin's psychology department discuss the susceptibility of blacks to tuberculosis, an infectious disease that no one suggests is psychosomatic. First, the researchers note that, although the tuberculosis-causing bacterium left traces discovered in neolithic man and was almost certainly known to the ancient Hindus and Egyptians, a protected rural lifestyle kept the disease out of sub-Saharan Africa until the mid-19th century. At that time, an influx of Europeans introduced the disease, particularly into communities of gold and diamond miners, whose crowded and unsanitary quarters were hotbeds of infection.

By the 1970s there were 12 to 17 times as many deaths from infectious disease among so-called colored people than among whites in South Africa, with up to 85 percent of the colored people's deaths attributed to tuberculosis. In contrast, tuberculosis accounted for only 1 percent of mortality among whites. Ryff and Singer believe that this huge discrepancy can't be explained entirely by differences in immunization and medical care, significant though they are. These researchers are interested in the psychosocial factors as well. They note that up to 80 percent of colored males lived away from home in makeshift communities rife with violent crime, suicide, alcoholism, drug abuse, and prostitution. The wives (often age 13 or younger) had to contend with managing households with absent husbands and little money. Children born to such families "grew up grossly deprived of food, shelter, instruction, nurturance, and attention . . . into rootless, alienated adolescents prone to crime and violence."

The United States, we hope, is a more egalitarian society than apartheid South Africa, but even here there are steep differences in the incidence of tuberculosis. Singer and Ryff note that 7 out of 10 tuberculosis victims in this country are minorities. Most researchers blame "environmental racism," chiefly substandard and overcrowded housing. But Ryff and Singer believe the figures call for further study of the psychosocial factors; their connection to all levels of health, including illnesses not generally considered stress related; and what interventions might be possible.

Income Versus Outlook

I hope that we will fine-tune our understanding of success in both its worldly and its allostatic aspects.

It's easy to think of allostatic load as a disease of the affluent, with businessmen and women in their BMWs with cell phones to their ears and suburban parents hurrying their kids into sport utility vehicles so that they can get to the mall before soccer practice. These are the people for whom the books and magazine articles tend to be written, because they're the ones who spend the most on books and magazines. In fact, people of lower socioeconomic status are more likely to suffer from allostatic load. I've talked about studies, like the Whitehall studies, that link low socioeconomic status to increased rates of illness and death. Newer research is beginning to show an inverse relationship between socioeconomic status and allostatic load. That is, the lower the socio-economic status, the higher the allostatic load.

In these studies a healthy allostatic response did not depend solely on the net worth of the participants. Singer and Ryff found data indicating that the joy is in the journey. Beginning with the Wisconsin Longitudinal Study, which followed a group of over 10,000 people from baselines established in the mid-1950s, the team of researchers examined a subset of 84 subjects, noting socioeconomic status as reported originally and in 1997. They checked the subjects' assessments of personal relationships (with spouses and parents) at both times. They also did something novel. Instead of looking for symptoms of specific diseases, such as hypertension, they measured the presence of allostatic load itself, using 10 of the warning signs, like urinary cortisol, that I talked about earlier.

Not surprisingly, lower levels of both socioeconomic status and the quality of one's personal relationships translated into higher allostatic load, and when the researchers looked at economic patterns alone, they found a direct linear descent, as might be expected. People who were on a "downward" pathway (those who had lower household income in both 1957 and 1997) were more likely to have an allostatic load score at or above 3, meaning that of the 10 biological signs of allostatic load measured, three or more were outside the optimal range; people on an "upward" pathway were less likely.

More intriguing is the way the picture changed when satisfaction with personal relationships was factored in. The researchers did find an inverse relationship between economic and personal satisfaction and allostatic load, but this time it wasn't a direct linear descent. Ryff and Singer checked for three things: economic status, satisfaction with relationships, and whether the subjects were on a positive or negative pathway for each of the two (whether one, the other, or both were better or worse in 1997 than in 1957). Not surprisingly, the people with negatives in money, relationships, and overall pathway fared the worst; 69 percent had allostatic load scores at or above 3. But the people who did the best (those with the lowest incidence of allostatic load) were *not* the ones who scored highest in all categories, as might be expected. This group came in at about the middle; 36 percent of them had allostatic load scores at or above 3. The people with the lowest allostatic load scores of all were the ones on a positive pathway despite negative reports in one or both categories. The first-prize winners were those on an upward path who gave a negative report on economic status but a positive one for their relationships. Among this group, only 20 percent had an allostatic load score at or above 3.

This finding strongly suggests, again, that a healthy attitude can confer a high degree of protection and resilience, despite one's circumstances. More importantly, it raises the possibility that resilience is the *reason* for the upward pathway and not just a consequence of it. Why didn't the people with positives in the money, relationship, and pathway columns do the best of all? Maybe the answer is that they had more luck than true resilience—maybe their allostatic potential was never put to the test. Being economically well off at both ends of a 40-year period hints at a fairly easy life, which in turn makes it easy to have good personal relationships. But the relationships might become less rewarding if the easy circumstances suddenly were to change! Instead of relying on socioeconomic status for our physical and mental health, we need to find out more about the resilience of people who struggle successfully. Sages and scientists have pondered the issue, but the Beatles put it most succinctly: "Money can't buy me love."

Positive Mental Health

I hope that mental health, like physical health, will become something more than the absence of disease.

Strong relationships remain some of the most powerful bastions against the trials of life. In the context of the Wisconsin Longitudinal Study, Ryff and Singer examined a subgroup of "resilient" women. These are women who experienced depression at some point in their lives but regained high levels of well-being in their early fifties. Some had difficult beginnings, such as growing up with an alcoholic parent or having to face in their childhood the death of a parent. But stable marriages, along with education and career satisfaction, and the ability to adapt restored positive health to these women. We need to know more about the processes—both psychological and neurobiological that make this possible—and to make this sort of resilience our definition of mental health.

Now the field of complications opens up even further. It's likely that a truly healthy mental outlook is one of the most important factors—maybe the most important—in achieving resilience and the ability to cope, providing the direction for whatever allostatic responses the body adopts. It's undeniably at the heart of people's willingness and ability to change their lifestyles. This would mean that achieving the best-possible allostasis for the greatest number of people will require a better understanding of positive mental health—thinking of mental health, not just physical health, as an ideal to achieve instead of a state characterized by lack of disease.

As long ago as 1948, the World Health Organization urged that mental health be viewed as something more than the absence of psychiatric illness (or "pathology" to make it sound even worse). But now, over 50 years later, we haven't made many strides in that direction. At this point we're not even doing such a hot job of treating the pathology. Both depression and anxiety are grievously underdiagnosed. Among the elderly, for example, one study showed that of patients who committed suicide, 20 percent had visited their primary care physician on the day of the suicide, 40 percent within one week, and 70 percent within one month. When patients do manage to get treatment, insurance companies are more likely to reimburse them for pharmacological interventions (meaning medications); the techniques and modifications recommended by psychotherapists, possibly more empowering in the long run, often remain unavailable.

How do we move from a somewhat spotty record of treating illness when and if it's noticed to a system of fostering positive mental health for all? This may be what our society needs most in order to fully embrace the philosophy of allostasis and make it work in our favor. It's a towering question, with no easy answers. Maybe in the future the primary care provider will be a psychologist, not an internist or general practitioner. Before that day comes, here are a few points to consider when regarding the possibilities of positive mental health.

We need a more sophisticated view of the relationship between emotions and health. Exploring the connections between "negative" emotions, such as hostility, and diseases such as hypertension is a good place to start. But if we are really to address allostatic load in a preventive sense, the best approach in the long term would be to emphasize positive mental health the way many medical practices and hospitals are beginning to work toward wellness. The resilience exemplified by the winners in Singer and Ryff's study has not yet been translated into biological terms. But these two investigators are working on it.

They are also trying to pin down the personal traits of those who exhibit positive mental health. Drawing on the writings of many psychologists, including Carl Jung and Abraham Maslow, they have determined that people who seem to have positive health—who handle stress, adversity, and aging well—have certain characteristics in common. These include self-acceptance; positive relations with others; autonomy, or the ability to regulate one's life according to personal standards and not the opinions and approval of others; the ability to choose and create environments that are conducive to happiness; having a purpose in life; and a strong sense of personal growth. And from surveying many lines of philosophical and scientific thought, Ryff and Singer have defined a good and healthy life as one that involves "setting and pursuing goals, attempting to realize one's potential, experiencing deep connection to others, managing surrounding demands and opportunities, exercising self-direction, and possessing positive self-regard."

Fine-Tuning the Connections

When ordinary mortals like ourselves feel besieged by stress it's hard enough to believe that there are such exalted beings in the world—cornucopias of admirable qualities who score high in all the categories mentioned by Ryff and Singer. Raising the rest of us up to that level seems like a tall order. But in the long run, achieving this type of positive mental health might be our best bet for optimizing our allostatic health as well. Trying to simply eliminate the negative, though an important step, has its limitations.

As Ryff and Singer point out in many of their papers, negative emotions have a place in life too; they're entirely appropriate reactions to negative or adverse circumstances. Let's go back to the high scorers in the allostatic load study, whose satisfactory relationships seemed to buffer them from economic adversity. It's unlikely that every one of them was a cockeyed optimist born lacking anger and anxiety, the way some people are born double jointed. Instead, they must have had some productive way of dealing with their feelings. Ryff and Singer also note that the breast cancer patients in David Spiegel's studies who attended support groups regularly and who lived a little longer on average worked through some of the most negative emotions that there are, including helplessness, rage, grief, and fear of death. Obviously, people with positive mental health aren't miraculously free of such emotions, and more research needs to be done to translate their coping ability into biological terms. It's a good start to document the connection between, say, hostility and heart disease, but we need to avoid the extreme—concluding that people succumb to illness because they failed to maintain a sufficiently positive attitude.

An analogous point could be made regarding another indicator of allostatic load—social isolation versus connectedness. Studies have shown that AIDS (acquired immunodeficiency syndrome) patients, for example, cope with their illness better and suffer less from their symptoms if they have a large number of social contacts. But, once again, their health advantages are probably due to more than just a laundry list of acquaintances. The ability to sustain meaningful and rewarding relationships is itself a sign of positive mental health; it's probable that the health and resilience of these patients are responsible for both the relationships and the improved health picture. This is another area in which personality, emotion, and lifestyle need to be better understood in biological terms.

The Courage to Change the Things We Can

I hope that we will all eliminate the "optional" stressors in our lives. Many of the groups studied by Ryff and Singer, and by many other scientists, are faced with worst-case scenarios, such as AIDS, ghetto life, cancer, and caring for loved ones with Alzheimer's disease. Other stressors, though just as capable of producing allostatic load, are more routine, and some may even be optional. Granted, there will be times when several unavoidable crises will converge at once and we have no choice but to shoulder up and cope with them. We can prepare our allostatic defenses by adopting the health measures discussed earlier. There's another strategy that we haven't discussed: we can decide, whenever possible, just which allostatic loads we're willing to try to carry. In other words, we can reject the stress outright.

Enormous burdens and challenges abound because of the complexities of life, and scientists and consumers must address this fact. But maybe life doesn't have to be quite as complex as it is. James Gleich has written a book, *Faster: The Acceleration of Just About Everything*, in which he argues that technological innovations supposedly designed to make our lives easier and save time for things we like to do have accomplished nothing of the sort. Instead they've made it easier for us to work all the time, while forcing a wholly unnecessary sense of urgency on us. Our scrambling now drives a good part of the economy. Gleich writes: "Federal Express and MacDonald's have created whole new segments of the economy by understanding, capitalizing on, and in their own ways fostering our haste. 'Tired of working overtime?' ask scores of advertisements. A medication is marketed 'for women who don't have time for a yeast infection'—as though slackers might."

We should do everything we can to resist the demands on our time. We may need to have cell phones so that we can call AAA on a rainy night if need be, but we probably don't need to take calls from the office—or check our messages—on weekends. (If such a change proves difficult to make, there's yet another new segment of the economy devoted to helping us: books about voluntary simplicity and catalogs full of soothing fountains, aromatherapy pillows, and other relaxation aids.)

Citizens of the 21st century also face tremendous pressure to make lots of money. A quick glance at the television bears this out. Anyone who watched *I Love Lucy* in the 1950s or in reruns can picture Lucy and Ricky's supremely ordinary apartment and Ethel's dowdy dresses. Such modest environs would be unheard of in today's world of television, where every commercial for floor cleaner is set in a state-of-the-art, zillion-dollar kitchen. The pressure to build up excess cash deposits is something else we need to resist. Don't forget the old saying that there are two ways to be rich—one is to have a lot, and the other is to want less. This isn't to say that everyone should live in a one-bedroom apartment like the Ricardos. But we should take a good look not only at what we really need to spend time doing but also at what we really need to possess. (Once again, if we're in doubt, we can always buy a book that will help us decide.)

The Neurobiology of the Future

Finally, I hope that scientists will keep on keeping on.

While the rest of us are ridding ourselves of stress and preparing our defenses for the challenges we can't avoid, scientists will continue trying to unearth the mental, emotional, and biological bases of life in the 21st century. We've already developed the philosophy of allostasis versus allostatic load; we've put together a fairly detailed picture of how the mind and body work together to produce the stress response and stress. The next challenge will be to work out the biochemical underpinnings of true health and well-being. Progress on that front may open up even wilder speculations: Is there a neurobiology of love, for example, or of happiness?

These questions haven't been addressed in a rigorously scientific way. But research into the nervous system may lead the advance. Already we're beginning to understand some of the processes that confer protection and resilience. In the future we will be able to unravel the skeins of biochemical connections that weave a well-adjusted life. From the standpoint of disease prevention alone, we'll have to do so, even if accepted scientific protocols aren't yet in place. And I have every confidence that we'll succeed. After all, the story of allostasis is the story of change in scientific thought.

Chemical Messengers of Allostasis, Their Receptors, and Their Protective and Damaging Effects

Allostasis is the body's way of remaining stable in a changing environment. Many chemical messengers in the body provide for this dynamic resilience, including hormones produced by major endocrine glands—such as the adrenals, thyroid, and pituitary—and neurotransmitters produced by nerve cells. Scientists classify these chemical messengers depending on where they act and on which cells. Indeed, the same chemical messenger can have different functions depending on its site of release and its site of action.

Chemical messengers that act on the cells that produce them are called autocrine factors (see Figure A-1). For example, nerve cells that produce dopamine, noradrenaline, and serotonin release these substances from the tree-like branches of neurons called dendrites, and each substance acts back on the dendrite that released it to regulate the electrical activity of the entire cell. In the case of serotonin, some re-

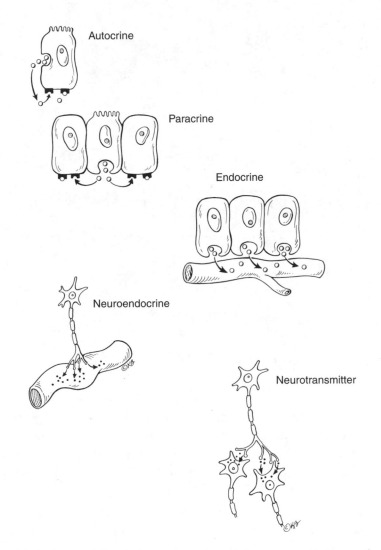

FIGURE A-1   Types of chemical messengers. Chemical messengers that act on the cells that released them are called autocrine factors; paracrine factors act on nearby cells. Endocrine factors (hormones) are released into the bloodstream and act on cells some distance away. Neuroendocrine factors are released from nerves into the bloodstream, whereas neurotransmitters alter the electrical activity of adjacent cells specialized to respond to them.

searchers believe that this auto-feedback mechanism helps to maintain mood and that when it malfunctions depression results. Sometimes autocrine chemical messengers also act in a so-called paracrine fashion—that is, they diffuse through the space between neurons and affect adjacent cells.

When a chemical messenger is carried through the bloodstream to a target some distance from where it was secreted, it is known as an endocrine factor, or hormone. The best-known hormones are produced by the endocrine glands (see Figure A-2). For example, cortisol from the adrenal gland acts on cells in the brain and also in the thymus gland and liver as well as other organs. But the brain also produces endocrine factors, such as the releasing factors produced by the hypothalamus, which tell other glands to produce their own hormones (see Figure A-3). A major phase of the stress response, the hypothalamic-pituitary-adrenal axis, is triggered when corticotropin-releasing factor from the hypothalamus signals the pituitary gland to produce adrenocorticotropic hormone (ACTH). This hormone, in turn, stimulates the adrenal glands to produce cortisol. Other endocrine glands that are controlled in this way include the thyroid and the gonads.

The pituitary gland produces hormones like prolactin and growth hormone that act on many body tissues and not just other endocrine glands. Likewise, the hormones vasopressin and oxytocin have important actions that affect body fluid balance and such processes as milk production and contraction of the uterus. All of these hormones are thought to influence mood and social behavior and may be key components in resilience and resistance to stress.

Although the pituitary is known as the master gland, not all hormones are under its influence. For example, the pancreas produces insulin in response to glucose levels in the bloodstream. In the immune system the spleen, thymus, and lymph nodes produce their own hormones and paracrine messengers called cytokines and chemokines. These hormones communicate with other cells in the immune system and affect the brain and other organs of the body. Feeling sick during a cold or flu is one consequence of the actions of excess cytokines produced by the body in response to the invading virus or bacteria. The

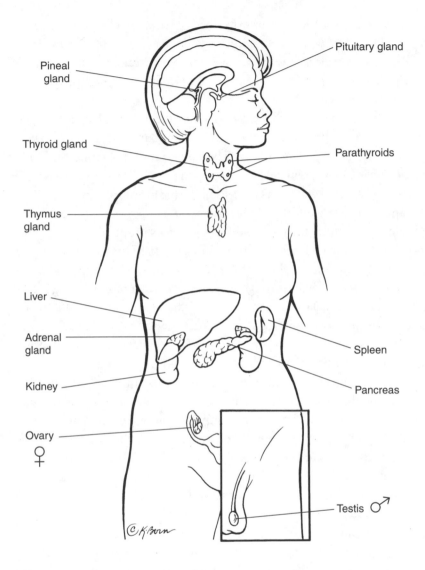

FIGURE A-2   The endocrine glands. The best-known hormones are produced by the endocrine glands. The hormones most important to the stress response are cortisol, produced by the adrenal cortex, and adrenaline, produced by the adrenal medulla and by sympathetic nerves.

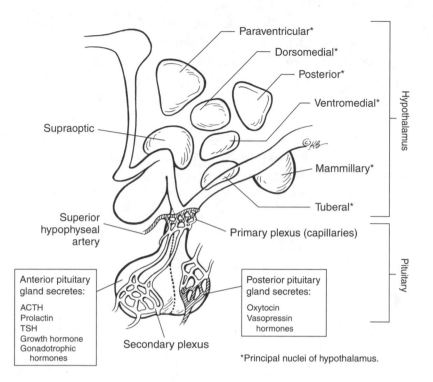

FIGURE A-3   Hypothalamus and pituitary glands. The hypothalamus supplies hormones to the posterior pituitary directly, through nerves. It also releases hormones into a network of blood vessels, called the primary plexus; these hormones act on the anterior pituitary to stimulate the release of other hormones, such as ACTH.

intestines also produce hormones that act elsewhere in the body to regulate feelings of being full or hungry.

Often, a chemical messenger originating from a neuron is released from the nerve ending of an axon instead of from the dendrite, and it then acts on the nearest cell that expresses a receptor for it. In this case, the messenger is properly known as a neurotransmitter. Neurotransmitters are a separate category of chemical messengers. Sequestered within the axons, they are released by electrical activity of the neuron that produces them, carrying signals that influence the activity of the receiving cells. Excitatory neurotransmitters, like glutamate and acetycholine, signal receiving neurons to increase their activity, while inhibitory neurotransmitters, like glycine and gamma-aminobutyric acid, tell the next cell in line to slow down.

Serotonin, dopamine, and noradrenaline can function as autocrine or paracrine factors (or both at once) or as neurotransmitters. Dopamine, for example, acts as an autocrine and paracrine factor when it is released from dendrites and regulates its own production from both the originating dendrites and the axons of nearby dopamine-producing cells. In this way the chemical messenger regulates movement (in the substantia nigra, a key movement area of the brain) and appetite, motivation, and response to drugs (in the mesolimbic area the so-called reward pathway). Dopamine acts as a neurotransmitter in the prefrontal cortex, where it plays a key role in some complex forms of memory. Finally, dopamine is a hormone when it is released from the hypothalamus to control the release of prolactin from the pituitary.

Another messenger that plays a dual role is adrenaline. A neurotransmitter widely used in the sympathetic nervous system, adrenaline is also a hormone when released by the medulla (or core) of the adrenal gland into the bloodstream, where it acts on the liver, blood vessels, and other organs and tissues that lie far away. Adrenaline is an important hormone in the fight-or-flight response.

All chemical messengers act on receptors in the target cells and tissues that respond to them (see Figure A-4). Receptors work through the lock-and-key principle and initiate cellular events that change the function, and often the structure, of the target tissues.

Chemical messengers of allostasis, exemplified by cortisol and adrenaline, are released during a stressful challenge or as a result of normal daily activity (see Figure A-5). They act on receptors found in many tissues. Cortisol receptors regulate expression of genetic information in the cell nucleus. For example, they bind to the DNA of cells in the hippocampus and help strengthen memories of dangerous things. Adrenaline also helps to enhance such memories but through a less direct route. Instead of entering the brain and binding to the DNA, adrenaline activates receptors on the surface of receiving cells near blood vessels, the "beta" receptors in the brain stem and other areas. Here adrenaline triggers a so-called second messenger system. Second messenger systems alter the chemical properties of proteins, particu-

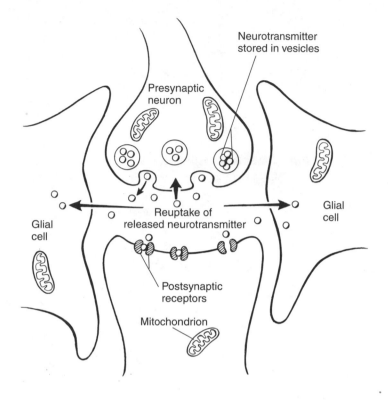

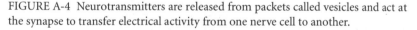

FIGURE A-4 Neurotransmitters are released from packets called vesicles and act at the synapse to transfer electrical activity from one nerve cell to another.

larly the receptors for hormones and neurotransmitters, and also the proteins that regulate the expression of genetic information in the cell nucleus. Through this relay, adrenaline acts on cells of the vagus nerve, which then transmits signals to the brain. So adrenaline, working indirectly through the second messenger system, also strengthens emotionally laden memories in the hippocampus and amygdala. Though adrenaline and cortisol affect different genes, the two hormones cooperate to help us remember the things we want to stay away from in the future—a valuable phase of the fight-or-flight response. The result of all these interactions is an entire "orchestra" of responses by many cells and tissues that shape how a person or animal is able to adapt to the

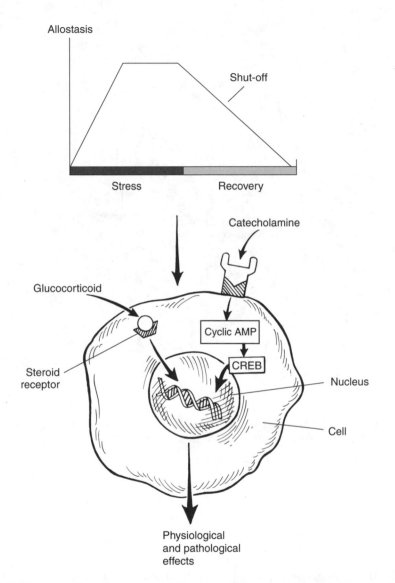

FIGURE A-5 Adrenaline and cortisol act on receptors on many cells throughout the body to alter these cells' activity and the expression of genes. AMP, adenosine monophosphate; CREB, cyclic AMP-responsive element binding protein.

conditions that caused the chemical messengers to be secreted in the first place.

The production of mediators of allostasis occurs according to two major patterns: in response to challenge or demand, as in stressful experiences, or as part of a routine "housekeeping" function that is governed by such things as the sleep-waking light-dark cycle (getting up in the morning, for example). One very important aspect of allostasis is that, after the mediators are secreted, they must be turned off. Cortisol has a built-in shutoff feature that regulates its own production, and for both cortisol and adrenaline there are nerve pathways that help turn off the whole response. Ideally, these self-regulatory pathways activate when the stressful experience is over. Sometimes, though, the shutoff mechanism fails, and the chemical mediators of allostasis are not supposed to remain in the "on" position. If they do, the consequences can be negative. Though the messengers of allostasis have protective effects in the short run, they can have damaging effects over longer periods if there are many adverse life events or if the hormonal secretion is dysregulated.

Healthy allostasis can give way to wear and tear, or allostatic load, in several ways (see Figure A-6). The simplest conceptualization is chronic stress, or "repeated hits" of allostatic mediators such as cortisol and catecholamines in response to novel threatening events (Figure A-6, panel B). People who have had excessive stress in their lives, as measured by multiple periods of poverty-level income, show earlier aging, more depression, and an earlier decline in both physical functioning and mental functioning. In many cases, chronic overexposure to cortisol may play a major role.

Repeated stress leads to impaired shutoff or an altered diurnal rhythm of cortisol or adrenaline production. Genetic factors, early developmental influences, or the effects of lifestyle may add to the influences of stress and increase the levels of cortisol and adrenaline.

Even if the number of stressful events is not excessive, the body may fail to efficiently manage the response to challenges or may fail to maintain a normal diurnal rhythm, as exemplified in panels C, D, and E of Figure A-6. Panel C illustrates a failure to get used to, or habituate to, repeated stressors of the same kind. Measurement of cortisol in a

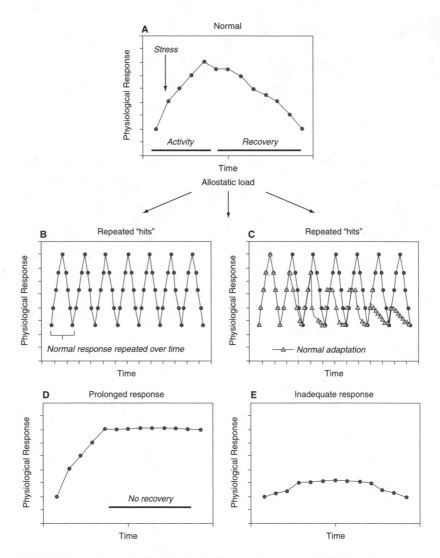

FIGURE A-6 Types of allostatic load. Chemical messengers of allostasis are normally turned off after a stressful event (A). But these hormones can cause damage through repeated activation (B), if the person can't habituate to the challenge (C), or if the stress response gets stuck in the "on" position (D). An inadequate response, of cortisol, for example, can result in overactivation of other allostatic players, which can then cause damage (E).

repeated public speaking challenge has revealed that about 10 percent of participants cannot get used to the "trauma"; these individuals, who also lack self-confidence and self-esteem, may well be overexposing their bodies to stress hormones under many circumstances in daily life that would not upset most other people. In these individuals the neural pathways that provide the shutoff are probably not as strong as those carrying the message of terror.

Panel D of Figure 6 refers to a failure to turn off each stress response efficiently or to show a normal diurnal rhythm. For example, individuals with a "genetic load" (two parents who are hypertensive) show prolonged elevation of blood pressure in the aftermath of a psychological stressor. Another example of the failure to shut off a response takes us into the realm of the housekeeping function of the mediators of allostasis, namely, the diurnal rhythm. Reduced amounts of sleep for a number of days result in elevated cortisol levels during the evening hours. Sleep deprivation and elevated diurnal levels of cortisol are also features of major depression. Elevated cortisol in the evening may lead to an undesirably high level of blood sugar overnight. Cortisol's first function is to stimulate the liver to generate glucose, and in addition to being exquisitely sensitive to cortisol it has its own inner clock that tells it to release glucose in the evening anyway. So high cortisol levels plus the liver's disposition to produce glucose at night—when we're asleep and not doing anything to use the excess glucose—mean that the glucose just circulates in the bloodstream. And idle glucose does the devil's work in the form of weight gain and insulin resistance, which set the stage for diabetes and other problems. Another scenario in which diurnal rhythms play a role is depressive illness, in which loss of bone mineral density has been linked to elevated diurnal glucocorticoid levels. Loss of bone minerals and loss of muscle protein are two of the recognized consequences of chronic elevation of glucocorticoids.

The "altered state" of allostasis occurs when a short-term or "acute" response is not sufficient to produce a long-term "adaptive" response. In this case the systems that are affected can themselves malfunction by overreacting. For example, hormones like cortisol operate to provide "checks and balances" to the other systems that are also turned on by many challenges. When the glucocorticoid response is inadequate, other allostatic systems such as the inflammatory cytokines, which are normally contained by elevated levels of cortisol, behave excessively (Panel E). The so-called Lewis rat provides the genetic explanation for this condition, having less corticosterone than the otherwise identical Fischer rat. Lewis rats are vulnerable to inflammatory and autoimmune disturbances, which can be overcome by giving injected glucocorticoids. Comparable human disorders in which lower-than-needed cortisol may play a role include fibromyalgia and chronic fatigue syndrome.

Thus, whether mediators of allostasis will protect or lead to damage is related to the dynamics of the response of the hormone, neurotransmitter, or other mediator. When turned on and off efficiently, the beneficial effects of allostasis predominate; when the allostatic responses are mismanaged (either not turned on in adequate amounts when needed or not turned off efficiently when no longer needed), the likelihood of harmful effects increases.

Notes

A New Way to Look at Stress

p. 11　**how best to relieve them** J. W. Mason, "A historical view of the stress field," *J. Hum. Stress* 1(1975):6-36.

p. 13　**whenever it is imperfect** H. Selye, *The Stress of Life*, rev. ed. (New York: McGraw-Hill 1976), p. 31.

p. 15　**increased by 50 percent** B. Guyer, M. A. Freedman, D. M. Strobin, and E. J. Sondik, "Annual summary of vital statistics: Trends in the health of Americans during the 20th century," *Pediatrics* 106(2000):1307-1317.

The Stress Response—or How We Cope

p. 20　**component of the pain experience** P. Rainville, G. H. Duncan, D. D. Price, B. Carrier, and M. C. Bushnell, "Pain affect encoded in human anterior cingulate but not somatosensory cortex," *Science* 177(1997): 968-971.

p. 27　**adrenals and some blood vessels** M. J. Blake, R. Udelsman, D. D. Norton, and N. J. Holbrook, "Stress-induced HSP 70 activation in adrenal cortex: A glucocorticoid-sensitive, age-dependent response," *Proc. Natl. Acad. Sci. U.S.A.* 88(1991): 9873-9877; R. Udelsman, M. J. Blake, and N. J. Holbrook, "The molecular response to surgical stress: Specific and simultaneous heat shock protein induction in the adrenal cortex, aorta, and vena cava," *Surgery* 110(1991): 1125-1131.

p. 31 **newly hatched salmon feed** W. W. Dickhoff, "Salmonids and annual fishes: Death after sex," in *Development, Maturation, and Senescence of Neuroendocrine Systems: A Comparative Approach* (New York: Academic Press, 1989), pp. 253-366.

p. 32 **elevated levels of corticosterone** J. C. Wingfield, M. C. Moore, and D. S. Farner, "Endocrine responses to inclement weather in naturally breeding populations of white-crowned sparrows," *Auk* 100(1983):56-62.

p. 33 **steeper rise in cortisol** Y. Cherel, J. P. Robin, O. Walch, H. Karmann, P. Netchotailo, and Y. LeMahor, "Fasting in the king penguin. I. Hormonal and metabolic changes during breeding," *Am. J. Physiol.* 12(1988):R170-R177.

p. 33 **avoidance behavior, and learning retention** J. C. Wingfield and M. Romero, "Adrenocortical responses to stress and their modulation in free-living vertebrates," in *Coping with the Environment, Neural and Endocrine Mechanisms*, B. S. McEwen, ed. (New York: Oxford University Press, 2000), pp. 211-234; R. M. Salpolsky, *Why Zebras Don't Get Ulcers: An Updated Guide to Stress, Stress-Related Diseases, and Coping* (New York: W. H. Freeman, 1998).

p. 34 **reading, writing, and arithmetic** P. D. MacLean, "A triune concept of brain and behavior," in *Hincks Memorial Lectures*, F. J. Boag and D. Campbell, eds. (Toronto: University of Toronto Press, 1973).

p. 35 **hippocampi revealed intense activity** E. A. Maguire, D. G. Gadian, I. S. Johnsrude, C. D. Good, J. Ashburner, R. S. J. Frackowiak, and C. D. Drith, "Navigation-related structural change in the hippocampi of taxidrivers," *Proc. Natl. Acad. Sci. U.S.A.* 97(2000):4398-4403.

p. 37 **amygdala the "low road"** J. E. LeDoux, *The Emotional Brain* (New York: Simon and Schuster, 1996).

Stress and the Emotional Connection

p. 40 **they are all under stress** H. Selye, *The Stress of Life*, rev. ed. (New York: McGraw-Hill, 1978), p. 3.

p. 43 **heartily commend it to you** W. B. Cannon, "The mechanism of emotional disturbance of bodily functions," *N. Engl. J. Med.* 198(1928):877-884.

p. 43 **pituitary gland just below it** G. W. Harris, "Electrical stimulation of the hypothalamus and the mechanism of the neural control of the adenohypophysis," *J. Physiol.* 107(1948): 418-429.

p. 44 **classic work,** S. Snyder, *Drugs and the Brain* (New York: Scientific American Library, 1986).

p. 47 **but the thyroid gland** R. Burgus, T. F. Dunn, D. Desiderio, D. N.

Ward, W. Vale, and R. Guillemin, "Characterization of ovine hypothalamic hypophysiotropic TSH-releasing factor," *Nature* 226(1970):321-325; Guillemin and Schally's research is described by N. Wade in *The Nobel Duel: Two Scientists' 21-Year Race to Win the World's Most Coveted Research Prize* (Garden City, N.Y.: Anchor Press, 1981).

p. 47 **kicks off the stress response** W. Vale, J. Speiss, C. Rivier, and J. Rivier, "Characterization of a 41-residue ovine hypothalamic peptide that stimulates the secretions of corticotropin and beta-endorphin," *Science* 213(1983): 1394.

Allostatic Load:
When Protection Gives Way to Damage

p. 56 **vessels that have become clogged** J. E. Muller, G. H. Tofler, and P. H. Stone, "Circadian variations and triggers of onset of acute cardiovascular disease," *Circulation* 79(1989): 733-743.

p. 57 **increased the risk of heart attacks** J. R. Kaplan, M. K. Pettersson, S. B. Manuck, and G. Olsson, "Role of sympatho-adrenal medullary activation in the initiation and progression of atherosclerosis," *Circulation* 84(1991):VI-23-VI-32.

p. 57 **highest among the rank and file** M. G. Marmot, S. G. Davey, and S. Stansfield, "Health inequalities among British civil servants: The Whitehall II study," *The Lancet* 337(1991): 1387-1393.

p. 57 **incidence of stroke, and cholesterol** J. E. Ferris, C. M. J. Shipley, M. G. Marmot, S. A. Stansfield, and G. D. Smith, "An uncertain future: The health effects of threats to employment security in white collar men and women," *Am. J. Public Health* 88(1998):1030-1036.

p. 58 **dropped from 64 to 59 years** M. Bobak and M. Marmot, "East-West mortality divide and its potential explanations: Proposed research agenda," *Br. Med. J.* 312(1996): 421-425; F. C. Notzon, Y. M. Komarov, S. P. Ermakov, C. T. Sempos, J. S. Marks, and E. V. Sempos, "Causes of declining life expectancy in Russia," *JAMA* 279(1998):793-800.

p. 59 **less than a month's duration** S. Cohen, E. Frank, W. J. Doyle, D. P. Sconer, B. S. Rabin, and J. M. Gwaltney, Jr., "Types of stressors that increase susceptibility to the common cold in healthy adults," *Health Psych.* 17(1998):211-213.

p. 59 **lower social status in both groups were** S. Cohen, S. Line, S. B. Manuck, B. S. Rabin, I. R. Heise, and J. R. Kaplan, "Chronic social stress, social status, and susceptibility to upper respiratory infections in nonhuman primates," *Psychosom. Med.* 59(1997):213-221.

p. 59 **physical and mental functioning** J. W. Lynch, G. A. Kaplan, and S. J. Shema, "Cumulative impact of sustained economic hardship on physical, cognitive, psychological, and social functioning," *N. Engl. J. Med.* 337(1997): 1889-1895.

p. 59 **death from a wide range of diseases** V. J. Felitti, R. F. Anda, D. Nordenberg, D. F. Williamson, A. M. Spitz, V. Edwards, M. P. Doss, and J. S. Marks, "Relationship of childhood abuse and household dysfunction to many of the leading causes of death in adults: The Adverse Childhood Experiences (ACE) study," *Am J. Prev. Med.* 14(1998):245-258.

p. 60 **low self-confidence and self-esteem** C. Kirschbaum, J. C. Prussner, A. A. Stone, I. Federenko, J. Gaab, D. Lintz, N. Schommeer, and D. H. Hellhammer, "Persistent high cortisol responses to repeated psychological stress in a subpopulation of healthy men," *Psychosom. Med.* 57(1995):468-474.

p. 60 **other things we are experiencing** K. A. Matthews, J. F. Owens, M. T. Allen, and C. M. Stoney, "Do cardiovascular responses to laboratory stress relate to ambulatory blood pressure levels? Yes, in some of the people, some of the time," *Psychosom. Med.* 54(1992):686-697.

p. 61 **let go of a stressful situation** W. Gerin and T. G. Pickering, "Association between delayed recovery of blood pressure after acute mental stress and parental history of hypertension," *J. Hypertens.* 13(1995):603-610.

p. 61 **more slowly than in normal animals** B. McCarty, "Sympathetic-adrenal medullary and cardiovascular responses to acute cold stress in adult and aged rats," *J. Auton. Nerv. Syst.* 12(1985):15-22.

p. 61 **don't work as well in the elderly** C. W. Wilkinson, E. R. Peskind, and M. A. Raskind, "Decreased hypothalamic-pituitary-adrenal axis sensitivity to cortisol feedback in human aging," *Neuroendocrinology* 65(1997):79-90.

p. 61 **decreased bone mineral density** D. Michelson, C. Stratakis, and L. Hill, "Bone mineral density in women with depression," *N. Engl. J. Med.* 335(1196):1176-1181.

p. 62 **often related to exercise extremism** R. M. Boyar, L. D. Hellman, and H. Roffwarg, "Cortisol secretion and metabolism in anorexia nervosa," *N. Engl. J. Med.* 296(1977):190-193; A. B. Loucks, J. F. Mortola, L. Girton, and S. S. C. Yen, "Alterations in the hypothalamic-pituitary-ovarian and the hypothalamic-pituitary-adrenal axes in athletic women," *J. Clin. Endocrinol. Metab.* 26(1989): 402-411.

p. 62 **noninsulin-dependent diabetes** K. Konen, L. Keltikangas-Javinen, H. Adlercreutz, and A. Hautenen, "Psychosocial stress and the insulin resistance syndrome," *Metabolism* 45(1996):1533-1538.

p. 62 **HPA axis and cognitive impairment** R. M. Sapolsky, *Stress, the Aging Brain and the Mechanisms of Neuron Death* (Cambridge, Mass.: MIT Press, 1992); R. M. Sapolsky, L. C. Krey, and B. S. McEwen, "The neuroendocrinology of stress and aging: The glucocorticoid cascade hypothesis," *Endocr. Rev.* 7(1986):284-301.

p. 62 **strong emotional significance** J. E. LeDoux, "In search of an emotional system in the brain: Leaping from fear to emotion and consciousness," *The Cognitive Neurosciences*, M. Gazzaniga, ed. (Cambridge, Mass.: MIT Press, 1995), pp. 1049-1061.

p. 62 **those associated with context** S. Lupien, A. R. Lecours, I. Lussier, G. Schwartz, N. P. V. Nair, and J. F. Meany, "Basal cortisol levels and cognitive deficits in human aging," *J. Neurosci.*14 (1994):1893-2903.

p. 62 **situation is not a threat** R. M. Sapolsky, "Stress in the wild," *Sci. Am.* 262(1)(1990):116-123.

p. 63 **legitimate reason to worry** J. Schulkin, B. S. McEwen, and P. W. Gold, "Allostasis, amygdala, and anticipatory angst," *Neurosci. Biobehav. Rev.* 18(1994):385-396.

p. 63 **shut off the stress response** L. Jacobson and R. M. Sapolsky, "The role of the hippocampus in feedback regulation of the hypothalamic-pituitary-adrenal axis," *Endocr. Rev.* 12 (1991):118-134.

p. 65 **underresponsive HPA axis** A. Buske-Kirschbaum, S. Jobst, A. Wustmans, C. Kirshbaum, W. Rauth, and D. H. Hellhammer, "Attenuated free cortisol response to psychosocial stress in children with atopic dermatitis," *Psychosom. Med.* 59 (1997):419-426.

p. 65 **though the patients certainly don't** L. J. Crofford, S. R. Pillemer, and K. T. Kalogeras, "Hypothalamic-pituitary-adrenal axis perturbation in patients with fibromyalgia," *Arthr. Rheum.* 37(1994):1583-1592; C. Heim, U. Ehlert, J. Hanker, and D. H. Hellhammer, "Abuse-related post-traumatic stress disorder and alterations of the hypothalamo-pituitary-adrenal axis in women with chronic pelvic pain," *Psychosom. Med.* 60(1998):309-318.

p. 66 **risk of both heart attack and stroke** P. Verdecchia, G. Schillaci, and C. Borgioni, "Cigarette smoking, ambulatory blood pressure and cardiac hypertrophy in essential hypertension," *Hypertension* 13(1995):1209-1215.

p. 66 **cardiovascular disease, stroke, and diabetes** P. Bernadet, "Benefits of physical activity in the prevention of cardiovascular diseases," *J. Cardiovasc. Pharmacol.* 25(1995):S3-S8.

Stress and the Cardiovascular System

p. 68 **heart attack or stroke** J. E. Muller and G. H. Tofler, "A symposium: Triggering and circadian variation of onset of acute cardiovascular disease," *Am. J. Cardiol.* 66(1990):1-70.

p. 69 **through which adrenaline acts** S. B. Manuck, J. R. Kaplan, M. F. Muldoon, M. R. Adams, and T. B. Clarkson, "The behavioral exacerbation of atherosclerosis and its inhibition by propranolol," P. M. McCabe et al., eds., *Stress, Coping and Disease* (London: Lawrence Erlbaum Associates, 1991), pp. 51-72.

p. 69 **removal of the ovaries** C. A. Shively and T. B. Clarkson, "Social status and coronary artery atherosclerosis in female monkeys," *Arterioscl.* *Thromb.* 14(1994):721-726.

p. 70 **also showed atherosclerosis** P. L. Schnall, C. Pieper, J. E. Schwartz, R. A. Karasek, Y. Schlussel, R. B. Devereau, A. Ganau, M. Alderman, K. Warren, and T. G. Pickering, "The relationship between 'job strain,' workplace diastolic blood pressure, and left ventricular mass index," *JAMA* 263(1990): 1929-1935.

p. 73 **in response to external needs** S. W. Porges, "Cardiac vagal tone: A physiological index of stress," *Neurosci. Behav. Rev.* 19(1995):225-233.

p. 73 **after the crisis had passed** F. L. Porter, S. W. Porges, and R. E. Marshall, "Newborn pain cries and vagal tone: Parallel changes in response to circumcision," *Child Dev.* 58(1988):495-505.

p. 75 **heart disease in a normal population** R. P. Sloan, A. Shapiro, E. Baliella, M. M. Myers, and J. M. Gorman, "Cardiac autonomic control buffers blood pressure variability responses to challenge: A psychophysiologic model of coronary artery disease," *Psychosom. Med.* 61(1999):58-68.

p. 76 **threefold evolution of the vagal system** S. W. Porges, "Orienting in a defensive world: Mammalian modification of our evolutionary heritage, a polyvagal theory," *Psychophysiology* 32(1995):301-318.

p. 78 **affect in a direct manner the heart** C. Darwin, *The Expression of the Emotions in Man and Animals* (1872; reprint, Chicago: University of Chicago Press, 1965).

p. 79 **removal of threat or danger** M. A. Samuels, "Voodoo death revisited: The modern lessons of neurocardiology," *Neurologist* 3(1997):93-304.

p. 79 **bradycardia observed in reptiles** C. P. Richter, "On the phenomenon of sudden death in animals and man," *Psychosom. Med.* 19(1957):191-194.

p. 81 **behavioral problems a few years later** S. W. Porges, J. A. Doussard-Roosevelt, A. L. Portales, and S. I. Greenspan, "Infant regulation of the vagal 'brake' predicts child behavior problems: A psychobiological model of social behavior," *Dev. Psychobiol.* 29(1996):697-712.

p. 82 **in readiness to deal with a challenge** M. C. Davis, K. A. Matthews, and C. E. McGrath, "Hostile attitudes predict elevated vascular resistance during interpersonal stress in men and women," *Psychosom. Med.* 62(2000):17-25.

p. 82 **heart attacks and strokes** J. H. Markowitz, "Hostility is associated with increased platelet activation in coronary heart disease," *Pyschosom. Med.* 60(1998):587-591.

p. 83 **risk factors, such as hypertension, were absent** J. E. Williams, S. C. Paton, I. C. Siegler, M. L. Eigenbrodt, F. J. Nieto, and H. A. Tyroler, "Anger proneness predicts coronary heart disease risk: Prospective analysis from the atherosclerosis risk in Communities (ARIC) study," *Circulation* 101(2000):2034-2039.

p. 83   **incipient heart disease** P. Verdecchia, G. Schillaci, C. Borgioni, A. Ciucci, I. Zampi, M. Battistelli, R. Gattobigio, N. Sacchi, and C. Porcellati, "Cigarette smoking, ambulatory blood pressure and cardiac hypertrophy in essential hypertension," *J. Hypertens.* 13(1995):1209-1215.

p. 83   **show left ventricular hypertrophy** Schnall et al., op. cit.

p. 84   **unusually excitable stress response** S. G. Matta, Y. Fu, J. D. Valentine, and B. M. Sharp, "Response of the hypothalamo-pituitary-adrenal axis to nicotine," *Psychoneuroendocrinology* 23 (1998):103-113.

p. 84   **more ACTH than males** K. Ogilvie and C. Rivier, "Gender difference in hypothalamic-pituitary-adrenal response to alcohol in the rat: Activational role of gonadal steroids," *Brain Research* 766(1997):19-28.

p. 84   **alcohol can blunt the HPA response** S. Lee and C. Rivier, "An initial, three-day-long treatment with alcohol induces a long-lasting phenomenon of selective tolerance in the activity of the rat hypothalamic-pituitary-adrenal axis," *J. Neurosci.* 17(1997):8856-8866.

p. 84   **twice as high during withdrawal upon recovery** B. Adinoff, D. Risher-Flowers, J. DeJong, B. Ravitz, G. H. A. Bone, D. J. Nutt, I Roehrich, P. R. Martin, and M. Linnoila, "Disturbances of hypothalamic-pituitary-adrenal axis functioning during ethanol withdrawal in six men," *Am. J. Psych.* 148(1991): 1023-1025.

p. 84   **response to experimental stimulation** G. S. Wand, D. Mangold, D. M. Ali, and P. Giggey, "Adrenocortical responses and family history of alcoholism," *Alcohol Clin. Exp. Res.* 23 (1999):1185-1190.

p. 84   **overstimulates the sympathetic nervous system and elevates cortisol** K. Kamara, R. Eska, and T. Castonguay, "High-fat diets and stress responsivity," *Physiol. Behav.* 64 (1998):1-6; L. Lapidus, C. Bengtsson, T. Hallstrom, and P. Bjorntorp, "Obesity, adipose tissue distribution and health in women—results from a population study in Gothenburg, Sweden," *Appetite* 12(1989):25-35.

p. 85   **fat is deposited in the body** S. B. Manuck, J. R. Kaplan, M. F. Muldoon, M. R. Adams, and T. B. Clarkson, "The behavioral exacerbation of artherosclerosis and its inhibition by propranolol," P. M. McCabe et al., eds., *Stress, Coping and Disease*, (London: Lawrence Erlbaum Associates, 1991), pp. 51-72.

p. 85   **according to a Swedish study** B. Larsson, J. Seidell, K. Svardsudd, L. Welin, G. Tibblin, L. Wilhelmesen, and P. Bjorntorp, "Obesity, adipose tissue distribution and health in men—the study of men born in 1913." *Appetite* 13(1989):37-44.

p. 85   **Whitehall studies** E. J. Brunner, M. G. Marmot, K. Nanchalal, M. J. Shipley, S. A. Stansfeld. M. Juneja, and K. G. M. M. Alberti, "Social inequality in coronary risk: Central obesity and the metabolic syndrome. Evidence from the Whitehall II study," *Diabetologia* 40(1997):1341-1349.

p. 86   **stress hormones can result in insulin resistance** D. N. Brindley and Y. Rolland, "Possible connections between stress, diabetes, obesity, hypertension and altered lipoprotein metabolism that may result in atherosclerosis," *Clin. Sci.* 77(1989):453-461.

p. 87   **overweight among adolescents has tripled** U.S. Department of Health and Human Services, *The Surgeon General's Call to Action to Prevent and Decrease Overweight and Obesity* (Rockville, Md.: U.S. Department of Health and Human Services, Public Health Service, Office of the Surgeon General, 2001).

Stress and the Immune System

p. 89   **encountered this foe before** R. Preston, *The Hot Zone* (New York: Random House, 1994).

p. 93   **stable, supportive environment** S. Cohen, E. Frank, W. J. Doyle, D. P. Skoner, B. S. Rabin, and J. M. Gwaltney, Jr., "Types of stressors that increase susceptibility to the common cold in healthy adults," *Health Psychol.* 17(1993): 214-223; S. Cohen, S. Line, S. B. Manuck, B. S. Rabin, I. R. Heise, and J. R. Kaplan, "Chronic social stress, social status, and susceptibility to upper respiratory infections in nonhuman primates," *Psychosom. Med.* 59(1997):213-221.

p. 93   **impair the immune system** J. Kiecolt-Glaser, W. Garner, C. Speicher, G. Penn, and R. Glaser, "Psychosocial modifiers of immunocompetence in medical studies," *Psychosom. Med.* 46 (1984):7.

p. 93   **stronger support systems** J. R. Dura, C. E. Speicher, O. J. Trask, and R. Glaser, "Spousal caregivers of dementia victims: Longitudinal changes in immunity and health," *Psychosom. Med.* 53(1994):345-362.

p. 93   **immune system activity, over the next 24 hours** J. K. Kiecolt-Glaser, R. Glaser, J. T. Cacioppo, and W. B. Malarkey, "Marital stress: Immunologic, neuroendocrine, and autonomic correlates," *Ann. N.Y. Acad. Sci.* 840(1998): 656-663.

p. 94   **coping with the death of a child** I. Levav, Y. Friedlander, J. Kark, and E. Peritz, "An epidemiological study of mortality among bereaved parents," *N. Engl. J. Med.* 319(1988):457.

p. 94   **participants did not live appreciably longer** P. J. Goodwin, M. Leszcz, and M. Ennis, "The effect of group psychosocial support on survival in metastatic breast cancer," *N. Engl. J. Med.* 345(2001):1719-1726.

p. 94   **thought to attack cancerous cells** Y. Shavit, G. W. Terman, F. C. Martin, J. W. Lewis, J. C. Liebeskind, and R. P. Gale, "Stress, opioid peptides, the immune system, and cancer," *J. Immunol.* 135(1994):834-837.

p. 94   **growth of tumors in rats** M. Visintainer, J. Volpicelli, and M. Seligman, "Tumor rejection in rats after escapable and inescapable shock," *Science* 216(1982):437-439.

p. 94   **rats more susceptible to tumors** R. Sapolsky and T. Donnelly, "Vulnerablity to stress-induced tumor growth increases with age in rats: Role of glucocorticoids," *Endocrinology* 117(1985):662.

p. 96   **once the stress was resolved** F. S. Dhabar, A. H. Miller, M. Stein, B. S. McEwen, and R. L. Spencer, "Diurnal and stress-induced changes in distribution of peripheral blood leukocyte subpopulations," *Brain Behav. Immun.* 8(1994):66-79.

p. 97   **cortisol into the bloodstream** F. S. Dhabar, A. H. Miller, B. S. McEwen, and R. L. Spencer, "Stress-induced changes in blood leukocyte distribution—role of adrenal steroid hormones," *J. Immunol.* 157(1996):1638-1644.

p. 98   **change is not irreversible** F. S. Dhabar and B. S. McEwen, "Acute stress enhances while chronic stress suppresses cell-mediated immunity in vivo: A potential role for leukocyte trafficking," *Brain Behav. Immun.* 11(1997):286-206.

p. 99   **genes that encode for these molecules** F. S. Dhabar, "Stress-induced changes in T-cell distribution are mediated by the selectin family of adhesion molecules." *Brain Behav. Immun.* 14(2000):90.

p. 101   **mental arithmetic causes the airways in the lungs to constrict** S. Cohen and R. Rodriguez, "Stress, viral respiratory infections, and asthma," *Asthma and Respiratory Infection*, D. P. Skoner, ed. (New York: Marcel Decker, 2000).

p. 102   **negative emotion, such as fear and anger** P. Lehereer, S. Isenberg, and S. M. Hochron, "Asthma and emotion: A review," *Asthma* 30(1993):5-21.

p. 102   **perceived stress in their lives** Cohen and Rodriguez, op. cit.

p. 102   **response to increased adrenocorticotropic hormone and to exercise** L. J. Croffond, N. C. Engleberg, and M. A. Demitrack, "Neurohormonal perturbations in fibromyalgia," *Baillieres Clin. Rheumatol.* 10(1996):365-378.

p. 103   **provocative nonetheless** C. Heim, U. Ehlert, J. Hanker, and D. H. Hellhammer, "Abuse-related post-traumatic stress disorder and alterations of the hypothalamo-pituitary-adrenal axis in women with chronic pelvic pain," *Psychosom. Med.* 60 (1998):309-318.

p. 103   **stress as well as the dermatitis** A. Buske-Kirshbaum, S. Jobst, A. Wustmans, C. Kirschbaum, W. Rauh, and D. H. Hellhammer, "Attenuated free cortisol response to psychosocial stress in children with atopic dermatitis," *Psychosom. Med.* 59 (4):419-426.

p. 103   **for the benefit of the individual** A. Buske-Kirshbaum, S. Jobst, and D. H. Hellhammer, "Altered reactivity of the hypothalamus-pituitary-adrenal axis in patients with atopic dermatitis: Pathologic factor or symptom?," *Ann. N.Y. Acad. Sci.* 840(1998):747-754.

p. 104   **decreased cortisol levels, to rheumatoid arthritis** K. Dowdell and C. Whitacre, "Regulation of inflammatory autoimmune diseases," in *Coping* *with the Environment: Neural and Endocrine Mechanism,* B. S. McEwen, ed. (New York: Oxford University Press, 2000).

p. 104   **only 50 percent of the others did** C. D. Lehman, J. Rodin, B. McEwen, and R. Brinton, "Impact of environmental stress on the expression of insulin-dependent diabetes mellitus," *Behav. Neurosci.* 2(1991):241-245.

p. 104   **higher risk of developing the disease** B. Hagglof, L. Blom, G. Dahlquist, G. Lonnbeerg, and B. Sahlin, "The Swedish Childhood Diabetes study: Indications of severe psychological stress as a risk factor for type I (insulin-dependent) diabetes mellitus in childhood," *Diabetologia* 34(1991):579-583.

p. 104   **chaotic family structure** G. M. Thernlund, G. Dahlquist, K. Hansson, S. A. Ivarsson, S. S. Ludvigsson, and B. Hagglof, "Psychological stress and the onset of IDDM in children," *Diabetes Care* 10(1995):1323-1329.

p. 105   **patients without the disease** S. Warren, S. Greenhill, and K. G. Warren, "Emotional stress and the development of multiple sclerosis: Case-control evidence of a relationship," *J. Chronic Dis.* 35(1982):821-831.

p. 105   **Persian Gulf war** P. Nisipeanu and A. D. Korczyn, "Psychological stress as risk factor for exacerbations in multiple sclerosis," *Neurology* 43(1993): 1311-1312.

Stress and the Brain

p. 107   **fear yet more for memory** H. R. E. Davidson, *Gods and Myths of Northern Europe* (London: Penguin Books, 1990), p. 147.

p. 111   **toxic effect on brain cells** K. Aus der Muhlen and H. Ockenfels, "Morphological alterations in the diencephalon and telencephalon following disturbances to the feedback mechanism adenohypophysis-adrenal cortex. 3. Studies on the guinea pig after administration of cortisone and hydrocortisone," *Z. Zellforsch.* 93(1969):126.

p. 111   **played a role in a hippocampal demise** P. W. Landfield and J. C. Eldridge, "Evolving aspects of the glucocorticoid hypothesis of brain aging: Hormonal modulation of neuronal calcium homeostatis," *Neurobiol. Aging* 15(1994): 579-588.

p. 111   **accelerated the aging of the hippocampus** R. M. Sapolsky, L. Krey, and B. S. McEwen, "Prolonged glucocorticoid exposure reduces hippocampal neuron number: Implications for aging," *J. Neurosci.* 5(1985):1221.

p. 111   **associated with many types of strokes** R. M. Sapolsky, "Why stress is bad for your brain," *Science* 273(1996): 749-750.

p. 113   **damage to the hippocampus of vervet monkeys** H. Uno, T. Ross, J. Else, M. Suleman, and R. Sapolsky, "Hippocampal damage associated with prolonged and fatal stress in primates," *J. Neurosci.* 9(1989):1709-1711.

p. 114   **hippocampus to provide the context** R. G. Phillips and J. E.

LeDoux, "Differential contribution of amygdala and hippocampus to cued and contextual fear conditioning," *Behav. Neurosci.* 106(1992):274-285.

p. 114   **recognizing it in others** S. B. Hamann, L. Stefanacci, L. R. Squire, R. Adolphus, D. Tranel, H. Damasio, and A. Damasio, "Recognizing facial emotion," *Nature* 379(1996): 497.

p. 115   **did not seem to involve the amygdala** S. B. Hamann, T. D. Ely, S. T. Grafton, and C. D. Kilts, "Amygdala activity related to enhanced memory for pleasant and aversive stimuli," *Nature Neurosci.* 2(1999):289-294.

p. 115   **adrenaline helps to develop memories of unpleasant things** R. E. O'Carroll, E. Drysdale, L. Cahill, P. Shajahan, and K. P. Ebmeier, "Stimulation of the noradrenergic system enhances and blockade reduces memory for emotional material in man," *Psychol. Med.* 29(1999):1083-1088.

p. 116   **link the shock with the place where it occurred** B. Roozendaal, G. Portillo-Marquez, and J. L. McGaugh, "Basolateral amygdala lesions block glucocorticoid-induced modulation of memory for spatial learning," *Behav. Neurosci.* 110(1996):1074-1083.

p. 117   **memory, cortisol, and stress all meet** M. Starkman, S. Gebarski, S. Berent, and D. Schteingart, "Hippocampal formation volume, memory dysfunction, and cortisol levels in patients with Cushing's syndrome," *Biol. Psychiatry* 32(1992): 756.

p. 117   **posttraumatic stress disorder from combat in Vietnam** J. Bremner, P. Randall, T. Scott, and R. Bronen, "MRI-based measurement of hippocampal volume in patients with combat-related PTSD," *Am. J. Psych.* 152(1995):973.

p. 117   **survivors of childhood sexual abuse** J. Bremner, P. Randall, E. Vermetten, L. Staib, and A. Bronen, "Magnetic resonance imaging-based measurement of hippocampal volume in PTSD related to childhood physical and sexual abuse—a preliminary report," *Biol. Psychiatry* 41(1997):23.

p. 117   **10 years previously** Y. Sheline, P. Wang, M. Gado, J. Cseernansky, and M. Vannier, "Hippocampal atrophy in recurrent major depression," *Proc. Natl. Acad. Sci. U.S.A.* 93(1996): 3908.

p. 119   **initially caused researchers to suspect** D. C. Blanchard, R. R. Sakai, B. S. McEwen, S. M. Weiss, and R. J. Blanchard, "Subordination stress: Behavioral, brain and neuroendocrine correlates," *Behav. Brain Res.* 58(1993): 113-121.

p. 121   **produce new cells in an area called the dentate gyrus** E. Gould, P. Tanapat, B. S. McEwen, G. Flugge, and E. Fuchs, "Proliferation of granule cell precursors in the dentate gyrus of adult monkeys is diminished by stress," *Proc. Natl. Acad. Sci. U.S.A.* 95(1998):3168-3171.

p. 121   **evidence of neurogenesis in humans** P. S. Eriksson, E. Perfilieva, T. Bjork-Eriksson, A. Alborn, C. Nordbord, D. S. Peterson, and F. H. Gage,

"Neurogenesis in the adult human hippocampus," *Nature Med.* 4(1998):1313-1317.

p. 121   **production of new cells by 15 percent** H. van Praag, G. Kempermann, and F. H. Gage, "Running increases cell proliferation and neurogenesis in the adult mouse dentate gyrus," *Nat. Neurosci.* 2(1999):266-270.

p. 121   **enriched environment increased the number of synapses in parts of the brain** W. T. Greenough and C. H. Bailey, "The anatomy of a memory: Convergence of results across a diversity of tests," *TINS* 11(1988):142-147.

p. 122   **these effects are reversible** E. Gould, B. S. McEwen, P. Tanapat, L. A. M. Galea, and E. Fuchs, "Neurogenesis in the dentate gyrus of the adult tree shrew is regulated by psychosocial stress and NMDA receptor activation," *J. Neurosci.* 17(1997): 2492-2498.

p. 123   **severely and permanently damaged** A. M. Magarinos and B. S. McEwen, "Induced atrophy of apical dendrites of hippocampal CA3c neurons: Comparison of stressors," *Neuroscience* 69(1995):83-88.

p. 123   **certain hippocampal neurons to decrease** K. Pham, J. Nacher, P. R. Hof, and B. S. McEwen, "Repeated, but not acute, restraint stress suppresses proliferation of neural precursor cells and increases PSA-NCAM expression in the adult rat dentate gyrus," *J. Neurosci.* (in press).

p. 125   **lower than normal cortisol levels** R. Yehuda, A. C. McFarlane, and A. Y. Shalev, "Predicting the development of posttraumatic stress disorder for the acute response to a traumatic event," *Biol. Psychiatry* 44(1998):1305-1313.

p. 125   **recovery from their traumatic distress** E. Aardal-Eriksson, T. E. Eriksson, and L-H. Thorell, "Salivary cortisol, posttraumatic stress symptoms, and general health in the acute phase and during the 9-month follow-up," *Biol. Psychiatry* 50(2001): 986-993.

p. 126   **restored neurogenesis activity to normal** B. Czeh, T. Michaelis, T. Watanabe, J. Frahm, G. deBiurrun, M. van Kampen, A. Bartolomucci, and E. Fuchs, "Stress-induced changes in cerebral metabolites, hippocampal volume, and cell proliferation are prevented with antidepressant tianeptine," *Proc. Natl. Acad. Sci. U.S.A.* 98(2001):12786-12801.

p. 126   **compared to men without the disorder** N. Schuff, T. Neylan, M. Lenoci, A. Du, D. Weiss, C. Marmar, and M. Weiner, "Decreased hippocampal *N*-acetylaspartate in the absence of atrophy in posttraumatic stress disorder," *Biol. Psychiatry* 50(2001): 952-959.

p. 127   **whereas 16 of the others developed the condition** G. Schelling, C. Stoll, H. P. Kapfhammer, M. Rothenhausler, T. Krauseneck, K. Durst, M. Haller, and J. Briegel, "The effect of stress doses of hydrocortisone during septic shock on posttraumatic stress disorder and health-related quality of life in survivors," *Crit. Care Med.* 27(1999):2678-2683.

p. 128   **two parents with hypertension** W. Gerin and T. G. Pickering,

"Association between delayed recovery blood pressure after acute mental stress and parental history of hypertension," *J. Hypertens.* 13(1995):603-610.

p. 129   **CREB in the nucleus of key hippocampal cells** D. Bartsch, M. Ghirardi, P. A. Skehel, K. A. Karl, S. P. Herder, M. Chen, C. H. Bailey, and E. R. Kandel, "Aplysia CREB2 represses long-term facilitation: Relief of repression converts transient facilitation into long-term functional and structural change," *Cell* 83(1995):979-992; C. H. Bailey, D. Bartsch, and E. R. Kandel, "Toward a molecular definition of long-term memory storage," *Proc. Natl. Acad. Sci. U.S.A.* 93(1996):13445-13452.

p. 129   **normal flies required 10 sessions** J. C. Yin, M. Del Vecchio, H. Zhou, and T. Tully, "CREB as a memory modulator: Induced expression of a dCREB2 activator isoform enhances long-term memory in *Drosophila*," *Cell* 81(1995):107-115; J. C. Yin, J. S. Wallach, M. Del Vecchio, M. Wildeer, E. L. Zhou, H. Quinn, W. G. Tully, and T. Tully, "Induction of a dominant negative CREB transgene specifically blocks long-term memory in *Drosophila*," *Cell* 79(1994): 49-58.

p. 131   **increase the neuron's level of excitability** N. G. Weiland, M. Orchinik, and B. S. McEwen, "Corticosterone regulates mRNA levels of specific subunits of the NMDA receptor in the hippocampus but not in the cortex of rats," *Abstr. Soc. Neurosci.* 21(1995):502.

p. 132   **happen to be cognitively impaired** S. Kerr, L. Campbell, M. Applegate, A. Brodish, and P. Landfield, "Chronic stress-induced acceleration of electrophysiologic and morphomeric biomarkers of hippocampal aging," *J. Neurosci.* 11(1991):1316-1324.

p. 132   **potential for damage and allostatic load** M. T. Lowy, L. Wittenberg, and B. K. Yamamoto, "Effect of acute stress on hippocampal glutamate levels and specrin proteolysis in young and aged rats," *J. Neurochem.* 65(1995):263-274.

p. 132   **lists of words with no problem** S. Lupien, A. R. Lecours, I. Lussier, G. Schwartz, N. P. V. Nair, and M. J. Meaney, "Basal cortisol levels and cognitive deficits in human aging," *J. Neurosci.* 14(1994):2893-2903.

p. 132   **more successfully aging counterparts** S. J. Lupien, M. J. DeLeon, S. DeSanti, A. Convit, C. Tarshish, N. P. V. Nair, M. Thakur, B. S. McEwen, R. L. Hauger, and M. J. Meaney, "Cortisol levels during human aging predict hippoc-ampal atrophy and memory deficits," *Nat. Neurosci.* 1(1998):69-73.

p. 133   **in normal wear and tear associated with aging** L. P. Reagan and B. S. McEwen, "Controversies surrounding glucocorticoid-mediated cell death in the hippocampus," *Chem. Neuroanat.* 13(1997):149-167.

p. 133   **did so in only a few days** H. A. Cameron and D. G. McKay, "Restoring production of hippocampal neurons in old age," *Nat. Neurosci.* 2(1999):894-858.

How Not to Be Stressed Out

p. 137   **twice as effective as the front-line medical treatment** Diabetes Prevention Program Research Group, "Reduction in the incidence of type II diabetes with lifestyle intervention or metformin," *N. Engl. J. Med.* 346(2002):393-403.

p. 137   **the risk of heart disease went down in accordance with the distance walked** A. A. Hakiim, J. D. Curb, H. Petrovitch, B. L. Rodriguez, K. Yano, G. W. Ross, L. R. White, and R. D. Abbott, "Effects of walking on coronary heart disease in elderly men: The Honolulu Heart Program," *Circulation* 100(1999):9-13.

p.137   **even if they began walking only later in life** J. E. Manson, F. B. Hu, J. W. Rich-Edwards, G. A. Colditz, M. I. Stampfer, W. C. Willett, F. E. Speizer, and C. H. Hennekens, "A prospective study of walking as compared with vigorous exercise in the prevention of coronary heart disease in women," *N. Engl. J. Med.* 341(1999):650-658.

p. 137   **possibly overcoming insulin resistance** G. Perseghin, T. B. Price, K. F. Petersen, M. Roden, G. W. Cline, K. Gerow, D. L. Rothman, and G. I. Shulman, "Increased glucose transport-phosphorylation and muscle glycogen synthesis after exercise training in insulin-resistant subjects," *N. Engl. J. Med.* 335 (1996):1357-1362.

p. 137   **white blood cells, such as macrophages and lymphocytes** H. Sugiura, H. Nishida, R. Inaba, S. M. Mirbod, and H. Iwata, "Immunomodulation by 8-week voluntary exercise in mice," *Acta Physiol. Scand. Mar.* 168(2000):413-420.

p. 138   **joggers scored 30 percent higher than their sedentary fellow subjects** T. Harada, S. Okagawa, and K. Kubota, "Habitual jogging improves performance of prefrontal tests," paper presented at the Society for Neuroscience Annual Meeting, Nov. 2001, San Diego, Calif.

p. 138   **significantly more newborn cells in the hippocampus** H. Van Praag, G. Kempermann, and F. H. Gage, "Running increases cell proliferation and neurogenesis in the adult mouse dentate gyrus," *Nat. Neurosci.* 2(1999):266-270.

p. 139   **more long-term potentiation** H. Van Praag, B. R. Christie, T. J. Sejnowski, and F. H. Gage, "Running enhances learning, neurogenesis, and long-term potentiation in mice," *Proc. Natl. Acad. Sci. U.S.A.* 96(1999):13427-13431.

p. 139   **encourage what scientists call food-seeking behavior** D. Brindley and Y. Rolland, "Possible connections between stress, diabetes, hypertension, and altered lipoprotein metabolism that may result in atherosclerosis," *Clin. Sci.* 77(1989):453-461.

p. 140   **speed up the accumulaton of abdominal fat** J. M. Mayo, C. A. Shively, J. R. Kaplan, and S. B. Manuck, "Effect of exercise and stress on body fat distribution in male cynomolgus monkeys," *Int. J. Obes. Rel. Metab. Disord.* 17(1993):597-604.

p. 140 **in the derriere** A. E. Moyer, J. Rodin, C. M. Grilo, N. Cummings, L. M. Larson, and M. Rebuffe-Scrive, "Stress-induced cortisol response and fat distribution in women," *Obes. Res.* 2(1994):55-261.

p. 141 **rats with impaired glucose tolerance** K. Kamara, R. Eskay, and T. Castonguay, "High-fat diets and stress responsivity," *Physiol. Behav.* 64(1998): 1-6.

p. 143 **evening blood glucose levels are elevated in the sleep deprived** L. Plat, R. Leproult, M. L'Hermite-Baleriaux, F. Fery, J. Mocke, K. S. Polonsky, and E. Van Cauter, "Metabolic effects of short-term elevations of plasma cortisol are more pronounced in the evening than in the morning," *J. Clin. Endocrinol. Metab.* 84(1999):3082-3092.

p. 143 **chronic fatigue and brain wave changes in EEG** H. Moldofsky, "Sleep, neuroimmune, and neuroendocrine functions in fibromyalgia and chronic fatigue syndrome," *Adv. Neuroimmunol.* 5(1995):39-56.

p. 144 **would become an alcoholic later in life** M. A. Schuckit and T. L. Smith, "An 8-year follow-up of 450 sons of alcoholic and control subjects," *Arch. Gen. Psych.* 53(1996):202-210.

p. 144 **family history of alcoholism** G. S. Wand, D. Mangold, D. M. Ali, and P. Giggey, "Adrenocortical responses and family history of alcoholism," *Alcohol Clin. Exp. Res.* 23(1999):1185-1190.

p. 145 **less able to mount an allostatic response** S. Lee and C. Rivier, "An initial, three-day-long treatment with alcohol induces a long-lasting phenomenon of selective tolerance in the activity of rat hypothalamic-pituitary-adrenal axis," *J. Neurosci.* 17(1997):8856-8866.

p. 145 **circadian rhythms of the stress hormones had been thrown off** G. S. Wand and A. S. Dobs, "Alterations in the hypothalamic-pituitary-adrenal axis in actively drinking alcoholics," *J. Clin. Endocrinol. Metab.* 72(1991):1290-1295.

p. 146 **put in the new situation together** D. Gust, T. Gordon, A. Brodie, and H. McClure, "Effect of companions in modulating stress associated with new group formation in juvenile rhesus macaques," *Physiol. Behav.* 59(1996):941.

p. 146 **lower cortisol levels than the males with fewer attachments** R. M. Sapolsky, *Why Zebras Don't Get Ulcers: An Updated Guide to Stress, Stress-Related Diseases, and Coping* (New York: W. H. Freeman, 1998), p. 216.

p. 146 **supportive friend in the audience** W. Gerin, C. Pieper, R. Levy, and T. Pickering, "Social support in social interaction: A moderator of cardiovascular activity," *Psychosom. Med.* 54 (1992):324.

p. 146 **patients with no social support** N. Frasure-Smith, F. Lesperance, G. Gravel, A. Masson, M. Juneau, M. Talajic, and M. G. Bourassa, "Social sup-

port, depression, and mortality during the first year after myocardial infarction,"
Circulation 101 (2000):1919-1924.

p. 147   **whose chief means of coping was denial** J. Leserman, J. M.
Petitto, R. N. Golden, B. N. Gaynes, H. Gu, D. O. Perkins, S. G. Silva, J. D. Folds,
and D. L. Evans, "Impact of stressful life events, depression, social support, coping, and cortisol on progression to AIDS," *Am. J. Psychiatr.* 157(2000):1221-1228.

p. 147   **social support can also ease the excruciating neuropathic pain**
J. A. Haythornthwaite and M. Benrud-Larson, "Psychological aspects of neuropathic pain," *Clin. J. Pain* 16(2000): S101-S105.

p. 150   **correlating with an improvement in the patient's OCD symptoms** J. M. Schwartz, P. W. Stoessel, L. R. Baxter, Jr., K. M. Martin, and M. E.
Phelps, "Systematic changes in cerebral glucose metabolic rate after successful
behavior modification treatment of obsessive-compulsive disorder," *Arch. Gen.
Psych.* 53 (1996):109-113.

p. 151   **if a rat has learned to push a lever to avoid receiving a mild
shock** H. Davis and S. Levine, "Predictability, control, and the pituitary-adrenal
response in rats," *J. Compar. Physiol. Psych.* (1982):393.

p. 152   **their blood pressure went back to a normal range** B. Melin, U.
Lundberg, J. Soderlund, and M. Grandqvist, "Psychological and physiological
stress reactions of male and female assembly workers: A comparison between
two different forms of work organization," *J. Organiz. Psychol.* 20(1999):47-61.

Positive Health

p. 156   **strong evidence of opiate receptors in cultured brain tissue** S.
Snyder, *Drugs and the Brain* (New York: Scientific American Library, W. H. Freeman, 1996).

p. 157   **produce one type of endorphin** R. Guillemin, T. Vargo, and J.
Rossier, "Beta-endorphin and adrenocorticotropin are secreted concomitantly
by pituitary gland," *Science* 197(1977):1367.

p. 158   **acupuncture triggers endorphin production** D. Mayer, D. Price,
J. Barber, and A. Rafii, "Acupuncture analgesia: Evidence for activation of a pain
inhibitory system as a mechanism for action," in *Advances in Pain Research and
Therapy*, vol. 1, J. Bonica and D. Albe-Fessard, eds. (New York: Raven Press,
1976), p. 751.

p. 159   **oxytocin may be a "bonding" hormone** T. R. Insel, B. S. Gingrich,
and L. J. Young, "Oxytocin: Who needs it?," *Prog. Brain Res.* 133(2001):59-66.

p. 159   **fail to recognize cage mates** J. N. Ferguson, J. M. Aldag, T. R.
Insel, and L. J. Young, "Oxytocin in the medial amygdala is essential for social
recognition in the mouse," *J. Neurosci.* 21 (2001):8278-8285.

p. 159   **in the brain of mother and child during breast-feeding** K.

Uvnas-Moberg, "Oxytocin may mediate the benefits of positive social interaction and emotions," *Psychoneuroendocrinology* 23(1998):819-835.

p. 159   **injected oxytocin lowers blood pressure** M. Petersson, P. Alster, T. Lundeberg, and K. Uvnas-Moberg, "Oxytocin causes long-term decrease of blood pressure in female and male rats," *Physiol. Behav.* 60(1996):1311-1315.

p. 159   **prolactin directly into the brains of rats** L. Torner, N. Toschi, A. Pohlinger, R. Landgraf, and I. D. Neumann, "Anxiolytic and anti-stress effects of brain prolactin: Improved efficacy of antisense targeting of the prolactin receptor by molecular modeling," *J. Neurosci.* 21(2001):3207-3214.

p. 162   **BDNF protects the brain against ischemia** D. Lindholm, G. Dechant, C-P. Heisenberg, and H. Thoenen, "Brain-derived neurotrophic factor is a survival factor for cultured rat cerebella granule neurons and protects them against glutamate-induced neurotoxicity," *Eur. J. Neurosci.* 5(1993): 1455-1464.

p. 162   **BDNF was increased in a part of the cortex** W. Tokuyama, H. Okuno, T. Hashimoto, Y. X. Li, and Y. Miyashita, "BDNF upregulation during declarative memory formation in monkey inferior temporal cortex," *Nat. Neurosci.* 3(2000): 1134-1142.

p. 163   **increases levels of both BDNF and NGF** S. A. Neeper, F. G. Gomez-Pinilla, J. Chois, and C. W. Cotman, "Physical activity increases mRNA for brain-derived neurotrophic factor and nerve growth factor in rat brain," *Brain Res.* 72(1996): 49-56.

p. 163   **shortly after the exercise period begins** H. S. Oliff, N. C. Berchtold, P. Isackson, and C. W. Cotman, "Exercise induced regulation of brain-derived neurotrophic factor (BDNF) transcripts in the rat hippocampus," *Mol. Brain Res.* 61(1998): 147-153.

p. 163   **higher on maze tests than their sedentary cage mates** L. Zhao, Z. Ying, V. R. Edgerton, and F. Gomez-Pinalla, "Inactivity reduces neurotrophin expression in the spinal cord," paper presented at the Society for Neuroscience Annual Meeting, Nov. 12, 2001, San Diego, Calif.

p. 163   **more of an increase in BDNF levels than rats that exercised voluntarily** D. B. Albeck, G. E. Prewitt, and L. Dalton, "Brain levels of BDNF are differentially affected by voluntary vs. forced running," paper presented at the Society for Neuroscience Annual Meeting, Nov. 13, 2001, San Diego, Calif.

p. 164   **raise the levels of BDNF in the hippocampus** P. S. Duman, G. R. Heninger, and E. J. Nestler, "A molecular and cellular theory of depression," *Arch. Gen. Psych.* 54(1997):597-606.

p. 166   **dedicating the cells to the memory of that event** T. J. Shors, G. Miesegaes, A. Beylin, M. Zhao, T. Rydel, and E. Gould, "Neurogenesis in the adult is involved in the formation of trace memories," *Nature* 410(2001):372-376.

p. 167   **found new cells in the prefrontal cortex** E. Gould, A. J. Reeves, M. S. Graziano, and C. G. Gross, "Neurogenesis in the neocortex of adult primates," *Science* 186(1999):548-552.

p. 167   **shown neurogenesis to occur in the mouse cortex** S. S. Magavi, B. R. Leavitt, and J. D. Macklis, "Induction of neurogenesis in the neocortex of adult mice," *Nature* 405(2000): 951-955.

p. 168   **have significantly more dividing cells in the hippocampus** J. E. Malberg, A. J. Eisch, E. J. Nestler, and R. S. Duman, "Chronic antidepressant treatment increases neurogenesis in adult rat hippocampus," *J. Neurosci.* 20(2000):9104-9110.

p. 168   **suppresses the formation of new nerve cells in the hippocampus** B. Czeh, T. Michaelis, T. Watanabe, J. Frahm, G. de Biurrum, M. van Kampen, A. Bartolomuccci, and E. Fuchs, "Stress-induced changes in cerebral metabolites, hippocampal volume, and cell proliferation are prevented with antidepressant tianeptine," *Proc. Natl. Acad. Sci. U.S.A.* 98(2001):12796-12801.

p. 168   **increased levels of acetylcholine in the basal forebrain** V. Luine, D. Park, R. Joh, D. Reis, and B. S. McEwen, "Immunochemical demonstration of increased choline acetytransferase concentration in rat preoptic area after estradiol administration," *Brain Res.* 191(1980):273-277.

p. 169   **changes in their memory** B. B. Sherwin, "Estrogen effects on memory in women," *Ann. N.Y. Acad. Sci.* 743(1994): 213-231; B. B. Sherwin and T. Tulandi, "Add-back estrogen reverses cognitive deficits induced by a genadotropin-releasing hormone agonist in women with leiomyomata uteri," *J. Clin. Endocrinol. Metab.* 81(1996):2545-2549.

p. 169   **key neurons in the hippocampus** A. H. Gazzaley, D. L. Benson, G. W. Huntley, and J. H. Morrison, "Differential subcellular regulation of NMDAR1 protein and mRNA in dendrites of dentate gyrus granule cells after perforant path transection," *J. Neurosci.* 17(1997):2006-2017.

p. 170   **"masculinization" of both the structure and the function of the hippocampus** E. Gould, A. Westlind-Danielsson, M. Frankfurt, and B. S. McEwen, "Sex differences and thyroid hormone sensitivity of hippocampal pyramidal neurons," *J. Neurosci.* 10(1990):996-1003.

p. 170   **female rats also seem to be resistant to the stress-induced atrophy** L. A. M. Galea, B. S. McEwen, P. Tanapat, T. Deak, R. L. Spencer, and F. S. Dhabhar, "Sex differences in dendritic atrophy of CA3 pyramidal neurons in response to chronic restraint stress," *Neuroscience* 81(1997):689-697.

p. 170   **rapid-fire cell death known as excitotoxicity** Y. Goodman, A. J. Bruce, B. Cheng, and M. P. Mattson, "Estrogens attenuate and corticosterone exacerbates excitotoxicity, oxidative injury, and amyloid B-peptide toxicity in hippocampal neurons," *J. Neurochem.* 66(1996):1836-1844.

p. 170   **destructive effects of this protein as well** P. S. Green, K. E. Gridley, and J. W. Simpkins, "Estradiol protects against B-amyloid (25-35)-induced toxicity in SK-N-SH human neuroblastoma cells," *Neurosci. Lett.* 128(1996):165-168.

p. 170   **the lower risk of the disease** V. W. Henderson, A. Paganini-Hill,

C. K. Emanuel, M. E. Dunn, and J. G. Buckwalter, "Estrogen replacement therapy in older women: Comparisons between Alzheimer's disease cases and non-demented control subjects," *Arch. Neurol.* 51(1994):896-900.

p. 170   **developed the disease did so much later** M. X. Tang, D. Jacobs, Y. Stern, K. Marder, P. Schofield, B. Gurland, H. Andrews, and R. Mayeux, "Effect of estrogen during menopause on risk and age at onset of Alzheimer's disease," *Lancet* 348 (1996):429-432.

p. 171   **women taking estrogen replacement therapy** C. Kawas, S. Resnick, A. Morrison, R. Brookmeyer, M. Corrada, A. Zonderman, C. Bacal, D. D. Lingle, and E. Metter, "A prospective study of estrogen replacement therapy and the risk of developing Alzheimer's disease: The Baltimore Longitudinal Study of Aging," *Neurology* 48(1997):1517-1521.

p. 171   **travel all the way to the cell's nucleus** P. B. Crino and J. Eberwine, "Molecular characterization of the dendritic growth cone: Regulated mRNA transport and local protein synthesis," *Neuron* 17(1996):1173-1187.

p. 171   **new events in the cell's environment** P. Crino, K. Khodakhah, K. Becker, S. Ginsberg, S. Hemby, and J. Eberwine, "Presence and phosphorylation of transcription factors in developing dendrites," *Cell. Biol.* 95(1998):2313-2318.

Where We Could Go from Here

p. 175   **disease or disorder at the time of the study** T. Seeman, B. Singer, J. W. Rowe, R. Horwitz, and B. S. McEwen, "The price of adaptation: Allostatic load and its health consequences," *Arch. Inst. Med.* 157(1997):2259-2268.

p. 176   **slower rates of brain aging when they grow up** M. Meaney, D. Atiken, H. Berkel, S. Bhatnager, and R. Sapolsky, "Effect of neonatal handling on age-related impairments associated with the hippocampus," *Science* 239(1988): 766-768.

p. 176   **to speed up brain aging** D. Lui, J. Diorio, B. Tannenbaum, C. Caldji, D. Francis, A. Freedman, S. Sharma, D. Pearson, P. M. Plotsky, and M. J. Meaney, "Maternal care, hippocampal glucocorticoid receptors, and hypothalamic-pituitary-adrenal responses to stress," *Science* 277(1998):1659-1662.

p. 177   **increase both aggression and alcohol consumption** J. D. Higley, W. W. Thompson, M. Champoux, D. Goldman, M. F. Hasert, G. W. Kraemeer, J. M. Scanlan, S. J. Suomi, and M. Linnoila, "Paternal and maternal genetic and environmental contributions to cerebrospinal fluid monoamine metabolites in rhesus monkey," *Arch. Gen. Psych.* 50(1993):615-623.

p. 177   **cognitive impairment in adulthood** J. D. Brenner, J. Licinio, A. Darnell, J. H. Krystal, M. J. Owens, S. M. Southwick, C. B. Nemeroff, and D. S. Charney, "Elevated CSF corticotropin-releasing factor concentrations in posttraumatic stress disorder," *Am. J. Psych.* 15(1997):624-629.

p. 177   **extreme obesity, skeletal fractures, and liver disease** V. J. Felitti,

R. F. Anda, D. Nordenberg, D. F. Williamson, A. M. Spitz, V. Edwards, M. P. Moss, and J. S. Marks, "Relationship of childhood abuse and household dysfunction to many of the leading causes of death in adults: The Adverse Childhood Experience (ACE) study," *Am. J. Prev. Med.* 14(1998):245-258.

p. 177   **illness and even antisocial behavior** D. L. Olds, J. Eckenrode, E. R. Henderson, H. Kitzman, J. Powers, R. Cole, K. Sidora, P. Morris, L. M. Pettitt, and D. Luckey, "Long-term effects of home visitation on maternal life course and child abuse and neglect," *JAMA* 278(1997):637-643.

p. 178   **children and adolescents are overweight** U.S. Department of Health and Human Services, *The Surgeon General's Call to Action to Prevent and Decrease Overweight and Obesity* (Rockville, Md.: U.S. Department of Health and Human Services, Public Health Service, Office of the Surgeon General, 2001).

p. 180   **even after correcting for education** Centers for Disease Control, National Center for Health Statistics," National Vital Statistics Report," 48(2000).

p. 181   **alienated adolescents prone to crime and violence** B. Singer and C. D. Ryff, "Racial and ethnic inequalities in health: Environmental, psychosocial, and physiological pathways," *Beyond the Bell Curve*, S. Fienberg et al., eds. (New York: Springer-Verlag, 1996).

p. 183   **allostatic load at or above 3** B. Singer and C. D. Ryff, "Hierarchies of life histories and associated health risks," *Ann. N.Y. Acad. Sci.* 896(1999): 96-115.

p. 184   **restored positive health to these women** B. Singer, C. D. Ryff, D. Carr, and W. J. Magee, "Linking life histories and mental health: A person-centered strategy," in *Sociological Methodology*, A. Raftery, ed. (Washington, D.C.: American Sociological Association, 1998).

p. 185   **"positive self-regard"** C. D. Ryff and B. Singer, "Psychological well-being: Meaning, measurement, and implications for psychotherapy research," *Psychother. Psychosom.* 65 (1996):14-23.

p. 187   **Just About Everything** J. Gleich, *Faster: The Acceleration of Just About Everything* (New York: Pantheon Books, 1999), p. 11.

Appendix

p. 199   **hormonal secretion is dysregulated** B. S. McEwen, "Protective and damaging effect of stress mediators," *N. Engl. J. Med.* 338(1998):171-179.

p. 199   **mental functioning** J. W. Lynch, G. A. Kaplan and S. J. Shema, "Cumulative impact of sustained economic hardship on physical, cognitive, psychological, and social functioning," *N. Engl. J. Med.* (1997):1889-1895.

p. 201   **would not upset most other people** C. Kirschbaum, J. C. Prussner, A. A. Stone, I. Federenko, J. Gaab, D. Lintz, N. Schommer, and D. H.

Hellhammer, "Persistent high cortisol responses to repeated psychological stress in a subpopulation of healthy men," *Psychosom. Med.* 57(1995):468-474.

p. 201   **aftermath of a psychological stressor** W. Gerin and T. G. Pickering, "Association between delayed recovery of blood pressure after acute mental stress and parental history of hypertension," *Hypertension* 13(1995):603-610.

p. 201   **during the evening hours** R. Leproult, G. Copinschi, O. Buxton, and E. Van Cauter, "Sleep loss results in an elevation of cortisol levels the next evening," *Sleep* 20(1997): 865-870; K. Spiegel, R. Leproult, and E. Van Cauter, "Impact of sleep debt on metabolic and endocrine function," *Lancet* 354 (1999):1435-1439.

p. 201   **diabetes and other problems** L. Plat, R. Leproult, M. L'Hermite-Baleriaux, F. Fery, J. Mockel, K. S. Polonsky, and E. Van Cauter, "Metabolic effects of short-term elevations of plasma cortisol are more pronounced in the evening than in the morning," *J. Clin. Endocr. Metab.* 84(1999):3082-3092.

p. 201   **elevated diurnal glucocorticoid level** D. Michelson, C. Stratakis, L. Hill, J. Reynolds, E. Galliven, G. Chrousos, and P. Gold, "Bone mineral density in women with depression," *N. Engl. J. Med.* 335(1996):1176-1181.

p. 201   **chronic elevation of glucocorticoids** R. Sapolsky, L. Krey, and B. S. McEwen, "The neuroendocrinology of stress and aging: The glucocorticoid cascade hypothesis," *Endocr. Rev.* 7 (1986):284-301.

p. 202   **injected glucocorticoids** E. M. Sternberg, "Neural-immune interactions in health and disease," *J. Clin. Invest.* 100 (1997):2641-2647.

p. 202   **fibromyalgia and chronic fatigue syndrome** A. Buske-Kirschbaum, S. Jobst, A. Wustmans, C. Kirshbaum, W. Rauth, and D. H. Hellhammer, "Attenuated free cortisol response to psychosocial stress in children with atopic dermatitis," *Psychosom. Med.* 59(1997):419-426; L. J. Crawford, S. R. Pillemer, K. Kalogeras, J. M. Cash, D. Michelson, M. A. Kling, E. M. Steinberg, P. A. W. Gold, G. P. Chrousos, and R. L. Wilder, "Hypothalamic-pituitary-adrenal axis perturbations in patients with fibromyalgia," *Arthr. Rheum.* 37(1994):1583-1592; A. M. Magarinos, K. Jian, E. D. Blount, L. Reagan, B. H. Smith, and B. S. McEwen, "Peritoneal implantation of macroencapsulated porcine pancreatic islets in diabetic rats ameliorates severe hyperglycemia and prevents retraction and simplification of hippocampal dendrites," *Brain Res.* 902(2001): 282-287; A. Poteliakhoff, "Adrenocortical activity and some clinical findings in acute and chronic fatigue," *J. Psychosom. Res.* 25 (1981):91-95; E. Ur, P. S. White, and A. Grossman, "Hypotheses: Cytokines may be activated to cause depressive illness and chronic fatigue syndrome," *Eur. Arch. Psych. Clin. Neurosci.* 241 (1991):17-322.

Index